D0398846

CREATIVE
CONVERSATIONS

CREATIVE
CONVERSATIONS

M I C H A E L
S C H U M A C H E R

Writer's
Digest
Books

Cincinnati, Ohio

94 93 92 91 90   5 4 3 2 1

Library of Congress Cataloging-in-Publication Data

Schumacher, Michael.
    Creative conversations: the writer's complete guide to conducting interviews / Michael Schumacher.
        p.   cm.
    ISBN 0-89879-396-3
    1. Interviews—Authorship.   I. Title.
PN171.I66S38   1990
808'.02—dc20   90-30638
                                                                                        CIP

This book is dedicated to
Adam Michael Schumacher
who's a pretty good talker himself

CONTENTS

ACKNOWLEDGMENTS

Contrary to the popular myth, writing is not the world's loneliest profession, nor is it necessarily a singular one. Writers, like painters, musicians, actors, and others engaged in the arts, depend upon the support, assistance, generosity, and kindness of numerous people in order to get a single work accomplished. The final work may bear only one person's name or signature, but it is almost always the result of some kind of collaborative venture.

This is certainly the case with this book. Many people shared their insights, ideas, and experiences with me, and I'd like to thank all of the people quoted in the book, especially Mark Dowie, Mary Kachoyeanos, Janet Kraegel, Tracy Kidder, Lawrence Linderman, George Plimpton, Gary Provost, and Studs Terkel. These interviewees, along with numerous others offering important background information or suggestions, made this book much stronger than it would have been if I had simply drawn from my own knowledge and experience.

I also wish to thank Bill Brohaugh, Tom Clark, and Bill Strickland of *Writer's Digest* magazine. Not only have these three gentlemen assigned and edited many of my interviews but, through their questions, suggestions, and insights, they have also greatly assisted in my development as an interviewer. A very special thanks to Sister Virginia Handrup who, in a mere year's time, taught me all the valuable principles that I hold dear today; everyone should have a teacher as devoted as she is.

For their assistance in various logistical concerns, my thanks to Peter Spielmann and Judy Hansen, Alvin and Diane Schumacher, Bill and Lorraine Landre, Keith Kahla, Meg Drislane, Bill Robbins, Michael and Jill Fargo, Jim Sieger, Ken and Karen Ade, Glen Puterbaugh, and Michael Seidman. All were very helpful in one way or another in the creation of this book.

To the people at Writer's Digest Books, particularly Nan Dibble and Jean Fredette, my appreciation for their patience and endurance.

Finally I must thank my wife, Susan, and three children — Adam, Emily, and Jack Henry — all of whom know how truly collaborative writing really is.

CREATIVE
CONVERSATIONS

THE INTERVIEW AND ITS USES

P eople.

It's difficult to imagine any work of nonfiction without them.

They add motion and sound and color and life to nonfiction. They flesh out the most skeletal of ideas. They give readers someone to listen to, empathize or disagree with, identify with, or believe in. They're measuring sticks, sounding boards. Even inanimate objects come to life when they are surrounded by people.

Tracy Kidder, author of the bestselling books, *The Soul of a New Machine, House,* and *Among Schoolchildren,* proved emphatically the importance of people in his first two books when he wrote compelling nonfiction about the technical details of computers and the building of a modern house. The computer and the house, inanimate objects for certain, were afforded character, dimension, and *life* by people who surrounded them.

"If you're interested in stories — which is what I like — you obviously have to have people in the narrative," says Kidder. "I feel very strongly that way. I really don't think that *House* is a book about a building; it's about something else. My three books are really books about ordinary people at work."

In journalism, a principal field of nonfiction writing, it's impossible to avoid the "people element." I've talked to a number of novelists who claim they originally intended to become journalists, only to move to fiction when they realized that they were uncomfortable in formal, day-to-day encounters with people. As novelists, they could remain in the shadows, observing the world around them — and the people in that world — without the intimate human contact that's obligatory in journalism. Novelists contend that their fiction is really the truth, and while I have no quarrel with that attitude, it should also be noted that "fictional truth" is much more filtered than law, ethics, or good writing practice will afford the nonfiction writer. In nonfiction, one doesn't—and *shouldn't*— bend or shape the truth (or opinion, for that matter) to one's own liking or design.

Interviews bring people into nonfiction. Through interviews we exchange information, listen to opinions, enjoy anecdotes, and learn more about other people's characters—all of which we are able to pass along to our readers. In every sense, interviews are literary conduits.

People can be exquisitely unpredictable. Their thoughts and actions delight, shock, anger, amaze, and educate. From seemingly simple conversations come great observations or stunning quotations. In nonfiction, the ordinary can become as extraordinary as anything you will encounter in fiction, and the most common voice in our midst can be heard with resounding clarity and purpose.

Truman Capote, one of this century's most gifted writers, understood this as well as anyone. His stories and short novels, widely recognized for their perception and stylistic eloquence, were accomplished character studies, but it is likely that he will be remembered more for one nonfiction book, *In Cold Blood,* and a few of his personality profiles than he will be remembered for his fiction. When it came to penetrating the psychological surface of a wide variety of people, few writers were Capote's equal. The reason? He genuinely liked people and could relate to them in ways that translated into noteworthy nonfiction.

"He knew so many people who were so entertaining," explains George Plimpton, the writer/editor who has compiled an oral biography of Capote. "He moved through many segments of society, from murderers to the highest social echelons. He knew almost everybody."

For Plimpton, these people helped identify and, to a large degree, define the man; for Capote, the writer, the reverse is probably just as true. He knew the value of lively conversation, and he was one of its best practitioners. When interviewer Lawrence Grobel asked him if remarks could be considered literature, Capote responded with the wit and perception for which he was known.

"No," he said, "but they can be art."

THE ART OF CONVERSATION

Meeting people and making some kind of art out of their remarks is what this book will be addressing. By art, I don't necessarily mean that you should be soliciting comments or quotations that are highbrow or stylistically mind-boggling; to enter into any conversation with those goals in mind is both arrogant and silly, and you are likely to leave the interview with the tinny echo of prepared or predictable statements ringing in your ears. What I mean is that there is an art to preparing for a formal interview, carrying on that conversation, and extracting from it remarks that reflect well upon you, on the person speaking, and on the topic being addressed.

USES FOR THE INTERVIEW

Writers use interviews in a myriad of ways, but for the purposes of this book we will be looking at interviews for four main uses:

- *support quotes* for news stories, features, magazine articles, and nonfiction books;
- *research and background information;*
- *personality profiles;* and
- *the question/answer interview.*

The greatest percentage of interviews are conducted for the first two categories on this list. For example, if you are a journalist assigned to write an article about a new method of cancer treatment, you will want to talk to a number of experts on every aspect of that treatment. Not only will those authorities provide you with important information that gives you a better understanding of the treatment itself, but you will also be able to use their words, in direct quotation, to support what you write about in the narrative of your text. No writer can possibly be an authority on every topic he or she chooses to write about, and even if it were possible, readers would demand a feeling of consensus — or, with controversial or provocative issues, a sense of argument — before they would accept what the writer was presenting in the article.

Support quotes provide that sense of consensus or argument. For example, before Mark Dowie wrote *We Have A Donor,* his study of organ transplantation practices today, he interviewed a number of internationally recognized authorities on numerous aspects of transplantation. Much of the discussion was used for research purposes — for gathering information needed for the author to discuss the history and nature of transplantation — but when Dowie addressed the controversial legal and ethical issues associated with transplantation in his book, he needed authoritative voices to passionately discuss the issues.

"Altogether, I talked to about one hundred people for the book," Dowie says, adding that many of his conversations were very brief, often amounting to his asking only a question or two. Using support quotes for a book, he says, is different from employing the same kind of quotes in magazine articles. "You have to be more selective when you're writing for magazines. You use fewer quotes. In the book, I used all of the quotes that were good."

In longer works, a writer is afforded such a luxury, whereas in magazine or newspaper articles, good support quotes — remarks that illuminate, or offer consensus or disagreement in an interesting way — must often be sacrificed, the unfortunate victims of space restrictions. Instead of using two or three strong support quotes, the writer may be forced to include only the best remark, and the choices can be tough.

In their published form, support quotes should be attributed to the speaker. Without attribution, the speaker's words lose much of their credibility and punch. Unfortunately, in the post-Watergate era of investigative reporting, attribution has become the focus of a major debate. Sources will occasionally agree to speak for the record only on the condition that their names not be used in the published article. This issue is problematic: editors, understandably squeamish about off-the-record or confidential sources at a time when journalists and publications are losing landmark libel cases, nevertheless encourage their reporters to bring back the BIG story, which so often hinges on information provided by a confidential source. For writers, this is a sticky dilemma, and it is an issue that will be addressed later in this book.

Unlike interviews conducted for support quotes, interviews intended for *research or background information* may result in a source's not being quoted at all. Let's say your local newspaper has asked you to write a feature story on the topic of growing raspberries. You don't know the first thing about raspberries (other than the fact that they're dark red or black, and you like them on French vanilla ice cream), so you decide to contact several area growers. For the most part, your interview will be conducted for the purpose of gathering information on where raspberries grow best, how one cultivates them, and so on. In writing your article, you will use the information you obtained in the interviews, but to attribute a direct quote of the obvious ("Raspberries taste good on French vanilla ice cream," says Mrs. Smith) is not only pointless, but it can undermine your story by making you look as if you're "talking down" to your readers.

On other occasions, you might be using these interviews as research for other interviews. If, for example, you've been asked to write a profile of rock star Mick Jagger, you might want to interview Keith Richards, his longtime band member and co-writer of most of his songs, for insights into Jagger's life and personality. Some of what Richards tells you may wind up being the foundation for the questions you would eventually ask Jagger himself. You may also quote Richards in your article (his love/hate relationship with Jagger has been the spice of many articles about Jagger, Richards, or the Rolling Stones), or you may agree to use him as "deep background," that is, an unattributed source of information. Either way, his insights would be invaluable to your article.

The third main use for interviews, the *personality or celebrity profile,* has become one of the most popular forms of nonfiction in the newspaper and magazine businesses. People seem never to grow tired of reading about the actions or thoughts of people in the public light. The profile focuses on one person, attempting to show as many sides of that person as is possible within a limited amount of space.

Writing a profile today can be quite a challenge, since editors are calling for short articles, such as those found in magazines like *People,* more than they are soliciting the lengthy, in-depth profiles featured in publications like *The New Yorker.* With television competing for coverage of the same profile subjects, the writer is put in the position of finding something original or new to say about a profile subject in very little space. As a result, the writer must be creative in approach, well versed on the person being profiled, and adept at gaining the kind of quotes necessary for a fresh, interesting angle to the profile.

A newspaper once asked me to write a 750-word profile of Norman Mailer for its Sunday book review section. As anyone who has interviewed this author can tell you, Mailer, an eloquent interviewee, is quite capable of spending more than 750 words in answering a *single question* in a clear, concise, and interesting way. The trick to my writing a successful profile for this paper was to find a very specific angle, interview Mailer on that angle, and break down his answers in a reasonable mixture of narrative, indirect quotes, and direct quotes, as well as to find a way to provide the color and setting to give the sense that the reader was sitting in on our conversation.

The *question/answer interview,* designed to read like a typescript of a conversation, was an immensely popular form of the published interview in the 1970s. Though it is not as favored today as it was during that decade, the question/answer interview still offers reader benefits that might be unavailable in the profile or feature article. For one thing, it is more direct, so the reader is seeing more of the person's words than would be the case if the writer were filling space with description and background. In longer Q&A's, the topic focus doesn't have to be so tight. Readers draw their own conclusions more in this format than in profiles, where author interpretation is an integral part of the writing.

To be effective, question/answer-style interviews must be conducted with people already in the public eye, or on topics already familiar to a majority of readers, since very little space in this format is devoted to introductory remarks or background information. Interviewers assume that their readers know something about their subject, and they proceed to use the interview to build upon what the public already knows, or to fill in the blanks in areas that may be unfamiliar to the reader.

Question/answer interviews present their own unique challenges to the writer. They have to flow smoothly and "sound" as if they are direct transcriptions of a single, relatively short conversation, even if they are the result of many hours of interviews involving several sessions. Transitions in the conversation have to be crisp, and each answer has to be complete. In this use of the interview, the writer employs an editor's skills as well as those of a writer.

How you intend to use the material you gather from your interview will influence the way you design and conduct the interview itself. For an in-depth profile, you would ask a broader range of questions than you might ask if you were looking for support quotes focusing on one topic. For a question/answer interview, you would probably solicit more detailed, quotable anecdotes than you might look for if you were gathering only background information.

Despite the different uses, the basic interviewing techniques vary only slightly from one use to another. The different variables will be addressed throughout this book, and in the final chapter we will look at special uses (oral history, biography, the "as told to" article, roundups, etc.) for the interview.

HOW INTERVIEWS ARE CONDUCTED

As we will see, how, when, and where interviews are conducted can greatly influence the information or quotes you gather during an interview. For the most part, interviewers have only a marginal say in these factors, but with good planning and experience, how you conduct your interviews should not affect your pursuit of strong, creative results.

Interviews can be conducted in three ways:

■ *In person.* The in-person or on-location interview finds the interviewer and interviewee meeting face to face at an agreed-upon location (or at the site of a news event) for the purpose of formally discussing topics of interest to a general readership. Because it affords the interviewer the opportunity to see as well as hear an interview subject in a given setting, the in-person conversation is the optimum method of conducting an interview. Unless special arrangements are made prior to the interview, it should be "for the record," with the mutual understanding that any information obtained by the interviewer will be used in one form or another for publication.

■ *Telephone.* The telephone interview employs the same basic techniques as the in-person interview and is usually conducted in lieu of an in-person conversation; it is preferable when time or distance factors make a personal visit impractical or impossible. In many cases, the telephone interview is ideal when the interviewer is checking facts, looking for a single piece of research, or searching for a brief quotation or two; it can also be employed when the interviewer is asking brief follow-up questions to those addressed during an initial in-person interview.

■ *Mail.* The mail interview, which may be written or taped, involves the interviewer's sending an interviewee questions to which he or she responds. Questionnaires and surveys, used primarily for research or roundup-style articles, are the most popular forms of mail interviews, although entire question/answer interviews have been conducted in this manner.

Unless specifically noted, all information in this book applies to all three methods of interviewing. In Chapter Five, special attention will be given to telephone and mail interviews, to the ways that they differ from the in-person interview, as well as how they can best be conducted.

An interviewer doesn't have to choose one particular method of conducting an interview for each article he or she is writing. It's quite common for a writer to use two or even all three methods when working on a single article. For example, I used all three methods in an interview I conducted with novelists Louise Erdrich and Michael Dorris. I talked with Erdrich in person for an hour in Chicago before we were joined by her husband, and then I talked with Erdrich and Dorris together for another hour. I followed up those conversations with separate telephone interviews. Finally, still needing to have another question or two answered and a few clarified, I mailed them the needed questions, as well as an edited transcript of our prior conversations for their review. Since I was not pressed by a tight deadline on the interview, I was afforded the chance to make the conversation, to be published in question/answer format, as in-depth and conclusive as possible. Using all three methods of interviewing gave me a chance to follow up my questions, and my subjects the opportunity to color in or clarify their answers. The result was an interview that was satisfactory to all of us.

TYPES OF INTERVIEWERS
Whenever you attend writers' conferences or seminars (or read books like this one, for that matter), you will find people searching

for common denominators. We search for similarities that unite us in our writing pursuits. In a way, this is an interesting paradox, inasmuch as writers—like painters, poets, photographers, moviemakers, and other artists—are attracted to the singularity of the creative arts, while at the same time they enjoy getting together, "talking shop," and comparing notes; in doing this, they find common ground.

The common ground/individuality paradox is important to bear in mind as you are reading this book, because all successful interviewers have their own styles of preparing for, conducting, and writing up interviews, those styles dependent upon factors such as the interviewers' personalities and the publications they are writing for. A writer for *The Saturday Evening Post,* for instance, might take an entirely different approach to interviewing a profile subject from that of a writer for *Mother Jones;* not only do the two publications take different approaches to the profiles they publish, but it could be argued that the publications attract different types of writers.

Some interviewers thrive on hard-line questioning and almost combative interviews, while others are loath to ask a semipointed question. An investigative reporter's approach to an interview will differ from that taken by a writer of "puff" pieces or soft news features; this will be quite evident when you're researching a potential interview subject and witness the different angles and approaches to that subject taken by different writers.

To be effective, it is crucial that you have as good an understanding as possible of who you are as an interviewer and writer. Part of this knowledge will be the result of your professional experiences, while another part will be inextricably connected to your personality and temperament, as well as to your values and goals as a writer. This is not to imply that you should be content to stand pat as a writer or person; the best writers are always seeking ways to expand their artistic and creative horizons by taking on new challenges in style and content. However, it's important that you know yourself and approach an interview on your own terms. If you're not the type of person who is able to pose tough questions, over and over, to reluctant or hostile interviewees, you should not propose and research an article on area politicians suspected of taking bribes; you may get the assignment, but you won't turn into a Mike Wallace overnight, and the interview you conduct will probably disappoint an editor. Editors have long memories and are quick to categorize their contributors, and if you disappoint them once, it's unlikely that you'll get a chance to redeem yourself. Conversely, if you satisfy them by submitting well-written pieces on topics that you're comfortable writing about, you will be on the way to a lasting, profitable relationship with those editors.

Take a hard, realistic look at yourself. Don't flinch or be too smug about what you see. Act upon what you learn. Your career will depend on it.

WORDS, IDEAS, COMMUNICATION

Edwin Newman, self-appointed watchdog of the English language and author of bestselling books on the topic, makes an excellent point in his book, *Strictly Speaking*, where he states: "If we were more careful about what we say, and how, we might be more critical and less gullible. Those for whom words have lost their value are likely to find that ideas have also lost their value."

Interviewers would do well to keep these thoughts in mind. Just because a person is talking as if he or she were being paid by the word doesn't mean that much is being said. In fact, pointless interviews in magazines, newspapers, or on television, have become the spiritual junk food for the late part of this century. We absorb countless "calories" of meaningless chatter, either unaware of or unconcerned about the damage that such talk can cause to our thought processes and the language itself.

Well-chosen words, stated precisely and eloquently, are the interviewer's goal. If you can make art out of someone's remarks, if you use conversation to further ideas, you have accomplished your task as a writer.

We call that task communication.

FINDING THE RIGHT VOICES

Although interviewers—and writers in general—would be the last to admit it, there are many parallels between successfully putting together a marketable newspaper or magazine article and the basic elements of salesmanship. In breaking down and analyzing the components of a successful sale, a salesperson will tell you that his or her work depends upon such steps as prospecting, preapproach, approach, presentation, closing, and following up. For successful interviews, the steps are similar. The interviewer prospects for potential stories and interview subjects, conducts preliminary research, approaches the subject with a request for an interview, conducts the interview, follows it up if necessary, and writes the story.

Salespeople, like all professionals, differ greatly in their methods of performing these various steps of their work, just as they vary in the emphasis they place on these steps; but if you were to poll the selling community, you would find that most salespeople place great significance on the relationship between their prospecting abilities and their sales records. The same principle applies to interviewing, although a large number of writers would balk at the notion of their considering a philistine dollar when art was at stake.

All highfalutin protests aside, a simple writing equation states that a writer is only as good as his or her work, and that work is only as good as the subjects and sources that support it. Tom Wolfe, author of *The Electric Kool-Aid Acid Test* and *The Right Stuff,* one of the great nonfiction stylists of the twentieth century, would have had a lot more trouble writing these bestselling books if he hadn't had people like Ken Kesey or Chuck Yeager as cornerstones to the books. Norman Mailer, who has enjoyed exceptional success as both a novelist and nonfiction writer, has built his nonfiction reputation on his ability to reach the core of such diverse people as hipsters and criminals, convicted murderers, movie sex goddesses, and Presidents. Mailer may have put it best when, talking about the characters and plots in his nonfiction, he noted that "God's a better novelist than the novelist."

For the interviewer, prospecting for interview sources is every bit as important as prospecting for topics to write about. "Where do you get all your ideas?" writers are asked constantly, usually by people who don't understand that there is a story in everything under the sun. The best writers recognize the potential for a story and find the right sources to tell that story.

Tracy Kidder readily admits that the topics of computers and housebuilding, by themselves, are not the types of subjects generally associated with entries on best-seller lists, yet his first two books focused on those topics and enjoyed time on those lists, as well as great critical acclaim and prestigious awards. For Kidder, selecting a subject to write about is a matter of satisfying his own sense of interest and curiosity in a way that appeals to a broad audience of potential readers.

"Choosing a topic is really an important issue because you're going to spend so much time and energy on it," he says. "The choice of subject is guesswork, but I generally have to feel that it's something I'm interested in. Then, of course, the next question is 'Will the people in the book turn out to be interesting?' "

Lawrence Linderman, author of scores of magazine profiles and interviews, agrees that the interviewer's personal interest in a topic or interview subject is crucial to the selection process. Like Tracy Kidder, Linderman emphasizes the importance of prospecting for interesting people to talk to.

"If you're going to be choosing your own interviews," he suggests, "you should really try to get people who almost have a friction in their personalities. I want some electricity, a sense that there's something behind those eyes that's inventive and not boring."

PROSPECTING FOR IDEAS

If you are a general assignment reporter for a newspaper, many of the story assignments coming your way will have been generated from the ideas of your editors; you will be handed an assignment, regardless of your interest in the topic. Many of your articles and interviews will be determined by news events. However, you might also keep lists of your own ideas, which you could work into your schedule of articles. These self-generated stories are the spices that keep the day-to-day tedium from becoming too constrictive.

Freelance writers are expected to generate their own article or interview ideas, and such freedom is one of the main attractions of this kind of writing. Unfortunately, too many freelance writers, particularly novices eager to publish, attempt to market work they feel an editor may be seeking, rather than work that interests them personally. Matching the right topic with the right editor is essential to selling your work, but you should never write any old thing simply for the sake of making a sale. Your work and self-respect will suffer if you do.

Prospecting for ideas and keeping topic files are two ways to stimulate development of writing projects. Ideas can be found almost anywhere.

Some of the most likely sources include:

■ *Newspapers and magazines.* These are the best places to prospect for ideas and start clip files. It's amazing how many ideas you can find in a single newspaper or magazine. National stories may have local interest, and vice versa. Newspapers publish the appearance schedules of celebrities passing through your area. Even the help-wanted ads or personals columns give clues to potential stories. When you're reading your newspaper or magazine, do so with a critical eye; if a story interests you or seems to be a likely topic for an article, clip it out and file it for future consideration.

■ *The library.* A weekly visit to the library should be part of every writer's schedule. In just an hour or two you can look at the newspapers and magazines on hand, as well as the new book arrivals. These sources will not only supply you with more article ideas than you could possibly pursue, but they will also give you a strong indication of the trends in book publishing and in the major newspapers and magazines.

■ *Bookstores.* Visits to bookstores are like visits to libraries: what better place to gauge trends than in the new-arrivals section of a well-stocked bookstore? When you are examining the books, read the flap copy. What topics are popular? What angles are being taken on these topics? Toward what readerships are these books being aimed? Books are excellent sources of newspaper or magazine article ideas. "Each week, we get more books than we could possibly review," says Roger Miller, book editor for *The Milwaukee Journal*. "If we can't review a book, I may send it to another section of the paper. It might be the start for a good idea for a story."

■ *Television.* As an industry, television is a slave to current topics and trends. Because of the immediacy of the medium, television is in a position to pounce upon anything of fast-breaking, current interest, whether it be absorbed in weekly programming or on the nightly news. From a single day's screening, you could come up with dozens of article ideas. As a bonus, you'll also come away with at least a minimal list of sources, since television news programs depend upon the same support quote methods as writers use. When you're watching such programs, jot down the sources that might work well in a newspaper or magazine article. Doing so can save you time when you're researching your story.

■ *Pamphlets, phone books, directories, junk mail, etc.* Article ideas can be found in the most unlikely places. A flyer that arrives in the mail can give you an idea for an interesting story to pursue. So can browsing through the Yellow Pages of your telephone book. People have unique or interesting jobs. Events are always being promoted. Unusual businesses exist. You can create a salable story idea from any of these.

■ *Hanging out.* Once the staple for ideas for newspaper columnists and reporters, hanging out has become a lost art in today's faster lifestyles. The competition between the print and electronic media has heightened the sense of urgency in the way the news is brought to the public. Instead of merely reporting the news as it occurs, or as it is brought to the attention of the media, reporters are now expected to uncover or "break" stories—to root around for stories hidden from the public or media. The uncovering of the Watergate scandal by Bob Woodward and Carl Bernstein, published in *The Washington Post,* is probably the most significant twentieth century example of reporters' breaking a news story of great consequence, and the success of that story has issued a challenge that the media have fervently pursued. As a result, there is an air of aggression in the way reporters pursue their stories.

But there is still much to say for the idea of sitting quiet and listening. Ideas and opinions are jostled around in conversations on the street, in restaurants and over drinks, and a fragment of overheard conversation, coupled with your inquisitive nature, may lead to a good article idea. Perhaps you can't wait for a story to come to you, but you can't ignore one that's in front of you either.

No matter where or how you prospect for ideas, you must always be on the alert. There's never a formal time to turn on creativity.

"You're never consciously or unconsciously looking for a story," says Bob Greene, syndicated newspaper columnist, occasional television reporter, and author. "Everything you see becomes a possibility. It's the idea that you never quit working."

Carry a small notebook or scrap of paper at all times, and make brief notations of any ideas that catch your fancy. Keep manila envelopes or file folders stocked with clippings. The ideas will build up and you will have to periodically sort through your lists and files, keeping the best of the ideas and discarding the rest. Since the average freelance writer or newspaper reporter is usually working on several writing projects at a time, the more ideas, the better.

DRAWING UP A LIST OF SOURCES

Once you have an idea that seems to be the skeleton of a good article, you'll need sources to help you tell your story and flesh it out. Finding the best available sources involves a process of selection. That procedure may take some time, as would be the case if you were writing an analytical piece on a topical subject with wide-ranging implications; or it may be determined very quickly, as would be the case if you were a reporter covering a specific news event; but you will find that you will always have choices in the sources you may interview. Sometimes the candidates are obvious; other times the candidates may not be readily apparent. The great story — as opposed to the average or poor story — depends upon the choices you make.

Pulitzer Prize-winning columnist Jimmy Breslin is a master of the good choice. Over the course of his career, he has written about scores of high-visibility news events, as well as hundreds of columns about the dramatic events that take place in the lives of average people, and he learned long ago that the best sources may be people who are at the margins of events rather than those who are actually at the center of them.

For his reportage of the nationally publicized execution of convicted murderer Gary Gilmore, Breslin repaired to the sporting goods store that had loaned the state the guns used to execute Gilmore. After talking to the store owner and patrons, Breslin was able to write powerful reportage that addressed his distaste for capital punishment and guns. In his coverage of the events surrounding subway vigilante Bernard Goetz, Breslin talked to a number of fringe observers, including the victims' friends, police officers, and even Breslin's own daughter, who was then working as a news assistant on the "CBS Morning News." His main source for his column on the murder of John Lennon was a police officer who drove the mortally wounded musician to the hospital.

"It's hard work," says Breslin, adding that many good storytellers prefer to go into television, where the money is better. Success in his medium, he says, involves a strong application to the most basic principles of the writing craft. "You can't do it without an awful lot of reporting," he asserts.

When you read one of Breslin's columns, you can see what he means. His sources are so strong that they appear to be the only reasonable ones for the story. The columns themselves are deceptively simple in their style. In reality, writing the column is a high-pressure job that requires Breslin to do hard legwork quickly, choose his sources, and write under constant deadline pressures.

In his typically brash style, Breslin explained the process when he wrote of the Lennon column: "I was home in bed in Forest Hills, Queens, at 11:20 P. M. when the phone and television at once said Lennon was shot. I was dressed and into Manhattan, to Roosevelt Hospital, the Dakota, up to the precinct, grabbed a cop inside, back to the Dakota, grabbed a cop outside, and to the Daily News. I wrote this column and made a 1:30 deadline. I don't think there is anybody else who can do this kind of work this quickly."

There is no doubt that much of Breslin's skill came from years of experience, from the almost countless number of times he's had to consider the available sources for a story and make instant decisions. It is a process that should be familiar to all writers, novice or veteran.

Before you conduct your interviews for an article or feature, you should draw up a list of potential sources. The list can be a formal written one, or it can be a list that you keep in your head, but it should be as comprehensive as your time and circumstances allow. The nature of these lists will vary. If you're a newspaper reporter with daily deadlines to honor, you'll be drawing up your lists and making your choices much faster than a magazine writer with two months to meet a deadline. If you're writing about an event, you'll be drawing up a list that's different from the type you would put together if you were writing about an issue.

Finding potential sources is a reasonably simple task, and your list of sources can be assembled in a number of ways; the main ones include:

■ *Prospecting.* Interview sources are everywhere, and you may find them by consulting a variety of reference materials, such as telephone books, city directories, magazine and newspaper indexes, court records, and so on. Potential interviewees become apparent while you're doing your initial research for a story (prior to the submission of a query letter), and more choices will present themselves as you go along. You'll find the names of experts in the newspaper or magazine articles you use for your research. If your article is on a topical issue, you'll see authorities interviewed on television. Any of these sources can be used in your article.

■ *Networking.* Many writers like to build a network of contacts who can help them locate sources or act as sources themselves. Networking is particularly effective for specialists, i.e., writers who focus on a specific field of interest. Sportswriters maintain contacts in Major League cities, while political writers develop intricate contact networks in Washington, D.C., state capitols, or city halls. These contacts are capable of answering questions the writer may have or, if they are not, they can point the writer in the direction of someone who is. It is not difficult to develop a network of useful sources on either a local or national level. What it does take is patience; networks are never developed overnight, and the best networks take years to put together.

■ *Recommendations.* One of the easiest ways to draw up a list of potential sources (and, in time, a network of sources) is to solicit recommendations from other reliable sources. You can also get ideas from editors, other writers, acquaintances, and even family members. When you're talking to an authority in a given field of interest, that person is certain to know other similar authorities—people who will add depth to your article. When you interview a person of this nature, never be afraid to ask for other potential sources. "When I'm interviewing someone for a book like *We Have A Donor,* the last question I always ask is, 'Who else?' " says Mark Dowie. "When I was working on that book, I wound up with a source list of three hundred to four hundred people. I attended a lot of meetings and conventions, and I learned about a lot of sources in those places."

■ *On the spot.* If you're covering a news event, your list of sources may have to be put together at the site of the event. At first glance, it may appear that your options are limited, either in actual numbers or in the quality of the available sources, but as we saw earlier in the Jimmy Breslin case, you will always have choices.

THE PERFECT SOURCE

The ideal source would be very knowledgeable—if not a recognized authority—on the topic you're writing about. This source would be a selfless individual devoted to the enlightenment of the world and would have no axes to grind. He or she would speak, without bias, in a manner that is compelling and exciting to the reader, and would be interested in addressing your issues without regard for personal gain.

The source: an eloquent saint. Interviewers dare to invent them in their dreams.

In the real world, sources bear the scars of flawed humanity. They can be petty or sullen, egotistical, devoted only to their own personal agenda, abrasive, vindictive, secretive, or protective of the very information you seek; they come in all shapes, sizes, colors, beliefs, and ages. They can possess many of the qualities of our eloquent saint, but you can wager that, given enough time, you'll be able to find characteristics that you don't like and never could admire.

Nevertheless, the fact that they are flawed, that readers can identify with (and therefore believe) them, that they share the interests or passions of the potential thousands of readers—this is what gives them the potential to add dimension and spin to your article.

Interviewers occasionally forget to expect flaws. In their zeal to secure their stories and meet deadlines, they hope for the ideal and are inevitably disappointed. They expect their sources to be open and frank. They want their preconceptions justified and, as the glut of libel cases would seem to indicate, if the sources don't fit into their preconceptions, they're willing to bend the truth or change it entirely. They pick the wrong sources for their topics, and then complain when the stories fail, as if the *sources* are at fault when things don't work out. In some cases, they fail to realize that some people just want to be let alone, that there are people out there who are not seduced by the modern idolatry of fame.

If this seems like a harsh indictment, consider the sliding reputation of the media in the minds of the general public. Writers, newscasters, reporters, and others are quick to point out that this indictment of the media is often a case of people's "shooting the messenger"; they also cite examples of the effective manipulation of public opinion against the media by recent political administrations. While there is truth in these defenses, it is also true that the media, in engaging in cutthroat competition that ultimately rewards the bottom line while rationalizing the body count added up along the way, has undermined its own reputation and credibility as much as any outside forces.

If we are indeed messengers, we must accept certain obligations that go with the message we carry, and this is where the importance of sources has its origin. The ideal source, as detailed earlier, may not exist, but we must nevertheless reach for the best sources available.

SELECTING THE BEST SOURCES

Whether you're prospecting for sources or choosing them from a list of candidates, you should consider a number of factors by asking yourself the following questions:

■ *Who is this person?* Readers demand credentials and are unlikely to accept what a person is saying, regardless of how intelligent or interesting, unless they believe the person is qualified to speak with authority on the topic. Credentials establish credibility. Job titles and positions are the type of credentials you're looking for, as well as any media exposure a source may have received. Readers want to be impressed. They enjoy hearing from someone they may have seen on the nightly news or read about in the newspaper. Notoriety can be as useful as fame, especially if you're writing an article on a controversial or debatable topic. Keep in mind that we're a "name-conscious" nation and, as deplorable at times as that may be, names sell stories.

■ *What does this person know?* Any interviewer you meet can tell you horror stories about interviews with people with impressive credentials but very little to contribute to a story. It's an interviewer's nightmare; too often, you won't discover this until your tape recorder is switched on and you are asking the questions. But you can diminish the odds of this nightmare occurring by asking yourself what a person can bring to a story that another person cannot. The best answer to this question? Experience. A good track record is as important as a person's name or position. Anyone can talk, and everyone has an opinion, but your best sources are going to be people with the breadth of experience necessary to underscore their statements. These are the people who are going to give you the anecdotes and examples that will further establish credibility and give color to your article.

■ *Why would this person want to talk to me?* It is the extremely rare interviewee who talks solely out of the goodness of his or her heart. Some agree to be interviewed because they enjoy seeing their names in print (yes, this is true even of famous people), while others may have personal agendas, such as the promotion of a product, in consideration. Some people just have an axe to grind. Some are dragged kicking and screaming into interviews, while others never seem to pause for breath. Everyone is motivated — even people who *refuse* to talk to you — so, if possible, it's a good idea to try to estimate what their motives might be *before* you contact or talk to potential sources. The best source is the one with either little or no apparent motive, or with a relatively harmless one (such as the promotion of a product); the least desirable sources will be the ones whose personal stakes in the interview are emotionally based (such as revenge). The former may keep you in the money, while the latter may bounce you into the courtroom.

■ *Why do I want to talk to this person?* This is the preceding question in reverse, and it's usually one that needs to be considered more by novice writers than by veterans. The worst motives you can have for choosing a particular source are personal motives, such as a desire to meet a celebrity. This certainly can be *one* of the reasons — many terrific articles and interviews have had their origins in a writer's personal interest in a source — but, generally speaking, you should be very cautious here. For one thing, you threaten the objectivity of your piece if you're "stargazing." (The same can be said about interviewing people you know — friends, acquaintances, or professional contacts.) You should also be very careful about choosing sources for whom you have strong negative feelings. You won't like all the people you interview over the course of your career, but it's dangerous to choose a source if you're hoping to make him look bad or show him up. You're always better off staying on neutral ground, as far as your feelings about a source are concerned.

■ *Does this person have something engaging to say?* The answers to the first three questions on this list can be used as indicators to the answer to this question. *How* something is said is almost as important as *what* is said, which is why people like Carl Sagan or Isaac Asimov are more interesting to listen to or read than others who may know as much or more about science than they do. As an interviewer, you'll want to talk to people who not only know what they are talking about, but who are also interesting to listen to. If you're going to the private sector for your sources — if you're interviewing people who have not been interviewed much before, if at all — you won't know how interesting they can be expected to be. However, it is something you can easily consider when you're thinking about the prospects of interviewing celebrities or authorities who have talked to the press on a number of occasions. When you're doing your research, keep this idea in mind. Does the person speak well? Does he or she have an interesting way of turning phrases? Do his or her statements bring out emotional responses in you? A colorful knowledgeable source is always better than a drab knowledgeable source, so the choices you make *before* you talk to people can greatly affect the effectiveness of your story, as well as the ease with which you'll be writing it.

OTHER FACTORS TO CONSIDER

Let's say that you've drawn up a list of potential sources and asked yourself all the previously mentioned questions about the candidates, and have come up with the best person (or persons) to talk to. You're convinced that you have a "can't fail" situation for your article.

Before you congratulate yourself too much — or even contact the source or sources—consider these last few factors:

■ *Availability*. Your ideal source may have spoken already at great length on the topic you're writing about and therefore may not care to discuss it further. Or the person might not wish to speak about it at all. Or maybe the person would like to discuss it but isn't in a position to do so. Or as is often the case with celebrities, some sources may not wish to speak until they have a product—a book, movie, record, etc.—to promote.

■ *Time*. Timing and availability can be inextricably joined. When choosing sources, you have to deal with a person's being available at the right time. The person may be busy, out of town, or otherwise inaccessible until too late to be included in your article. There are going to be occasions when your deadlines will eliminate certain sources from consideration, mainly because you cannot work a given source into your schedule or time frame.

■ *Geography*. Source location is especially important when you are writing for a national audience. Readers like to feel a proximity to the article they read; it gives them a sense of involvement. Unless the story itself depends upon your sources' being from a specific area, you're always better off selecting sources from different parts of the country than from one region alone. Try to establish a strong geographical cross section. The more diverse the geographic locations of the sources of your story, the better your odds of appealing to a wide audience of readers.

■ *Expenses*. The costs of using sources are all too often overlooked by freelance writers with good intentions but limited budgets. Many publications don't have budgets that accommodate lavish expense vouchers submitted by their contributors, and even those that do rarely pay expenses until after a story has been submitted. This means that you will have to foot the bill either entirely or until you're reimbursed. Expenses become a major consideration when you find yourself having to travel to interview your sources. The telephone isn't always a remedy, either, since long-distance interviews can be quite expensive, especially if you must conduct numerous interviews for your project. It's best to consider expenses *before* you propose an article to an editor, but if you don't and you subsequently find yourself assigned an article that forces you to budget your money, you'll have to make expenses a factor in your ultimate choice of sources for that article.

You can prepare yourself for some of the snags just listed by including alternate sources on your list of potential interviewees. When you are prospecting for sources — or for article ideas, for that matter — you can set priorities, but you should try to avoid placing yourself in the position where the success of your article depends upon the cooperation of a single source. In some cases, such as Q&A's, and to a lesser extent, profiles and news features, you will have to interview specific individuals, but even so, you can prepare for disappointment.

"I always take the point of view that most people are available to you," says Gary Provost, author of numerous magazine articles and books. "I query an editor on the assumption that I'll be able to talk to a person, but once in a while I can't. If I have to call an editor to say that I couldn't get to a person, I try to be ready with another name. I'm prepared to make a little trade."

KEEPING SOURCES AND TOPICS FRESH

While looking for topics to write about and sources to interview, you should keep your publication's lead times, as well as your deadlines, at the front of your mind. The span of time between an assignment deadline and the time an article is published is crucial, since much can happen between the time you turn in your story and the day readers are looking at it. People change jobs. Events occur in the time between the submission and publication of your article, shedding new meaning on the topic you're writing about. A topical issue can lose its freshness or shine.

This is not usually a major concern if you're writing for daily newspapers. They accommodate last-minute changes much more easily than magazines, which generally work with four- to six-month lead times. (In fact, it is not uncommon for a year to pass between the time a completed article manuscript is submitted and the time in which a magazine publishes it.) How you work with lead times will determine the freshness and, ultimately, the marketability of your article.

Good planning eliminates many potential snags. Look ahead when you are planning stories or lining up interviews; try to calculate the time it will take you to write an article and add six months to your estimated finishing time. Ask yourself if the story will be fresh at that time. For example, let's say you want to write a profile of a basketball player, and you would like to see the piece published at a time near the end of the regular basketball season, just before the playoffs begin. You estimate the profile will take six weeks to write. Using these figures, you would have to turn in your profile in late August or early September, since the playoffs begin in April, which probably means you would have to propose the article to an editor in May or June. That way, you would be giving the editor ample time to consider your query and respond, plus you'd be giving yourself a little extra breathing room to research and write the article.

Such planning isn't a hard-and-fast rule, of course, but it's a workable one. You will probably find that you won't need quite this much time to write and market your article, but by allowing yourself a little extra time, you're also 1) getting a jump on other writers who may be proposing a similar article; and 2) affording yourself time to submit your query elsewhere if it's turned down by your preferred market.

To keep your sources fresh and relevant, also use time projections when you're drawing up your list of sources. Is it likely that your source will be prominent six months down the road? Will he or she be in the same job or position? (You probably won't want to interview a lame duck senator two months before he leaves office — not if his position is a crucial part of your article.) Will your source even agree to discuss your topic in six months?

Successful prognostication is one of the most important aspects of capturing an editor's interest in an article query. By asking yourself a few questions about the future, you will also be helping yourself plan the questions you'll wish to ask an interviewee.

STAY REALISTIC

One day several years ago, I was having lunch with an articles editor of a large-circulation magazine, and while we are eating we batted article and interview ideas back and forth. I'd come to the meeting with a fairly substantial list of ideas that I wanted to sound off of this editor, but none of these seemed to click with him.

He finally asked me if I might be interested in interviewing a well-known baseball player for his magazine.

"You mean nobody's ever proposed an interview with this guy?" I asked, finding the notion difficult to believe.

"Oh, we get queries about him all the time," the editor replied. "There's one writer out there who's probably sent me a dozen queries over the years. There's no way I'm going to assign him the story."

The problem, this editor continued, was that any writer can submit a query, and any writer can propose an interview with the biggest-name celebrities in the business, but there were never any guarantees that the writer could produce the kind of story he was looking for. He went on to explain that his office was flooded with queries, submitted by writers who had never published an article in their lives, proposing interviews, profiles, or articles on people and topics that would tax the endurance and skills of some of the country's finest established writers. The editor's inevitable rejections were based on his feelings of skepticism, tempered by his belief that there was a reasonable risk in his assigning an inexperienced writer to such a story. He questioned that writers of such queries could even secure the interviews, and even if they did, he wasn't certain they could handle the material. When I reminded him that even his regular contributors had started somewhere at some time, he countered with the idea that most of the magazine's regulars began their relationships with his magazine with modest assignments and moved up the proverbial ladder.

"A person's going to have to have very special access to one of these high-visibility celebrities before I'm going to assign him the piece," the editor concluded.

This is not the kind of news that novice writers want to hear, but unfortunately it's true in all too many cases. There is, to varying degrees, a pecking order in every magazine or newspaper in the business. Editors prefer to work with writers they know of or have successfully worked with before, and they will offer assignments to those writers before they assign the same articles or interviews to novices or unknowns.

The same bias is found, though to a lesser degree, in interview subjects' willingness to be interviewed by novices or unknowns. Celebrities prefer to talk to writers they know or have heard about; they want their thoughts and statements published in the best publications. Faced with a huge number of interview requests, they winnow out for consideration those writers and publications that they believe will best serve their interests.

This is not to suggest that you shouldn't pursue the highest standards and goals in the articles you write or the people you interview. However, you should be realistic when you're prospecting for ideas or drawing up a list of potential sources for your articles. If, for example, you have never interviewed a politician, it's unlikely that you will be given an audience with the governor of your state. If you don't have impressive clippings or an assignment with a highly regarded newspaper or magazine, you probably will not land an interview with some of the top box office attractions in the motion picture industry. If your only writing experiences have been a few articles for your weekly newspaper, you'll probably have trouble selling an in-depth article query on a hot topic to the editors of *The New York Times Magazine*.

A realistic attitude, tempered by patience, will take you far. Start off modestly. Build up your list of published credits. Challenge yourself a little more, with tougher topics and better-known sources, in each new article you write. In time, you will have the credentials necessary to convince an editor that you are qualified to pursue a major story. Well-known interviewees will be more inclined to give you their time.

Interviewing is not simply a matter of turning on a tape recorder and asking questions; it's also a matter of opening doors. To be successful, you won't be aiming to get your foot in the door; you'll be working to have the door opened for you. You want to be invited in.

If you don't believe it, ask any salesperson.

RESEARCH AND PREPARATION

'll admit it: when it came to the topic of the importance of re-searching for interviews, I was naive until I was interviewed my-self.

I'd always taken the researching aspects of interviewing very seriously and I assumed that others did as well. The importance of solid researching is a principle that is drilled into aspiring writers as early as high school and introductory college courses in journalism. Instructors tell you that research is the foundation upon which the good interview is built, that being prepared for an interview — knowing something about your interviewee and preparing ques-tions in accordance with that knowledge — is as essential an element to bring to the interview as a notebook or tape recorder. Most stupid questions, we're told, are the result of poor researching and planning.

I could go on and on, but the bottom line is that researching is something that I've always taken for granted, and I always assumed that others did as well.

Until I found myself on the other side of the microphone.

Mind you, this was not a seat-of-the-pants interview. I was not a part of a fast-breaking news event, nor was I being interviewed for my reaction to one. Many interviews are conducted in quick-flash style, where preparation for the interview is impossible. This was not the case with my interview. A local paper wanted to profile me for a future Sunday edition, and I was contacted by a reporter more than a week before we sat down to talk. I was even given the focus of the profile in advance: the reporter was interested in (and perhaps amused by) the fact that I specialized in interviewing well-known writers, and he wanted to talk to me about those experiences. At that time, I was also working on a book about poet Allen Ginsberg. The reporter wanted to know how this local boy, this writer from a medium-sized Midwestern town, wound up talking to some of the most renowned writers in the country.

I should have known I was in trouble when I noticed that he preferred to take notes, rather than tape, our conversation. (More on that later in the book.) The interview took a sudden turn southward when he looked at his legal pad, upon which he had scribbled a handful of questions, and asked: "What writers have you interviewed?"

In my mind, I was in the interview's anticlimax when I answered his very first question.

THE IMPORTANCE OF PREPARATION

My problem with that reporter's first question was two-fold. First of all, the question indicated that he had done no research whatsoever. Granted, I'm not a lengthy entry in this year's *Who's Who,* but in the one-week-plus that he had from the time he called to line up the interview and the time we got together, he could have checked the magazine index at the local library and obtained a partial list of my published author interviews. He might even have looked up one or two of them and read them. Such minimal research is not, as the cliché goes, rocket science.

My second complaint about the reporter's question was in the way it was worded. Perhaps he *had* been too busy to spend those ten minutes at the library, but he didn't have to broadcast his ignorance by asking his question the way he did. He might have found some discreet way of getting me to talk about some of my interviews, a way which would have found me volunteering some information without his having to ask for it specifically. That sort of thing isn't rocket science, either.

Since that experience, I've conducted an informal survey on research practices. I've talked to people on both sides of the microphone, and I've heard an appalling number of horror stories — tales that brought me to the conclusion that I was naive in assuming that interviewers take the researching step of interviewing for granted.

"I haven't got the time for it," one interviewer, a reporter, told me. "I can get the information from the person I'm talking to. That's why I'm interviewing him in the first place."

That may be true to a certain extent, but many of the interviewees I talked to expressed resentment at the lack of preparation that was so obvious when they were interviewed. They were fed up with being asked questions they had answered numerous times and in great detail before. They complained of being asked "stupid questions." Many were concerned about the way an unprepared interviewer would handle their conversation in the published article.

"If the interviewer's not concerned about the facts before he comes in to talk to me, what's he going to do with them later?" one interviewee wondered.

Sound research and preparation assure you of the chance to carry on an intelligent, informed conversation with the interviewee. Research helps you design your interview, develop your line of questioning, and find a slant to your article. Good research is a compliment to the person you're interviewing; it tells him or her that you cared enough about the interview to look into the important details of the person's life, work, or interests. By showing a person you care in this way, you're encouraging the development of the confidence necessary to any good interview.

BEGINNING YOUR RESEARCH

Depending upon the nature of the piece you're writing, research can be a formidable task, requiring weeks or even months of work, or it can be quite simple, involving only a couple of phone calls and minimal library time. If you're working on an in-depth article on a topical issue or a profile of a celebrity who has been interviewed hundreds of times, you'll find a wealth of available research material just at your local library. Other research sources exist elsewhere. The task of researching will seem overwhelming if you don't organize your approach to it. Even if your research is minimal, you will want to organize in a way that helps you use your time to its best advantage.

The first thing you should do is determine the actual method you'll be taking at the beginning of your researching. That approach will probably fall into one of three categories:

- Scattershot research;
- General research; or
- Specific research.

The amount of time you have to conduct your research and preparation, along with the type of article you're writing, will help determine the best of these three approaches for your initial research.

For example, when you're conducting *scattershot research,* you will be gathering any information you can find on a person or topic. Generally speaking, you would use this approach if you know little or nothing about the subject you're researching, and your deadlines would have to be such that you would have plenty of time to sift through all information, relevant or irrelevant, that you gather. Biographers are fond of using this approach, as are writers working on in-depth profiles or lengthy articles. They photocopy or take notes on any printed materials they can find, and they conduct informational interviews well before they talk to their main sources. If you're working on an article or profile and have yet to pinpoint the angle you want to take in your piece, scattershot researching, with the variety of information that it provides, might be the best approach to take.

General research is similar to the scattershot approach, with the main distinction being that you'll have some idea of what you're looking for when you begin. You may have an idea of an angle or two that you want to pursue, and you would then address your research to all the general information you can find that is pertinent to those angles. You will have some sense of direction before you begin. Writers conducting research for Q&A style interviews often take general researching approaches, as do writers checking backgrounds before they conduct interviews for oral histories. You might find this approach useful if you were researching an article for which you would need a number of support quotes on several distinct topics.

Reporters often employ a *specific research* technique when they are working on the background for their stories. Strapped for time and usually working on very focused stories, reporters will make several calls to check on one specific angle or fact, or they might drop by the library or their newspaper's own clip files for a few pieces of information that will help them with their interviews. Other writers use this approach if they're looking for very specific information on a single topic, or clarification of information they've already obtained. This type of researching is fast and undemanding, and it prepares the writer for a similar type of interview.

On occasion, you will find yourself using more than one method of researching on a single article or interview. If you start out researching in the broad, general sense, you'll probably wind up focusing your research as you learn more about your topic and the angle you'll be taking in your article. Or you might find that a specific topic has broad implications; if this occurs, you will probably fan out your research.

The important thing is to know where to begin. Once you've started, you can always move in the direction in which your research takes you.

THE RESEARCH/WRITING METHOD

Many writers working on long projects (such as books, or multipart newspaper or magazine articles) prefer to research, interview, and write almost simultaneously. These writers "block" their projects into chapters or sections and approach each section as if it were a self-contained article. The research/interview/writing cycle is accomplished in each section and then repeated in the next. The theory behind this practice is that you learn while you're writing, and what you learn in an early section of a writing project will affect the way you research or interview for a later section.

Other writers take a two-pronged researching approach: they research for their interviews, conduct them, and then research further to add dimension or color to what they learned from their interviews.

Tracy Kidder has taken the two-pronged approach in his three books, and the method has worked well for him. "I often make a gesture toward learning something about a subject in general by doing some reading," he says about the beginning of his researching, "but I usually find that my interest sort of flags and then becomes intense once I've gotten ahold of the story. For *Among Schoolchildren,* I did all of the research and then I did the writing. With *Soul of a New Machine,* I was researching and writing almost simultaneously. With *House,* I did some writing early on and then brought in the material I call the 'exteriors' — the library research — into the stories. Exteriors are the materials that lie outside the actual story, the things that give a subject its historical or national context. It's mostly library research. I do the library research while I'm writing, when I feel I need it."

This simultaneous research/writing method enables a writer to gather further information as it is needed for a particular section of a project. It is a building-block approach to writing an article. To employ this method, you must be very organized and have a strong sense of the direction your article or book is taking. Without such organization, the method can be disruptive to the flow and pacing of your writing, causing you to spend more time on revising and reworking a piece than you would have spent if you did all your research before you conducted your interviews or began your writing.

WHERE TO FIND INFORMATION

There used to be a time when research meant legwork. Getting information was time-consuming, occasionally expensive, and often frustrating. Reporters didn't even know that some of the published information existed, let alone where and how to secure it. People would have to run themselves all over the map just to obtain a few pieces of critical information.

Today, there is still plenty of legwork involved in researching, but data bases, FAX machines, telephone modem, and other information storage, retrieval, and transfer systems have cut back the amount of time, expense, and frustration a researcher encounters in a search for information. It's quite realistic to say that if something exists and has been documented, it can be located by a vigilant researcher. With such an abundance of existing informational sources, there is little excuse for an interviewer's being unprepared for a conversation.

There is no way that one could possibly list all existing sources of information available to writers, but there are many that are easy to locate, accessible, useful, and to use some of today's computer jargon, user-friendly. Some of these sources give you the research information you're seeking, while others will direct you to the sources. The following are some that you should be familiar with and employ whenever you're preparing for an interview.

For general information:

- *Encyclopedias.* All libraries have general encyclopedias (*World Book, Encyclopaedia Britannica,* etc.) which can be used for thumbnail sketches on almost any subject imaginable. Encyclopedias dealing with specific fields of interest are also available. Both types are excellent sources of quick information and are a good place to begin your research.

- *Current Biography.* A monthly publication, bound at the end of each year into annual yearbooks, *Current Biography* features brief (two-four pages) though reasonably detailed portraits of people in the public eye. Also listed at the end of each entry are other published articles about the person being profiled.

- *Who's Who.* There is a large variety of volumes under the "Who's Who" publishing umbrella (*Who's Who, Who Was Who, Statesmen's Who's Who,* etc.), and these books offer basic information about prominent people in all fields of interest. Accomplishments, published credits, and important dates are included. An excellent source for general background information.

- *Newspaper and Magazine Indexes.* Indexes have long been the staple of research sources. The *Reader's Guide to Periodical Literature,* along with the *Magazine Index,* list recently published articles about people, events, and issues in a great variety of publications. Newspapers such as *The New York Times* and *The Wall Street Journal* publish their own bound directories of the articles they published. Libraries carry many of these indexes, and if your public library doesn't have them, you can usually find them in a nearby university library.

- *Books in Print.* Published in volumes devoted to subjects, authors, and titles, the *Books in Print* series will give you the information you need to look up published books on a topic or by a particular author. All libraries keep these books in stock.

- *Miscellaneous directories.* Most library reference shelves have an assortment of directories that are very useful when you are prospecting for sources or doing background checks in your research. Associations and organizations publish their own directories, as do universities and businesses. These directories supply you with names, addresses, phone numbers, positions, and other critical information about experts who can help you with your research or serve as sources in your articles.

- *Newspapers.* Back issues of local newspapers are generally available either in paper copies or microfilm. Back issues of nationally distributed newspapers (*The New York Times, The Washington Post,* etc.) can be found on microfilm in libraries in large cities or on college campuses.

■ *Library catalog files.* The subject listings in your library's catalog files should offer you a representative listing of books on topics you'll be writing about. These files will not only tell you of the books the library has on hand, but they will also give you a better indication of the scope of your article's research and ultimately, writing.

The best way to acquaint yourself with available reference books is to spend a few hours in your library's reference books section when you're beginning your research. If you live in a large city, you'll find hundreds of available reference books. If you can't find what you're looking for, ask for assistance. Many libraries keep important reference books and documents behind counters for their own reference service librarians, and just because a book isn't sitting on a shelf where you can see it doesn't mean a library doesn't have it on hand.

For specific research—facts, dates, and other specific information—there are an equally large number of sources available. Those sources include:

■ *Reference services.* Libraries in many large cities provide, free of charge, reference services that can save you a trip to the library, as well as the time it takes to look up a fact or two. Ask a question and a reference librarian will find the answer. A single phone call will get you the fact you're looking for.

■ *Blue Books.* State and city governments publish "blue books" that list statistics, figures, names, and positions of all kinds of public servants and government-related topics. Need a figure for the population of an upstate city? The name of an alderman in that city? General census information? Blue books provide these statistics.

■ *Statistical abstracts and yearbooks.* Terrific sources for figures and statistics, these books gather a wealth of information taken by the Census Bureau and other government agencies.

■ *Public documents.* Birth and death records, court reports, arrest records, marriage applications, and real estate records—

all are available to the public, as are the minutes of public hearings.

- *Government pamphlets.* Government agencies issue pamphlets and brochures on their organizations, and many of these publications offer statistics and information useful for issues-oriented articles and interviews.
- *The Congressional Record.* This periodical is a must if you're researching for an interview dealing with hot, topical, political issues.
- *Almanacs.* Every year, several publishers issue inexpensive paperback almanacs that are crammed with useful information and statistics. An almanac, along with a dictionary, atlas, and desk encyclopedia are essentials for every nonfiction writer's desk reference library.
- *Annual reports.* Many corporations make their annual reports available to the public, and these reports are filled with statistics on the corporations' financial dealings, as well as listings of their officers and transactions from the preceding year.

How you use these and other sources will depend upon the extent of your research, the time in which you have to do it, and the approach you're taking. When preparing for an interview, you should be conscious of gathering both general and specific information. General research will help you with your overall discussion, while specific information will help you underscore or fine-tune that discussion. Perhaps most important, the combination of general and specific information will be very useful when you organize your interview and design the questions you want to ask your interviewee.

USING RESEARCH TO DETERMINE AN ANGLE

If you are thorough in your research and inquisitive about what you learn, you'll find that what has previously been recorded about a person or topic will accentuate what *hasn't* been written. There will be holes or unanswered questions in the research materials you read, as well as topics of discussion that were either ignored or not explored as fully as they could have been. Recent events may have created a situation where an updating is needed.

By paying close attention to what has and has not been written, you can accomplish two tasks. First, you will know what questions and angles have already been addressed in other interviews, profiles, and articles, so you'll be prepared to avoid repetition in the questions you ask and the article you write. Second, you'll be able to add depth or spin to your article. Your research should give you ideas about what angles to pursue in your piece.

While you're researching, take plenty of notes. Look for patterns. What topics has your interviewee addressed most often? What questions does he or she answer the most? What angles have other writers taken in their articles? What could you add to what is already known about a person or topic?

Newspaper columnist and author Bob Greene remembers a time when he pursued an interview with former President Richard M. Nixon. Like so many people of his generation, Greene had detested Nixon while he occupied the White House; years later, however, as a professional writer, Greene found that his anger with Nixon had been replaced by a sense of curiosity. Who, Greene wondered, was this man, once so capable of eliciting such powerful emotional responses from millions of people?

If given an interview opportunity with Nixon, most reporters would have zeroed in on the major issues of the former president's era, particularly the Vietnam War, Watergate, and a fall from grace that saw Nixon moving from the height of a huge election victory in 1972 to the depths of his resignation from the presidency in disgrace two years later. These topics had been written about extensively, but it is unlikely that readers or critics would have accused Greene of rehashing if he'd gone back over that familiar territory. It's not often that one is granted an audience with a former president and, given the time restrictions of such interviews, a reporter is likely to move directly to the highlights or lowlights of the president's career.

Greene avoided the temptation. Feeling that Nixon "had been through something no one else had," Greene decided to talk to Nixon on a human, rather than political, level. The resulting interview made national headlines. "I think he liked the idea that I approached him in a human way," Greene says of Nixon. "It's funny. We didn't talk about politics at all. We talked about Nixon the man. To me, if I can reach the humanity in an interview subject, I don't want to talk about anything else."

Reaching for the humanity in someone is Greene's journalistic signature, and finding such angles *before* the interview is an important aspect of the craft of interviewing. Before you call a potential interviewee or turn on your tape recorder, look at your research and see if you can form an idea of what you hope to accomplish in the interview itself. How do you intend to tell your story? From what angle? How can you devise questions that accomplish this?

Answering these questions will help you plan your interview and place the questions you want to ask in perspective. Sometimes, as in a situation where you're covering a news event, answers will unfold at the scene; at other times, such as a scenario that finds you interviewing a subject for a long period of time over several sessions, the interview itself will direct you toward some of the answers.

Still, you should have an idea of what you're looking for prior to your interview. Your research will help you in this area.

TOO MUCH RESEARCH

Although it seems improbable that you could know too much, that you could gather too much research, there are ways in which your research can work against you. You can spend too much time researching and threaten your deadline. Worse yet, you could jeopardize an interview itself. George Plimpton, who has conducted a number of interviews for *The Paris Review* and edited them all, remembers two occasions in which too much research cost his publication an important interview.

"One has a fear of being not quite well enough prepared and going in there and wasting an interviewee's time," Plimpton admits. "So you keep putting the interview off. We did that with Somerset Maugham and then all of a sudden he died. The same thing happened with J.P. Marquand. We decided we hadn't done enough homework—there were three or four more books to read—and we lost an opportunity to see him. I've always regretted that terribly."

Those examples, of course, are drastic ones. You normally don't have to consider an interviewee's health when you are conducting your research. On the other hand, if you've put in a reasonable amount of time on your research and feel as if you could carry on a decent, even if not definitive, exchange with a person, you shouldn't let what you don't know stand in the way of your conducting the interview.

As we'll see in Chapter Five, there are occasions during an interview when ignorance works in your favor. Knowing too much might translate into your taking some issues for granted — issues or events that your readers may not be aware of. You may settle for less than a complete answer to a question to which you know part of the answer. You may feel too secure with your knowledge.

Interviewees don't expect you to know everything about them; if you did, you wouldn't be interviewing them in the first place. If it's apparent that you've done homework before the interview, the person you're talking to will be happy to fill in some of the blanks for you. After all, by supplying you with information, he's showing off his expertise.

When you're beginning your research, set a schedule for the time you'll be spending in gathering information. Adhere to that schedule. If you use all your interviewing skills, your conversation will provide you with the rest of what you need.

DESIGNING THE INTERVIEW

Research and background checks aren't the only ways that you prepare for an interview. You'll also want to design the interview itself. You'll want to know what questions you should ask and how you should ask them. Such preparation will keep you from wasting your and your interviewee's time.

The trick, however, is to keep from seeming *too* formal. You need answers, but you won't get the best answers if you come across as a robot. You need to connect with your interviewee in a way that transcends the professional obligations you both feel.

The best interviews are both controlled *and* spontaneous. As the interviewer, your job is to guide the conversation along, to direct it to those areas of greatest interest to your readers. However, you should never be so intrusive as to dam the flow of an interviewee's thoughts. You must be willing to improvise.

Studs Terkel compares his method of interviewing to the way jazz is played. That style, he claims, affords a person the opportunity for creative expression within a prearranged framework.

"Jazz is improvisatory," says Terkel. "There's a skeletal framework — a beginning, a middle, and an end — but it allows for *creating* as well as interpreting. Say Ernie Wilkins wrote a song for Count Basie. When Joe Newman got up to blow the trumpet for his solo, he had a framework, but he was also improvising.

"So it is with a conversation. I have an idea in the beginning —

I don't just shoot blindly. I have ideas, but I make adjustments. You adjust; sometimes you change the sequence of questions. Suppose a person says something that I didn't think he was going to say. He leads me to something else. It's like jazz: you improvise. If a person says something that's unprepared for, it's *right*. I just go on to something else."

For those who have enjoyed Terkel's books or radio program, the effects of his interviewing philosophy are delightful: Terkel's interviews are compelling, unpredictable, and often emotionally charged. Interviewees are willing to say anything to Terkel, where they may hold back when talking to interviewers who insist on strictly following a preset list of questions.

The key to this success, as Terkel suggests, is to take a *creative* approach to interviewing. This can be done regardless of the type of article you're writing or the circumstances you're writing under. You can be creative while interviewing a celebrity for a magazine article or while talking to a survivor of a natural disaster for a news story. In all interviews, what you want to avoid is *predictability*.

Predictability is the greatest enemy of any interview. Readers despise it and interviewees have come to almost expect it. An interviewer moves in and asks the same tired questions or, just as bad, questions that can be answered with pat, prepared answers. We've all suffered through "how did you feel?" interviews ("How did you feel when the flood wiped out your home and left you and your family totally destitute?" "How did you feel when you won the Olympic Gold Medal?"), as well as interviews that are little more than a rehash of every other interview with a given individual. Far too often, just obtaining an interview with a "name"—newsmaker or celebrity—overshadows in the minds of interviewers and editors what that person has to say.

There is certain to be an element of predictability in any interview. When an actress tours the country to plug her latest movie, she's going to want to address questions about the movie. (She may even insist upon that being the only topic of discussion.) A politician running for office will want to address certain issues central to his campaign. Readers *will* be curious to hear how a disaster survivor feels about his plight. Still, by incorporating good interview planning with solid researching, a dash of common sense, and a sense of creativity, any interview can avoid the predictability that plagues so many of the published interviews on the market today.

HOW TO DESIGN AN INTERVIEW FRAMEWORK

Once you have an idea of the angle you hope to pursue, you can focus your attention on designing an interview that increases your chances of getting the information you're seeking. This is generally a two-step process:

- Designing the framework of the interview itself; and
- Preparing specific questions that fit into the interview's framework.

The framework of an interview is the actual approach you'll be taking in gathering your information during the interview. This step can be compared to a photographer's choosing a lens with which to take a picture. Sometimes you'll want to concentrate on a broad field of vision, while at other times you'll be focusing on something at close-up range; very often, you'll find yourself moving from the broad to the specific, or vice versa. To achieve the desired results, your choice of interview framework can be as important as a photographer's choice of camera lens.

The nature of your article, as well as the amount of time you have with which to write it, will determine the framework of your interview. General assignment reporters for daily newspapers use a different framework for their articles from the ones used by magazine writers who have a greater, more flexible choice in angles and more time to write their stories.

A general assignment reporter, for example, would probably use a *tunnel framework* for the majority of his or her interviews. This framework, as its title implies, is very focused and narrow in scope, inviting quick, informative responses to queries about a single event. As interviewer, you're soliciting specific information or brief reactive responses:

Q. *This was the third home run you've hit this month, after going the first two months of the season without a round-tripper. Is this a matter of your settling in and overcoming rookie jitters?*

A. I don't know. Maybe . . . I'm finally getting to the

point where I'm seeing pitchers for a second or third time. That helps a lot. You get used to pitching on the Major League level.

Q. *What kind of pitch did you hit for the homer tonight?*
A. It was a fastball, up around the letters. I'd fouled off a couple of curveballs before he came in with his heater. I was sitting on the fastball all the way.

Q. *Were you surprised to see a fastball when he was ahead of you in the count?*
A. Yeah. He probably figured he'd fool me.

Q. *Which he did the last time you faced him: you struck out twice and grounded out once. Tonight, you were two-for-four. That must do wonders for your confidence.*
A. No question about it. I always knew I could hit Major League pitching, but knowing something and going out and doing it are two different things.

The framework for the line of questioning in this interview excerpt is very tight — the focus, technically, being on a single pitch in one baseball game. The interviewer will only be using a couple of the hitter's quotes in his coverage of the game, and he's chosen to use the occasion of the home run to elicit a few remarks about the young player's confidence in his ability to play baseball on the Big League level. Using a tunnel framework for the interview is the best approach for this interviewer, because he's reporting about a single event.

A feature writer for the same newspaper, however, might take a different approach. Let's say you've been assigned a medium-length feature on the same rookie ballplayer for your Sunday newspaper. You have more room in which to tell your story, your focus isn't as tight, and your deadline isn't as tight as the daily reporter's. For this article, you might use a *funnel framework* for your interview with the player. In this framework, you begin with a broad line of questioning and focus as you go along. You might begin with a general discussion of the player's first three months in the

Major Leagues, your questions designed to obtain general information on the difference between life in the Major Leagues and Minor Leagues, the changes in lifestyle, and so on. After the player has given you his general assessment, you would begin to question him in more specialized areas, angling for specifics to color in the anecdotes he gave you in the general discussion. This framework is good for the interviewer for several reasons: first, it allows the interviewee the opportunity to relax and tell his story before the questions become more demanding and specific; second, by doing so, the interviewee is providing the interviewer with ideas for further questioning; finally, framing an interview in this manner helps keep the questioning organized.

Investigative journalists are fond of using the funnel interview framework because it is a natural way of setting up tough questions. By addressing the general topics first, you're setting the table for the hard, specific questions you'll be asking later, much the way attorneys operate when they are questioning witnesses in court.

The *inverted funnel* framework works in the opposite way: you start with a specific question and work your way out. This framework works well for "issues-oriented" articles or personality profiles. If, for example, you were writing a profile of Stephen King, the popular horror novelist, you might want to begin your interview with specific questions about his most recently published book. From there, you could fan out to a general discussion about horror fiction. Once again, you're letting your interviewee help design the tone and direction of the conversation. Stephen King has been interviewed countless times on the topic of horror fiction, so starting the interview with a general discussion may find you rehashing old material, whereas a discussion of a specific book may give you an idea or two on how to work in a fresh angle on this general topic.

As previously mentioned, time and the type of article you're writing will act as strong factors in your determination of the framework to use for your interview. Your research will also play a role, as will the circumstances of your interview and the personality or nature of your interviewee. Through trial-and-error experience, good interviewers develop an instinct for finding the proper framework for their interviews, just as good photographers seem to have an instinct for the best lens to choose for a particular picture.

With a good framework, you'll be prepared to improvise in your interview.

BLOCKING OUT THE INTERVIEW: AN ORGANIZATIONAL OPTION

If time allows, many interviewers like to "block out" their interviews before they prepare the actual questions they want to ask. After deciding upon the framework for the interview, they outline the topics to be discussed in the interview, along with the probable sequence in which the various headings are likely to be addressed. (See sample on page 224.)

Blocking out the interview helps you organize. If you have been thorough in your research, you already have a number of topics and question areas in your head, but by putting them on paper you're making the preparation of questions easier and more organized — much more so than if you were to sit down and simply begin to write down the questions that come immediately to mind.

USING OPEN-ENDED AND CLOSED QUESTIONS

The way you word a question is as important as the question itself. The difference between a thoughtful, properly worded question and a sloppy, poorly worded question is the difference between a clear, complete answer and a vague or incomplete answer. An interview should be neither a cross-examination nor an elusive, pointless encounter; instead, it should be a conversation consciously designed to elicit general *and* specific responses. As the person responsible for keeping an interview within a given framework, you should know when and how to ask questions that allow your interviewee to speak freely, as well as when and how to ask questions that clarify points or bring you specific information. To do this, you will be using a mixture of open-ended and closed questions. Each type of question has characteristics that invite very different types of responses.

Open-ended questions encourage lengthy answers, such as overviews, descriptions, opinions, and anecdotes. These questions often start with the words "how" or "why," and in asking open-ended questions, you're encouraging your interviewees to explain. People reveal much about themselves when they're answering open-ended questions and, if you're listening well, you will be given more clues for follow-up, and for more specific questions. However, asking too many open-ended questions can be hazardous to the interview. You may want your interviewee to talk, but you don't want him or her to ramble or meander all over the map. Too many open-ended questions can lead to that effect; they can also be intimidating to people who are accustomed to dealing with the precise, or to people who are shy or untalkative.

Closed questions seek brief, specific answers. If you're trying to gather facts for a news story or magazine article, closed questions will help you gain much of the information you need. ("Who was there?" "How long did the meeting last?" "What color was her coat?" These are examples of closed questions.) Asking too many closed questions can make an interviewee feel as if he or she were being interrogated and it may be irritating, such as this exchange I overheard at a local fast food restaurant:

Customer. I'd like a cup of coffee.

Q. Large or small?
Customer. Large

Q. Caffeinated or de-caf?
Customer. Caffeinated.

Q. Cream or sugar?
Customer. Black.

Q. To stay or to go?
Customer. To go.

Q. Anything else?

In this case, each question was necessary for the counter worker to determine what the customer wanted, but this particular worker fired the series of closed questions at the customer in such a rapid-fire sequence that the customer was beginning to show irritation by the time the brief encounter had ended. The necessary questions were sounding too much like a cold interrogation. The same impression can be given by interviewers who string too many closed questions together.

Ideally, you should mix your open-ended and closed questions in accordance to the framework of your interview. If, for example, you are working within an inverted funnel framework, you would begin with a few select closed questions and use the answers to direct you to open-ended questions that expand upon the facts you've been given. With a funnel interview framework, you would do the opposite.

Control of the interview itself can be determined by your mixture of open-ended and closed questions. By eliciting lengthy responses, open-ended questions give the interviewee more control of the interview, while closed questions put you, the interviewer, at the proverbial helm. Bearing this in mind will help you guide the direction and pace that your conversation is taking.

PREPARING QUESTIONS

Open-ended and closed questions can be worded in a large variety of ways, and while the wording of these questions will depend largely upon the person you're interviewing, time-tested, trial-and-error interviewing has proven some types of questions to be much more effective than others.

Some questions, for example, are surefire giveaways of an interviewer's preconceptions and therefore should be used with extreme caution, if at all. Others are vague or confusing to the interviewees and thus produce inadequate responses. There are even questions that discourage any response at all.

Among the problem questions:

■ *Leading questions.* There is a subtle but very real distinction between the leading *question* and the leading *comment.* The leading question ("Aren't you angry about the way the critics have treated your latest play?") compromises your sense of objectivity and might invite a hostile response, while a leading comment ("You must have been very pleased to win such a prestigious award"), if worded with sensitivity and used sparingly, can gently prod an interviewee into clarifying an answer or expanding upon a response. If nothing else, these leading comments can keep a conversation going. But *both* forms are manipulative and risk the scorn of the interviewee who resents the notion of being patronized or being pulled through the conversation. In fact, some interviewees resent this so much that they wind up responding more to a perceived attitude than to a question. You might even find yourself being "put on" by your interviewee's response; an obvious or half-serious leading question may be greeted with an obvious, half-serious, or put-on, answer.

■ *Obvious questions.* Obvious questions (queries to which the answer is either known or can be assumed) get obvious answers — if they're answered at all. Interviewers who ask this kind of question are usually biding time or are unprepared. "How did you feel?" questions, with few exceptions, fall into this category. ("How did you feel when you won the Nobel Peace Prize?" What is the interviewee to say, that he or she felt lousy?) For every situation there is an obvious question, and it should be avoided. By all means, get that person's reaction to winning the Nobel Peace Prize, but do so in a way that doesn't insult your interviewee's — and your readership's — intelligence. In many cases, just encouraging the person to continue talking will lead to a reflection of that person's feelings, or to an opening you can use to inquire about them. Let the conversation lead you into questions of this nature, rather than leading the conversation into them yourself.

■ *Multiple choice questions.* By offering your interviewee a choice of answers ("When did you decide to join the priesthood? When you were a boy? As a teenager? A young adult?"), you are again asking a person to tailor an answer to one of your preconceptions. It may be that one of your preconceptions is correct, but you should ask the question in a manner that entices your interviewee to volunteer his own answer. In the first case, you're placing words or ideas into your interviewee's mind before he has had the opportunity to consider the question and, by doing so, you risk getting a less than complete, truthful, or thoughtful response — much less than you might have received if you'd simply let the interviewee answer.

■ *Stupid questions.* Contrary to the idea that there is no such thing as a stupid question, there are a number of questions that are ill-advised, inappropriate, or just plain stupid. It would be inappropriate to ask private citizens questions about private affairs that have no bearing upon the article you're writing, just as it would be a bad idea to ask an actress to list the titles of her films; in the former, you're delving into areas that are none of your business, while in the latter you're admitting that you didn't care enough about a person's public business to research it prior to the interview.

Hypothetical questions ("If you could be any kind of rodent, what would it be?") can be stupid, although some carefully worded "if" or "what if" questions can produce interesting, telling responses. Most interviewers have horror stories about the stupid questions they've asked—it happens to the best of interviewers—but these questions usually surface in the heat of the battle and are not planned before the interview. Avoid hypothetical questions when you're planning your interview, as well as questions that have little or nothing to do with the article you're writing. Doing so will decrease the risk of your asking a stupid question.

■ *Comment questions.* During the course of any interview, you are likely to ask a few questions that are not questions at all but, instead, are statements or comments. ("And after the election, you drove directly to Washington D.C.") These comments can be very useful in their ability to move a conversation along and show that you are familiar with the interviewee's story, but an abundance of such comments undermines the interview. An interviewee may wonder why you are bothering with an interview if you know so much already. He may assume that you know more than you do and therefore not volunteer useful or complete responses to your other questions. Some comment questions, designed by interviewers as probes or icebreakers ("It's good to see your book at the top of the best-seller list") produce no quotable responses at all ("Right. I'm happy about it"). Keep your questions in the interrogative structure, and word them so they command a response, rather than another comment.

■ *Dualistic questions.* Like multiple choice questions, dualistic questions—questions that give a person two opposites to consider for answers—can bring a multitude of problems. "Whether or not" questions fall into this category; "Do you know whether or not you'll be healthy enough to run in the Boston Marathon next month?" (If the person says "yes," you still don't know exactly what he means.) Either/or questions have the same pitfalls. There are almost always more than two choices to any answer, and by offering only two choices to an interviewee, you might find yourself receiving a response that's vague or not exactly true.

■ *Apologetic questions.* Interviewers will sometimes use an apology as a prefix to a tough question ("I hate to ask, but . . ." "I know it sounds stupid, but . . ."). These apologetic prefixes are intended to take an edge off the question itself — to hint to the interviewee that you're on his side — but they can produce a boomerang effect. An interviewee may agree with you ("Yes, it *is* a stupid question") or he may worry about what you intend to do with his response ("If he hates asking the question, why is he asking it?"). In using an apology as a lead-in to your question, you are tipping off your interviewee. You're telling him that what follows your apology is going to be a question that will be difficult to answer; furthermore, you're saying that the tough question must be important because you're proceeding with it, even though you hate asking it.

Red flags should be going up in your mind every time you find yourself drawing up a question that falls into one of the above-mentioned categories. These questions can block the flow of good conversation. They can cause your interviewee to pause and wonder why you're asking some of your questions. They may even irritate or anger the person.

While you're working on the wording of your questions, you should also be aware of three other types of questions that may stymie a conversation. These questions may not have the adverse effect on the interviewee that the earlier-mentioned types may have, nevertheless they do invite inadequate or incomplete responses. Be very cautious about asking:

■ *Questions that are too long.* Don't spend too long in framing or introducing a question — certainly no longer than two or three sentences. The longer you talk, the less clear the point of your question will be to your interviewee. If you have a major question that needs framing, set it up through a series of shorter questions that lead logically to the main inquiry.

■ *Questions with several parts.* In press conferences, interviewers will often ask two-part questions (a main question, with a follow-up), but two-part or multipart questions can be confusing in one-on-one conversations, resulting in your interviewee's addressing only one of the questions in his or her response. Keep your questions simple. Break down your multipart questions into a logical sequence of shorter questions. Doing so will give you better, more complete answers.

■ *Questions that can be answered with "yes" or "no" or with other one-word responses.* These kinds of questions may be asked if you're looking for a definitive response or a lead-in to another question, but by themselves, they can put the brakes on a smooth-running conversation, especially if you ask a couple of these questions in succession. If you're looking for quotable material, a simple "yes" or "no" won't do.

THE BEST QUESTIONS

Unlike the types of problem questions just cited, the most effective questions you can ask will either solicit specific information or encourage your interviewee to give you examples, anecdotes, details, or opinion. They are posed in such a way as to make you look inquisitive yet objective, firm but fair. They compel an exchange of ideas.

When you are preparing your interview questions try to work in as many questions that fit into the following categories as possible.

■ *Questions that begin with "how" or "why."* Some questions serve two purposes. First, they call for examples, anecdotes, and, generally, more detailed answers; second, by answering the questions, your interviewees are engaging in a type of self-analysis that will beef up your interview or article. These questions work nicely for interviewers because there is a built-in sense of objectivity in the way the questions are worded. You're asking an interviewee to tell his or her side of the story; you're stepping aside for the voice that matters. In an indirect sense, you're deferring to your interviewee.

■ *Questions that call for specific answers.* There's still much that can be said for "who, what, where, and when," as well as "how" and "why" questions. Facts, figures, dates, and locations are important. They form clear pictures in readers' minds. Readers want specific information, and you should ask plenty of questions that call for that information. "I ask a lot of questions that seem trivial to the people I'm asking," says Gary Provost. "I might ask what kind of cigarettes a person was smoking or what kind of car he was driving, and while those questions may seem trivial or out of context to people, they don't realize that I'm trying to create a picture for the reader. I may have just finished a scene and I've got everything I need except the color of the car. That's why I have that question."

■ *Questions that expand upon what's already known.* When

you're conducting an interview, the last thing you want to hear is an answer you've already seen or heard elsewhere. People who are interviewed often tend to repeat themselves. They answer the same questions over and over, and after a while they have slick, stock responses to the questions they are asked most often. However, this does not mean that you cannot go over familiar territory — indeed, some editors will demand it and interviewees will expect it. When you're designing your interview questions, go over your notes and research. Ask yourself how you can expand upon what you already know. Then design a question that poses that angle to your interviewee.

∎ *Questions that clarify*. Not only will you want to expand upon existing information, but you'll also want to clarify any past statements that may not be clear. You'll also want to get clarification of any vague answers an interviewee may give you during the interview. Experienced interviewers can almost predict when they're going to receive vague answers, and they're always prepared to ask "What, exactly, do you mean by that?" "In what way?" or similar questions that call for explanation. Prepare ahead of time to ask for examples for clarification.

∎ *Questions that probe*. Like questions that expand or clarify, probing questions are designed to dig deeper into a topic of discussion. Some probes are aimed at reaction ("What do you think of the President's decision to send more troops to Central America?"), while others are designed for further explanation ("I'm not sure I understand what you meant when you told *The Boston Globe* that you'd be happy to support gun control legislation. In the past you've always opposed it.") Probes, like "how" and "why" questions, produce responses that tell you something about your interviewee's character, and they're especially useful tools for writers working on profiles or Q/A-style interviews.

∎ *Questions that display your objectivity*. When you're preparing tough questions, try to find a way of wording them that isolates you from any negative criticism your interviewee may have heard. You're usually safe by putting the blame for such criticism on someone else ("Your critics say that . . . ." or "It's been said that . . . ."), but be prepared to cite your sources if your interviewee challenges you with a *"Who* said that?" response. Careful phrasing of challenging questions makes you look objective, rather than aggressive, and it will encourage a better response than an intentionally pointed question. (We'll address this issue further in Chapter Five, when the topic of asking tough questions during the interview is discussed.)

■ *Questions that present location or sequence of action.* Before each of my interviews, I try to prepare an accurate chronology of the events that put the person I'm interviewing in the public light. If I'm writing a profile, I put together a thumbnail sketch of important events, complete with dates; if I'm talking to someone who's a newsmaker or who has been reluctantly thrust into public events, I try to reconstruct the news event in as strong a chronology as I can piece together. Invariably I will find "holes" in my chronology—areas that have been ignored or are unaccounted for. I will also find that some events have been skimmed over. These are areas I'll want to explore in an interview. I'll take what I know and build off of it, designing questions that sequence events with the appropriate locations, dates, and times.

Naturally, many other questions will occur to you while you're conducting your interview. An interviewee may surprise you with a disclosure that leads you into an entirely new area of discussion, or he may disappoint you by having very little to say about a topic you were certain would be important to him, but it's always best to enter an interview with as many prepared questions as possible. Know what you want to ask and how you want to ask it. The ideal situation is to enter the interview with more questions than you could possibly ask, but be reasonable; you can overprepare questions as easily as you can conduct too much research. Establish priorities based on what you need for your article or interview, prepare questions in those areas, and be prepared to let the interviewee dictate any of the "bonuses" you may receive.

PUTTING YOUR QUESTIONS ON PAPER

Taking a list of written questions to an interview session can have a mixed effect on the conversation. For the interviewer, having written questions can be reassuring, yet paying too much attention to those written questions can stymie the flow of conversation. For interviewees, the notion that the interviewer has taken time to draw up and type out questions may be encouraging, a sign that the interviewer has given the conversation plenty of prior thought;

that very effect, however, can backfire if the interviewee grows apprehensive about what might be on that list. (Interview subjects have demanded to see these lists of questions and have rejected questions they don't want to answer.)

When practical or possible, it's always best to prepare a list of written questions to take to the interview—the more questions, the better. Written questions act as insurance against things going wrong during the interview. You may spend many hours preparing for an interview, only to find after the interview that you forgot an important question or two in the heat of the conversation. Or you may find yourself running out of questions if the ones you have in your head are quickly answered. Written questions insure you against both of these situations.

One way to avoid the minor pitfalls of the written list of questions is to type up a complete list and then memorize the first half-dozen or so questions that you intend to ask. (Some interviewers like to memorize more questions than this, but the danger here is that you'll concentrate on the memorized questions at the cost of the interview's spontaneity.) By memorizing the first questions on your list, you can make the opening of the interview look more spontaneous and free-flowing than it actually is, and this can put your interviewee at ease. Once the conversation is rolling along, you can steal occasional glances at your written questions and replenish the questions you're holding in your mind.

SEQUENCING PREPARED QUESTIONS

If you've blocked out your question areas before you prepared your questions, you'll have a good idea of the sequence in which you'd like to pose your questions. The key to sequencing prepared questions is your anticipation of an interviewee's responses, as well as your set of priorities regarding what you want to bring out of your interview. If you have been thorough in your research, you probably can make an educated guess on how your interviewee will answer some of your questions, but you have to be careful in doing so. If you rely too much on preconception or anticipated answers you might find yourself knocked back on your heels by a surprising response or, worse yet, you may not hear or recognize the person's response and make the mistake of carrying on with your line of questioning in total disregard for what was said.

Still, preparing a logical sequence of some of the questions you'll be asking offers you another sense of organization that can be useful during the interview, especially if it promises to be a long one, or if you're conducting an interview that you intend to eventually present in the Q/A format. In both of these instances, you want the interview — during the conversation itself and in print — to seem natural, logical, and complete, and by having a preset sequence of questions, even if only for a few of the subject areas you intend to pursue, you can guide yourself along this path.

THE IDEAL AND THE PRAGMATIC

The various aspects of research and preparation presented in this chapter are the ideals. Every reporter would like to have unlimited time to research a story. Any freelance writer would love to work on question preparation until the perfect interview could be constructed.

In the real world, however, reporters are sent to the location of breaking news stories and are expected to conduct thoughtful or provocative interviews on the spur of the moment. Deadlines can be measured in minutes. Research materials on a person or subject may not be readily available. An important interview may pop up without warning, and the writer would have to conduct a "seat of the pants" interview and hope for the best.

Experience is the interviewer's greatest teacher. You learn the best methods of phrasing questions through trial and error, by asking every kind of question imaginable and learning which types bring you the best responses. You learn how to mix your open and closed questions by interviewing people, looking at the results of the interviews, and gauging your successes and failures. Sometimes the only way to learn the value of preparation is to enter an interview ill-prepared and suffer the consequences. (It's an experience any interviewer can tell you about.) You learn how to work under the gun.

Good research and preparation, when possible, will spare you from the worst scenarios. In fact, solid research and preparation will give you the ultimate reward: when you conduct your interview, you'll look and sound knowledgeable, and the conversation will appear to be extemporaneous, even if it's been planned to its finest details.

HOW TO LINE UP INTERVIEWS

Imagine yourself sitting quietly in your home. Someone will be arriving in a few moments, and you're not entirely certain that you are pleased to be accepting this visitor into your home. You look around you at all the things that make you feel comfortable — at the things that reflect largely upon who you are — and you wonder what your visitor will think. Maybe he won't like the paintings you have on the wall, or your choice of books on the shelf. Maybe he'll envy the furniture you have in your study. One thing is certain: he'll steal more than a passing glance at your environment; he'll gauge everything around you and whatever impressions he finds noteworthy he will pass on to others.

You tell yourself that there is no rationale for your feeling this way. This is *your* home, and you've always felt good in it. What does it matter if he or anyone else doesn't find it to his liking? Besides, he should remember that you invited him into your home — you weren't obliged to see him.

The doorbell rings. You straighten a picture on the wall as you head toward the front hall. You pause briefly at a mirror, check the way you look, push down a few stray hairs. You pause briefly when you get to the door. On the other side of the door is a total stranger, a person you have spoken to only twice in your life. You don't know if that person is a friend, enemy, or neutral. What you do know is that when you open the door and admit him, it will be like admitting thousands of people into your living room. This person is going to sit down, open a notebook or turn on a tape recorder, and begin asking you questions you may not want to answer. This stranger is going to ask you questions about your life — queries you wouldn't dream of asking a stranger yourself. He's going to ask these questions and then, based on what you tell him in the next two hours, he's going to sit down at a word processor and pretend he knows you well. He's going to write down his version of who you are.

Then he's going to share those thoughts with thousands of other people.

THE "UNKNOWN" ELEMENT

Not all interviewees, of course, are so apprehensive about meeting their interviewers. Some are confident that they can manipulate the conversation and the person asking the questions. Others are combative. Some are indifferent; they'll answer whatever questions you ask and go about their business.

As an interviewer, however, you have no precise way of knowing the disposition of the person you're talking to. On many occasions you can make an educated guess, based on what you know or see, or upon the reason you're interviewing the person in the first place. You shouldn't have much difficulty in understanding the state of mind of a person standing in the street and watching her house burn down. You won't have to stretch your imagination too far to predict how a politician, about to be indicted for graft, might feel about being interviewed for the daily newspaper. You won't be taxing your powers of prognostication when you try to gauge the mental state of the wide receiver who just caught the game-winning touchdown pass at the Super Bowl.

In Chapter Two we touched briefly on this issue when we addressed the topic of selecting sources. Trying to estimate why a source will talk to you is a vital part of the interviewing process. It's important not only because it helps you measure and frame the quality of the person's responses to your questions, but also because it prepares you for the time when you meet that person or call to line up an interview. Finally, your estimations will be handy when you are working on the wording of your questions: if you can put yourself in your interviewee's shoes, if you're able to place yourself on the other side of that door and feel the interviewee's emotions about the prospects of being interviewed, you will be in a much better position to word your questions in a manner that encourages quotable responses.

Only a tiny percentage of the public feels at ease when meeting total strangers. We fear the unknown and since, with every conversation, a person is revealing something about him- or herself, there is a measure of jeopardy involved in confronting this unknown element in the interview, especially if there is any hint that the stranger might bring up private, personal, or embarrassing affairs during the course of the conversation. Put yourself in that position. Imagine, say, that you've recently gone through a painful divorce, and a stranger approaches you at a party and asks for the intimate details of the divorce. Now imagine that, as soon as you open your mouth to speak, even if to tell the person that it's none of his business, the room falls quiet and everyone present waits for your response. In a sense, this is what happens when a person is interviewed, and this is why the great percentage of interviewees have, at best, mixed feelings about talking to you. For all they know you are going to grind them, along with their thoughts, into hamburger meat.

If we're to judge by the proliferation of profiles, interviews, and features in today's magazines and newspapers, added to everything we see on television or read in the daily newspapers, more people are talking than ever before. People hold press conferences for the flimsiest reasons imaginable. If a major star has a new movie coming out, you will probably see his or her face plastered across a dozen or more different magazine covers in newsstands from coast to coast. People have axes to grind, products (including themselves) to hype.

Nevertheless, the converse to all this is also true: people are refusing to talk to the press more than ever before, and even those who do talk will only agree to be interviewed if certain conditions are met. People demand to see manuscripts before they're submitted, interviewees ask to see lists of questions and topics of discussion before the interview. Many refuse to address sensitive personal details or issues. The fear of the unknown has turned normally agreeable people into disagreeable interviewees.

What does all this mean to interviewers? It means that you will have to consider a few ideas *before* you meet your interviewee or call to line up an interview. You will have to contemplate the best way to approach a person with a request for an interview, and you'll have to set in your mind what interview conditions, if any, you may be willing to concede to a person. Failure to consider these ideas could cost you a good interview. Or it could cost you the interview itself.

ASSIGNMENT OR INTERVIEW FIRST?

Should you line up or conduct an interview before you have a guaranteed assignment for the piece you're writing, or should you secure the assignment before you contact an interviewee?

Freelance writers have been debating this question for ages but, unfortunately, there is no absolutely correct answer to the question. Instead, it takes on a "chicken or egg" quality. If you can tell an interviewee you have an assignment with a reputable publication, you will probably have less trouble lining up an interview than you would encounter if you told the same person that you had no assignment or were working on "spec"; on the other hand, an editor may not feel comfortable about assigning you an important story unless you already have an interview lined up or conducted, or can assure him that you can obtain one. Editors regularly make assignments based on faith, but you always stand a better chance of having your proposed article or interview accepted if you can tell an editor that you've already conducted the interview, or that you have special access to the interviewee.

From the interviewee's standpoint, the issue is also problematic. Busy people aren't inclined to invest valuable time on speculation; they want to be assured that their efforts are being put to good use. Celebrities, always aware of where their names are appearing, want to be assured that their interview or profile will be published in the right newspaper or magazine. If you are unable to tell a potential interviewee that you have an assignment for a reputable publication, you may have difficulty in getting the person to talk to you.

Although there is no final word on this topic, a general consensus exists on several points:

■ Always secure an assignment before you embark on a project that promises to be more complex or time-consuming than your average articles. This would include issues-oriented or investigative reports, as well as long, in-depth profiles or interviews. As it is, you will be devoting a substantial amount of time in researching for your query letter; it is wasteful to invest more time, when there are no guarantees that your article proposal will be greeted with enthusiasm.

■ Consider your sources. If your interview is with a well-known person, you are safer to conduct an interview before you have an assignment than you are with an unknown. You can make valid assumptions about the marketability of celebrities, and you can probably conduct the interview with the confidence that you will be able to place your interview *somewhere*. A word of caution, though: be brutally honest in your assessment of a person's appeal to a large readership. Just because *you* like someone doesn't mean a large segment of the reading population shares your enthusiasm.

■ When you're lining up an interview for which you have no assignment, be honest with your interviewee. Don't tell a person that you have an assignment if you do not. Don't misrepresent yourself or the publication you're writing for (if you have an assignment), either when you're lining up the interview or actually conducting it.

HOW TO CONTACT AN INTERVIEWEE: DIRECT AND INDIRECT APPROACHES

Depending upon your potential interviewee and the circumstances of the interview you are proposing, you can take either a direct or indirect approach in setting up your interview.

The direct approach finds you contacting the person and lining up the interview yourself, with little or no assistance from third parties. You can approach the interviewee in person, call him or her on the telephone, or establish contact by mail.

The indirect approach involves your getting in touch with your subject through that person's assistant, agent, manager, publicist, or through some other third party. The third party should have direct access to the interviewee and enough influence to persuade the person to talk to you.

Your methods of arranging for an interview will vary from interview to interview. If you are a reporter covering daily news stories, most of your interviewees will be approached directly at the location of the news event you are writing about; you will be walking up to the interviewee, introducing yourself, and moving immediately into the interview itself. For news features, you will take the most pragmatic approach: you will either call the interviewee directly to set up an interview appointment, or you may arrange the interview with the help of the person's assistant. If you are writing a celebrity profile for a magazine, you almost always will be working with a third party in setting up your interview.

Regardless of the method you use, the way you present yourself when you contact a potential interviewee can be a determining factor in your getting an interview.

SOME GENERAL RULES

When you approach an interview subject, whether directly or indirectly, you should employ the following procedure:

■ *Identify yourself.* This seems obvious enough, but interviews are lost on a regular basis because interviewers hem and haw when they are trying to identify themselves. Never start a conversation with "You don't know me, but . . ." or "I was reading about you in the paper the other day . . ." or some other vague lead-in that has nothing to do with your request but only serves to remind the interviewee that he or she may be dealing with a nonprofessional. Be straightforward but warm, keeping in mind that you are well within your rights to request an interview, while bearing in mind as well that the interviewee has every right on earth to refuse you. Don't worry about whether or not you have the necessary "name" for the interview. The interviewee may not have heard of you, but that shouldn't be a factor in the person's agreeing or refusing to grant an interview.

When you are identifying yourself, you will also want to mention the publication that assigned you the article, provided you are working on assignment. An assignment from a reputable publication can help you secure an interview, but whatever you do, don't misrepresent yourself. Don't tell an interviewee that you are writing an article for *The New York Times* if you are actually writing it for your local weekly newspaper. Don't say you have an assignment if you don't. If you are working without a formal assignment, you can take one of two approaches: you may mention a couple of the publications you've worked for in the past, without linking one of them directly to your present project ("I'm a freelance writer and have sold my work to *Playboy, The New York Times,* and *Ladies Home Journal.* . . ."), or you may avoid the issue altogether ("I've been working on a story about. . . ."). Either way is preferable to your volunteering the fact that you haven't yet marketed your story. If the interviewee asks about your market, you should tell the truth, though you can also list a couple of the markets you're aiming your article for.

■ *State your business.* Before you contact a person to line up an interview, you should have devised a way to state your business in a brief, concise manner. "It's difficult to explain" is not the kind of answer you should offer when any interviewee asks about your article. Be prepared to state your article's purpose in a couple of sentences. Tell your potential interviewee, to the best of your ability, what your article is about and how he or she fits into your plans. If you are working under strict or tight deadlines, be sure to say as much. Provide as much information in as little time as possible, but do so without showing *too* much of your hand. For example, if you know that your interview is going to involve your asking a lot of tough questions, you're better off taking an "I'd like your side of the story" approach than an "I'll be asking pointed questions" attack. Be ready to answer questions about your article, and research enough beforehand so you will be able to prove that you are authoritative — or at least well versed — on the topic you're writing about.

■ *Offer appropriate credentials.* If, in your recent past, you have published articles similar to the one you are now writing, or if you have published articles you think your interviewee will find interesting, you should mention them to your potential interview subject. If you haven't done so when you were introducing yourself, you may also list a few of the publications you have worked for, but be reasonable: an interviewee doesn't want to hear your life story or a long litany of your published credits. Use common sense. Mention two or three of the most influential publications, or those that publish similar types of articles, and avoid mentioning any credits that may bring pause to the interviewee. (For example, if you're approaching a minister, it's not necessarily wise to bring up your *Penthouse* credits, though those credits will probably serve you well if you are interviewing, say, an athlete or actor.) Be modest about your credentials — offer them as you might offer a business card. Listing too many credentials — or mentioning them in a boastful way — will make you look arrogant, not professional, and no interviewee wants to feel as if he or she will be playing a game of matching wits during an interview.

■ *Volunteer any information that helps your cause.* There are times when name-dropping can be useful in helping you obtain an interview. Suppose you are conducting a survey of university presidents on the topic of recent housing trends on college campuses. If you have talked to several university presidents prior to your calling another president with an interview request, it might not hurt to mention the people you have already spoken to. Volunteering this sort of information will put your potential interviewee more at ease; he or she may like the list of other university presidents in your story, and the fact that he or she is not the first — or only — voice appearing in your story will be reassuring as well. This idea also applies to other information you may have: if you have information that will put a person at ease or may prompt that person to agree to an interview, don't be afraid to present it when you call to request an interview.

In a sense, formally requesting an interview is similar to writing a query letter to an editor: it's a business transaction that commands the right touch. A light touch is usually better than a heavy-handed one when you're setting up an interview, although, as we'll see later, there are times when you'll have no other choice than to play hardball with an interviewee. In taking a light touch, you will be telling your potential interviewee that, in effect, your article will be a worthwhile adventure for you, the interviewee, and the readers, but it is not so important that it must stand as the interviewee's final word on the subject. You shouldn't overstate your case or intimidate your interviewee by making the interview look too formal (or even grave). You don't want to be either an interviewee's pal or adversary, but you do want to come across as professional, unbiased, and genuinely interested in what the person has to say. If you project these qualities when you contact your interviewee, you stand a good chance of securing the interview.

THE DIRECT APPROACH

To be an effective interviewer, you need to be skilled at meeting people. Even if the only contact you'll have with a person turns out to be a conversation on the telephone, when you call someone to request an interview, you will be "meeting" that person, just as you would be meeting the person if you were to walk up to him or her on the street and begin talking. Initial meetings are introductions, and from these introductions come impressions that will determine your chances of securing the interview, as well as a tentative trust level that will greatly influence the way your questions are answered.

By its nature, the direct approach to lining up interviews carries an element of improvisation; you don't just walk up to someone and begin reading a typed request off a sheet of paper. The direct contact of an initial meeting has built-in risks. You might trip over your words, poorly phrase your request, or form a bad first impression. If you get off on the wrong foot by representing yourself poorly, you're going to experience difficulty with your interview — if you get one at all.

The method you choose to directly approach someone will be based upon both your personality and the circumstances of your interview. If you find it easy to meet people, you will probably prefer to approach a potential interviewee in person; if such meetings are difficult for you, you will probably prefer to contact your interviewee by telephone or through the mail. If you're a reporter covering a news event, your approach will take place at the location of the event; if you're a freelance writer with two months to piece together your article, you may take a slower approach. Regardless of your method of contacting an interview subject, you will have to concern yourself with meeting a person, introducing yourself, and forming a good first impression.

IN-PERSON MEETINGS

Under the best of circumstances, making a "cold call" — approaching a person, introducing yourself, and either trying to arrange an interview or actually conducting the interview on the spot — can be difficult; under trying circumstances, it can be almost impossible.

Newspaper reporters face these circumstances on a regular basis. They are dispatched to the scene of a tragic occurrence and are expected to return with good, quotable material. They are expected to talk to people at times when those people are least inclined to talk, and for their efforts they are often greeted with suspicion, scorn, anger, confusion, or silence.

A good many of these responses are well earned. I recall a particularly tragic story that involved a young mother who, in a state of deep depression, killed her three children and then took her own life. Those events took place in a very small, politically conservative town, and the news media swarmed all over the story. On the day of the burial of the woman and her three children, a reporter walked up to her parents' front door, identified himself to the woman's brother, and said he wanted to interview the woman's grieving parents. He was nearly punched in the nose for making the request.

The reporter's problem was not in his hoping to talk to the parents per se — in the technical sense, he was just trying to do his job — but in the insensitivity, poor judgment, and bad timing he displayed when he tried to interview the people. We've all seen reporters swarming on newsmakers, and there is something unsettling about the sight. In far too many cases, the reporters appear to be arrogant, insensitive, bothersome, or just plain cold. Ironically, we depend upon — and relish — the quotes garnered by those same reporters. We would be incensed at the reporter who backed away from an important story because he or she had misgivings about interviewing the people involved.

We've also heard stories about the persistent reporter who camped out in a newsmaker's office and waited for the person to come out at the end of the day. Or of the investigative journalist who spent months in pursuit of an important, newsbreaking interview, facing the person's rejection day in and day out until the interviewee finally caved in and agreed to talk. At times, reporters appear to have more audacity than good common sense.

In fact, approaching a person to line up an interview requires both ingredients — audacity and common sense. You must have the nerve to address a person and state your case, and you must show good common sense while you're doing so.

When you are approaching a potential interview in person, you should:

■ *Consider the circumstances.* How would you react to a request for an interview if you were in your interviewee's position? Would you be inclined to grant an interview? If not, what would it take to change your mind? If you can put yourself in your interviewee's position, you will be better prepared to use your most persuasive approach when you request an interview.

■ *Know what you want to say before you approach the person.* This point has already been touched upon in our discussion of interview preparation, as well as in the general rules concerning the lining up of interviews, but it cannot be overstated. Know what you want to say to the person before you approach him or her. If you have the time, you might want to rehearse the finer points of your presentation. Doing so will give you confidence when you approach the person, and it will also help you state your case in a way that seems spontaneous.

■ *Take a low-key approach.* People don't like to feel as if they are being pressured or bullied into an interview. Formalities can give them that sense. Use the word "interview" sparingly; you're better off if you say something like "I'd like to talk to you about . . . . " This approach will look less formal to those accustomed to being interviewed, less imposing to those who are not.

■ *Appeal to the person's sense of self-importance.* All of us want to feel important or useful, and if you are able to convince your interview subject that he or she is helping you out by talking to you, and that he or she is the best, most authoritative, or most crucial voice in your article, you are more likely to gain an interview than you would be if you made the same person feel like just another voice in the crowd. If the interviewee has a unique position or perspective, know what it is and use it to your advantage.

■ *Be courteous.* Reporters and freelance writers occasionally forget that society's rules of etiquette apply to *them,* as well as to the rest of the world. Avoid pushing your way into a person's life. Don't interrupt conversations, pull interviewees away from their personal or professional business, or become an imposition. Be polite, regardless of the circumstances.

■ *Be aware of how you are presenting yourself.* Do you look and sound professional? Do you appear to be the kind of person a stranger would trust? What kind of first impression are you making? See yourself in your mind's eye; be aware of what you're saying.

■ *Don't talk too much.* Overstating your case, or talking too much in general, can cause unwarranted suspicion in the person you are talking to. Too much talk can be intimidating to people who do not often grant interviews and annoying to those who do. Talking too much can also make you look desperate. State your case briefly and give your potential interviewee plenty of time (and silence) in which to respond.

■ *Be prepared to restate your case, but not to argue.* People will listen to a persuasive person, but not to an argumentative one. If the person seems negative or skeptical about participating in the interview, you'll need to be ready with a persuasive way of underscoring the points you made when you explained your article the first time around.

■ *Whenever possible, try to get the person to agree with you on the points you're making.* This is an old salesperson's trick, and while it can seem manipulative if it's used too often or indiscriminately, it can be quite effective, when you are trying to line up an interview, if you can get a person's agreement on the finer points of your presentation. It implies that you're both on the same side, that you think alike, that mutual trust is possible.

■ *Have an alternative plan.* On occasion, you will discover that you've picked the worst possible time to approach a person with a request for an interview. For example, it's always difficult if your potential interviewee is standing in a group of people—it's easier to be ignored, rejected, or taken less seriously. The same applies to a cold call at a person's place of employment. You might have to make the request anyway, as would be the case if you were covering a news event, but if you know that you'll have another opportunity to talk to the person, and if your deadlines afford you the luxury of putting off the request until you find a better opportunity, you might be better off using your meeting to simply establish contact. Introduce yourself, tell the person you have a matter you'd like to discuss with him or her in private at another time, and ask if it would be acceptable for you to call or drop by in the near future. People may not be enthusiastic about the prospects of such a meeting, but they'll rarely turn you down.

TELEPHONE MEETINGS

When you're lining up interviews over the phone, you should employ all of the tactics you'd use if you were meeting the potential interviewee in person, but keep in mind that the telephone has a way of flattening out your personality. The person you're calling cannot see your face, feel the grip of your handshake, see your smile or gestures. If you've never met him or her before, you are just another voice, an unsolicited interruption. You should also remember that it is easier for a person to reject a request when it's made on the telephone than when it's taking place in person.

Because of all this, you will have to be especially sharp when you call. If you must, have notes (but not a written script) in your hands when you call; use the notes for organization, as an aid to your presentation. When you speak to the person, mix warmth with professionalism. Be enthusiastic, and make sure that your enthusiasm is present in your voice. Exude confidence: act as if you have every reason to believe that the person will grant your request. If the response seems uncertain or negative, suggest that the person think it over; say that you'll call back. Be aggressive, but not offensively so. Remember: you're selling yourself as well as your project, and the potential interviewee is unfamiliar with both.

CONTACTING AN INTERVIEWEE BY MAIL

There are advantages and disadvantages to contacting a person and requesting an interview through the mail. On the negative side, time works against you. There are no guarantees that people will respond to your letters. Mail is easy to ignore or forget about. Busy people place a low priority on answering unwelcome, unsolicited, or unexpected mail.

On the positive side, your request will almost always reach the person you're writing, with little interference from third parties. A well-written letter can impress a potential interview subject and convince him or her that you will do well with your article. You can be more precise with your wording than you might be on the phone or in person.

Newspaper columnist Bob Greene secured three of his biggest interviews (Richard Nixon, Patricia Hearst, and Richard Speck) by approaching his subjects by mail. Getting these interviews was a journalistic coup for Greene, since all three interviewees were avoiding the press at the time in which Greene approached them.

"Each of those interviews started out with a letter from me to the person," Greene says. "I realized that, while they were huge names in the news, they were still people. What I do best is write, and I thought that if I wrote them a good letter, maybe they would respond."

They did, and Greene had three interviews that drew national attention.

When contacting a person by mail, follow the same general rules mentioned earlier in this chapter. Since you won't be speaking directly to the potential interviewee, it is important that you treat your letter as a very important surrogate. After all, it will be speaking for you, and your securing an interview will depend upon how your interviewee reacts to the relatively few sentences you put on paper.

The most effective procedure is a package that includes:

■ *The letter.* Keep the letter brief and to the point—no more than one and one-half single-spaced, typed pages. Always type the letter, and if you have it, use letterhead. Identify yourself and state your business, as you would if you were speaking directly to the person. Since the letter is a sample of your writing, as well as a proposal, make each word count. Include a brief description of the article you're writing, along with a word or two about how that person can help make your article successful. Mention your deadline and propose a time and place for the interview, leaving the door open for a counterproposal from your interviewee. The letter does not have to be complicated or extensively detailed to bring you the results you seek; in fact, the outline form of the letter may rouse the person's curiosity more than if you were to spend a half-hour on the phone in discussion of the project. Neatness counts—send a letter free of strikeovers and typos, as if you were submitting a query letter to an editor.

■ *Clippings.* A *few* clippings of your recent or related published work can be very useful in displaying your professionalism and knowledge on a topic. Photocopies are preferable, since you should not expect or ask to have your clippings returned. Limit yourself to two or three articles. Busy people lack the time or inclination for reading career perspectives coming from unknown sources.

■ *SASE.* Always include a self-addressed, stamped envelope for the person's response. (A standard business envelope will do.) Failure to enclose an SASE is an invitation for no response to your letter, since it not only shows you to be less than professional, but it is also annoying to the person who would have to use his or her own time and money for postage.

Obtaining a person's address is not as difficult as it may seem. You can reach many potential interviewees through their work offices; you'd be surprised by how many have their home addresses listed in the telephone book. For celebrities, you may want to make contact through agents, publicists, or work offices, though there are no guarantees that you'll get their home addresses through these people; they will probably suggest that you send the package to the person through them. You will also find many celebrities' work or home addresses listed in the annual *Who's Who* publications, available in libraries, or in *The Address Book,* an annually updated book that lists hundreds of celebrity addresses. Don't overlook other contacts, either: friends, relatives, and business associates of a potential interviewee will often provide you with an address.

Mail your package of materials in a manila envelope. Some writers prefer to send such packages via registered or overnight mail, but doing so doesn't guarantee that your package will get any more special or quicker attention than a first class package would receive. Allow an adequate amount of time (three to four weeks) for a response. If you have not heard from the person in that time, you may follow up your package with a letter or postcard inquiring about the status of your proposal. Be patient. People are no more obliged to answer their mail than they are to grant interviews. A soft touch will increase your odds of getting a response from a busy or forgetful person.

THE INDIRECT APPROACH

One of the "perks" (if you can call it that) of being famous, wealthy, powerful, or influential is the capability and position to place barriers between yourself and the people you don't want to be bothered with. Busy people hire secretaries or assistants to screen their calls and line up appointments that are subject to their approval. Answering services also accomplish the former task, while agents and publicists often handle the latter. If you are a freelance writer trying to get in touch with celebrities, corporate officials, politicians, or other well-known or busy persons, you probably won't be any more successful in trying to contact them by walking into their offices, than you'd be if you tried to find their numbers listed in the telephone book. The direct approach to contacting them may be out of the question. To get in touch with these people, you'll have to go through a third party.

The indirect approach to contacting an interviewee often requires a certain amount of savvy and a lot of patience. You will have to understand *two* minds (the interviewee's and the third party's) instead of one, and you will have to carefully gauge how you can use one to get to the other. You'll probably have to play a waiting game that will frustrate you or deflate your ego in order to inflate the ego of the person you want to talk to.

The indirect approach is rarely easy, though it can be rewarding if you base your actions on a few reasonable assumptions:

■ *Assume that the person is very busy and would prefer not to talk to you.* This doesn't mean that he or she *won't* talk to you, or won't give you a good interview once you've lined it up and started, but the assumption will aid you when you are preparing your case. If you take for granted that the person doesn't want to be bothered, you are going to construct a more persuasive case for why that person should meet with you. This assumption will also prepare you mentally for the runaround you might receive when you're trying to line up the interview.

■ *Assume that you are only one of many potential interviewers making the same request.* If you're hoping to talk to a newsmaker, celebrity, or otherwise well-known person, this will probably be a valid assumption, especially if that person is rooted to a topical issue or event. By making this assumption, you will again be recognizing the importance of building a strong case in your favor: your proposal will have to stand out from the others.

■ *Assume that the third party has a stake in passing along (or not passing along) your request.* A third party's interests in your interviewee's professional welfare may be marginal or strong, but it is very real nonetheless. An agent has financial stakes in a client. An assistant or secretary may have strict orders about screening calls or lining up appointments. Publicists measure their success by the quality and quantity of interest they can garner for the person they're representing. If you can understand the stakes the third party has in handling your request, you'll be better equipped to present yourself in accordance with those stakes.

■ *Assume that your request will be greeted with at least a small amount of skepticism, indifference, or even cynicism.* Assessment is a two-way street: just as you will be trying to assess the stakes and interests a third party has in the person you're trying to contact, that third party will also be trying to determine your interests and intentions in making the request. Agents, publicists, assistants, and secretaries deal with the public every day; they've heard every story there is to hear, and they generally possess a type of radar that helps them gauge a writer's involvement in an interview. That involvement may be measured by the publication the writer is representing, or by the familiarity that the third party has with the interviewer, or by the type of article that's being written. If you assume that the third party will be hard to impress, you will find yourself focusing on those areas that set you apart from all the other people that person has to deal with in the course of a workday.

■ *Assume that your request for an interview is merely a business transaction.* Don't take success or failure personally. It's always possible that a third party will take a liking to you and will assist you in obtaining an interview—the opposite is also true—but, in most cases, your request will be treated like any one of the other requests the third party receives. Priorities will be established, protocol will be followed; unless you are a well-known interviewer or are representing a top-priority publication, your name will be added to a list or you'll be put through the paces that any other person experiences. If you prepare yourself mentally for such eventualities, you won't feel inordinately good or bad about the results of your request.

At first glance, there appears to be an element of negativism, a "prepare for the best while assuming the worst" attitude in the above-listed assumptions; but it should be noted that, in preparing yourself mentally for the task of dealing with a third party when you are trying to make an appointment for an interview, you are by no means conceding probable defeat or betting on a losing hand. Instead, adopt the attitude that you are strengthening your position by building a strong defensive stance. In trying to predict a third party's state of mind, sense of business, and reaction to your interview request, you are recognizing the many realities that may determine your success in obtaining the interview, and in recognizing those factors, you will be mentally prepared to build your case. Most third parties, you'll discover, are not the enemy; in fact, they tend to be as interested in your interviewee as you are. Like you, they are professionals with jobs to do. By understanding their jobs, you'll be better set to accomplish your own.

ARRANGING INTERVIEWS THROUGH PRESS AGENTS, PUBLICISTS, AND AGENTS

Lining up interviews through people with vested interests in your interviewee—press agents, publicists, managers, agents, etc.—is, at best, a mixed bag. Writers complain about the ways in which these people meddle in the business of the interview; put them through the paces when it comes to contacting the interviewee and arranging the interview; refuse to return phone calls; and make unacceptable or ridiculous demands as terms for the interview itself (I'll discuss these later in the chapter). Some of these people insist upon being present during the interview, while others ask to see stacks of your published clippings or the questions you intend to ask—or anything else, just short of your donating a pint of your blood to the cause. The enigma of such representatives is the fact that they can be quite generous and useful if they feel you can help their client, while they also can be cold and abrupt when you are the one asking the favor.

"PR people are always ready to get me interviews with people nobody wants to read about, but as soon as you toss out a familiar name, they act like they don't know you," objects one writer who has sold his work to dozens of publications, adding, "Agents are even worse. You get the impression that they're totalling up figures on their calculators while they're talking to you. If they can't justify an interview in terms of eventual dollars and cents, they'll pass right over you and look for someone else."

To a degree, one cannot blame agents or publicists for taking this stance. Their jobs focus on getting money and publicity for their clients. Their success can be measured both qualitatively and quantitively. Like salespeople, they are accustomed to having doors slammed in their faces, and their day-to-day tasks can take on characteristics of the extreme: on one day, they may be futilely attempting to generate publicity for clients with little popular appeal; on the next day, they may be fielding dozens of requests for interviews with their hottest, nationally known and admired clients. Furthermore, as middle people, they are obliged to report their successes and failures to their clients—a demanding chore when you assume that bruised or inflated egos are often the results of those reports.

When you consider the duties of an agent's or publicist's job and pit those duties against the complaints voiced against those representatives, you can see why you must have devised a solid request when you make your approach for an interview. Because you are dealing with busy professionals, you should implement your request in a businesslike manner. Call during business hours. Eliminate the small talk, unless you know the representative well. Be thorough but to the point when you detail your writing project, and make certain you emphasize any points (the magazine or newspaper you're working for, your experience, etc.) that might impress the third party. Show enthusiasm for your article or interview—enthusiasm can be contagious, especially when you are dealing with people whose own enthusiasm is dulled by the monotony of their day-to-day routines. Be complimentary toward, by not patronizing of interview subjects (representatives know the difference, and they despise the latter). Emphasize the interviewee's importance to the project you're working on.

Above all, don't take personally any of the questions the agent or publicist is certain to have, the responses you receive (pro or con) to your request, or any of the demands a representative may make of you. Business is being conducted, and you will be respected for your professional behavior. By all means, be prepared to answer questions or negotiate the terms of the interview, but do so in a straightforward, positive manner.

Despite the complaints against them, agents, managers, publicists, and press agents are not ogres to work with. I've dealt with them on scores of occasions, and while I have a few horror stories of my own as a result of those encounters, the number of those tales is vastly exceeded by the number of times I've dealt with decent, agreeable people. The key to success is understanding the importance of the professional exchange that is taking place: you are offering good publicity in exchange for an interview. Few third parties will frown upon that exchange.

TWO STANDARD PUT-OFFS

Besides "hello" and "goodbye," the two lines you're likely to hear most often when you call a third party to line up an interview are "He's in a meeting" or "She's away from her desk at the moment." More times than not, there will be no truth to either of these claims; chances are, the person is in his or her office but is unwilling or unable to be interrupted. Inexperienced journalists or writers may find these lines annoying—"How dare these people lie to me like that?"—while more experienced interviewers tend to regard these words as kinder alternatives to a person's saying "He won't talk to you now." Regardless of what you think of these little white lies, the end-result will always be the same: you won't be talking to the person at that moment.

When you are given one of those lines, never show irritation, even if you're feeling it; doing so will only jeopardize your further attempts to contact the interviewee. Instead, remind yourself that the person screening your call is only performing his or her duty. Be polite. Ask what time would be best to call back or, if you're so inclined, play along with the game and inquire about when the person will be out of the meeting or back in the office. (If accomplished in a light-hearted way, with a sort of "wink" in your voice, this method could pay off its own dividends: people screening calls put up with their own fair share of guff on any given day, and they are more likely to be sympathetic—and, thus, ultimately cooperative—with a person who winks at their little lie than with someone who confronts it.) Whatever you decide to do, stay professional. Don't snarl, whine, show indignation, or complain.

On the other hand, if your attempts to contact a person are still producing one of these two lines after several calls, you are justified in taking a more aggressive approach. Remind the person you're talking to that you've made repeated attempts at contacting the person, and mention that time is becoming a factor in your completion of your article. Under these circumstances, you might get better results if you suggest that the potential interviewee call you—collect, if the call is long distance. Stay patient. You can be assertive without losing your cool. Restate your case, underscoring the importance of the interviewee's voice in your article.

"I'LL CALL YOU BACK"

Almost as common as "He's in a meeting" or "She's away from her desk" is the promise of the return call. Quite often, this promise is used in conjunction with one of the two put-offs.

The promise of a return call seems both logical and sincere when it's made: you call a person's office, speak to his or her assistant, are given a standard put-off, and you provide the assistant with the correct spelling of your name and your telephone number. "I'll have him call you as soon as he returns," the assistant tells you. Not wanting to miss the call, you hang around your house or office, listening for the sound of the phone, only to give up after a few hours, when it's obvious that you are not going to get the call.

Handling this situation is similar to handling the two standard put-off lines: stay patient, be persistent, and try to impress upon an assistant or secretary the urgency of your having your call returned. Some journalists like to speed up the return call process by telling an assistant that they are only going to be in their offices until a specified time, but this ploy doesn't guarantee the return call.

MESSAGE SERVICES

For those who are away from their offices, too busy to take phone calls, otherwise predisposed, or desirous of the ultimate call screening device, the message service must seem like a godsend. In this system, calls and messages are taken, logged, and passed along by hired professionals. Unlike personal assistants or secretaries, these professionals may not even know the person for whom they are taking messages. They cannot arrange appointments, speak for the person receiving the message, hand out any kind of useful information, or even assure callers that their calls will be returned. All they can do is take a message and promise to pass it on.

Which they do, despite naysaying or professed befuddlement by people who don't return your calls or claim they never received your messages.

In reality, message services are highly efficient screening services. With message services, one of three things generally happens:

- The message service passes all messages directly to the person on the receiving end;
- The message service passes the messages to a person's assistant, who then sorts the messages into high priority or low priority calls; or
- The message service sorts the calls into priorities and passes them along.

In principle, dealing with a message service is similar to dealing with other third parties, with a few exceptions. For one thing, since the service is employed by, but not a part of, the office you're seeking to contact, it will do you little good to seek information about the person you're trying to contact. Message services generally have no idea when their clients will be picking up their messages, when (or if) they will be back in the office, when they might return your call, and so forth. "He'll be calling in for his messages" or "She checks with us every few hours" are common responses to queries about when messages are passed along; any other questions will be answered with one form or another of a verbal shrug. Your telling the service that your message is urgent means very little to the person you're talking to: *all* messages are urgent, or so it seems to them, and even if you tell the message service that you're only going to be in your office, at the number you're leaving, for a specified time, you will find that nothing you say will guarantee your placement in a high-priority list of messages. The message service may note that you said your call was urgent, or that it needed to be returned within a specified time, but that doesn't necessarily mean that you'll be hearing from the person you are calling.

The best method of leaving messages largely depends upon your familiarity with the person you want to contact. If the person knows you, you should leave your name, phone number, and a brief description of what you want to talk about. If the person doesn't know you, or if he or she has met you but may not remember who you are, you'll want to leave a message that compels the person to return your call. Leave your name and phone number, but don't show much of your hand. Instead of detailing your reasons for calling, leave a message that might catch the person's curiosity. If you are on assignment for a prestigious publication, you might mention the publication in lieu of a message ("This is Jane Doe, and I'm calling in reference to an article I'm writing for *Woman's Day*."). Some interviewers like to call, ask for a person by his or her first name (implying that they know the person), and then refuse to leave a message, confidently insisting that the person already knows what the call is all about. On some occasions, leaving no message, other than your name and number, is effective.

Whatever you choose to do, keep your message short. The people working for message services have their own form of shorthand that, in a few words, outlines a caller's message, so any detailed message is likely to be condensed to a few words. Present yourself in a self-confident tone, as if you and the person you're leaving a message for are old acquaintances; this attitude might land you in the top-priority message pile. Above all, be polite and patient, even if you find yourself leaving several messages in one day.

NEGOTIATING TERMS

An interview should be an even trade between interviewer and subject; the latter provides information or viewpoints with the understanding that his or her offerings will be used in publication; in exchange, the interviewer promises to employ the subject's words in a fair, useful way, in context and without distortion. This agreement is an unspoken, unwritten contract; without it, the level of the interviewer/interviewee trust — and, therefore, the conversation itself — is threatened.

Unfortunately, trust is a disappearing social element, and the more it vanishes, the less likely such unspoken contracts become. Today, it is not at all uncommon for interviewees to insist upon or to negotiate various terms for the interview before they agree to be a part of it. They want a degree of control of the interview and the way their words are used in print.

When you are setting up an interview in advance, you will have to reach an agreement with your subject on where and when you'll meet, as well as on how long you will be talking. That much is the given in any prearranged interview. Besides those issues, you may also be required to address an interviewee's demands for script approval, or the person may ask to see a list of questions or topics to be covered in the interview *prior* to the interview. You may be told that certain topics are off limits. The interviewee may even ask for the right to edit his or her remarks. None of these demands are rare—in fact, they are becoming more and more commonplace, especially if the interviewee is a celebrity, public figure, or person whose words are otherwise measured carefully by the reading public. The silent contract has suddenly become very vocal.

AGREEING UPON A PLACE TO MEET

The setting for an interview is enormously important. It influences the tone of the conversation, as well as its direction and overall effectiveness. It even affects its length. In many cases, the location of the interview will determine how much information you are able to gather or the honesty of an interviewee's responses.

Carl Bernstein, who, along with fellow reporter Bob Woodward, broke the Watergate story for *The Washington Post*, emphasized the importance of location in an interview with Tony Swartz published in *Playboy*. Bernstein claimed he and Woodward were more successful in their interviews because they knew where to conduct them.

"You look [a name] up in the phone book; she lives in Rockwell, you go to Rockwell; you go at night, not when she's working at her office and her boss is going to see you talking to her.

"That's exactly why the Federal prosecutors didn't get a . . . thing the first time around. They interviewed people in their offices, with attorneys for the Nixon people around. The subjects were under duress. We got them at home. Common sense. Then you work your way up."

Conversely, some interviews conducted at a person's office or workplace fail because the interviewee feels *too* secure, too powerful, in that environment. To a corporate executive, an office is a place where business is conducted and deals are struck; it is a control environment that discourages any signs of weakness, indecision, or vulnerability — characteristics that are consciously masked or guarded. To interview a person in this environment is to risk the construction of a facade in front of an interviewee's words.

Unfortunately, interviewers have little to say about where they conduct their interviews; they are at the whim and mercy of the person doing the talking. Clever interviewers might find ways to circumvent location problems, much the way Woodward and Bernstein did, but for most of us, the bulk of our interviewing will be accomplished by our showing up at an appointed place at an appointed time.

This doesn't mean that you cannot offer counterproposals to an interviewee's suggestions of meeting places. Many times, an interviewee will have no definite preference, but will offer the first location that comes to mind. If the interviewee sounds open to suggestions, don't be afraid to offer one of your own. If you can, suggest a neutral location — a place where the person can devote full attention to the interview and not feel influenced by the surroundings.

For example, here are a few ideas you might want to consider:

■ Try to choose a place where distractions will be minimal. When you are interviewing someone, you don't want to be competing with a lot of externals, whether they be other people moving about, background noises, or things that might otherwise catch your interviewee's eye. An empty room is preferable to a bench in a crowded park.

■ If possible, avoid scheduling interviews over lunch or dinner. It's awkward to conduct an interview and eat at the same time, and you will generally find yourself shutting off the tape recorder or putting down your notebook while you're eating, which means you'll be spending a period of unproductive (in terms of taped or formal conversation) time with an interviewee. You can't take notes while you're eating. You will also be periodically interrupted by waiters, waitresses or, if the person is a celebrity, gawkers, autograph seekers, or people eager to meet the person. A meal has a beginning, middle, and ending, and you don't want the meal's structure to determine the structure of your interview. In today's fast-paced world, a lot of business is conducted over lunch or dinner; formal interviews, however, should not be, if they can be scheduled for other times.

■ Try to avoid scheduling interviews at the office of an interviewee's representative. Agents and publicists might not interfere with the interview itself, but their presence can influence what your interviewee tells you. If a person's representative must be present, you might suggest that you, the representative, and the interviewee meet on neutral ground, even if that means conducting the interview over lunch, backstage, or in some other locale that is generally not a preferred place for formal conversations. Along these same lines, try to isolate your interviewee from others who may be sitting or standing around. If you are at the scene of a news event, guide your interviewee off to the side, to a nearby location where people won't be as apt to listen in or observe your conversation. This gentle, yet very noticeable relocation sends a message to the other people present: "We're conducting formal business here — please do not disturb."

■ If you are going to be talking to a person more than once, you might suggest that you switch locations for interviews following your initial conversation. For example, if you are writing a profile of a football player, you may very well find yourself conducting the initial interview in the team clubhouse. To follow up that interview, you might suggest that the next one be conducted elsewhere. Tell the player that you'd like to talk to him somewhere else — at home, at a neutral location, or if the player is on the road, a hotel lobby or room — all in the interest of a better-rounded portrait. You will probably find that, away from his teammates and the *macho* bravado typical of locker rooms, you'll see an entirely different side of the player.

■ More than anything else, it is important that your interviewee be comfortable in the interview's setting. If the person seems nervous or tentative about doing the interview, don't offer a counterproposal to that person's suggestion for the interview's location. Neutral turf might be intimidating to such a person, and you will only damage the quality of your interview — or you might lose it entirely—if you suggest any location other than the interviewee's stated preference.

Ultimately, the decision of interview location belongs to your interviewee, and while the location might be negotiable from time to time, you should never argue about it. If you feel you can, make your counterproposal; if it is refused, accept the person's location, without displaying reluctance, disappointment, or irritation.

AGREEING UPON THE LENGTH OF THE INTERVIEW

The amount of time you're allotted to talk to an interviewee is important to know before an interview, not because it is negotiable (generally, it is not), but because it allows you to plan in a way that utilizes your time to its fullest. As we'll see, pacing a conversation is fundamentally important to a successful interview, especially a lengthy one, and knowing how much time you'll have to conduct the interview will help you with your pacing.

If you are covering news stories, you won't have as much opportunity to agree on interview lengths as will the person who is working on a long magazine profile, who can call an interview subject weeks before the conversation. Nevertheless, it is a good idea to ask a person how much time you'll have to talk, because you don't want an interview to end unexpectedly before you've asked all your important questions.

You will also want to make certain that you have been given enough time to get the information you need. If you've been assigned an in-depth profile or Q/A interview with a celebrity, a half hour of that person's time will probably be insufficient for you to gather the kind of material your project requires. In that case, you will have to inquire about the possibility of a follow-up interview, and if this is impossible, you will have to decide on the chances of your writing an adequate story based on your one encounter.

Publicists or agents are infamous for "low-balling" interviewers in the amount of time they allot to interviews. To a large degree, this is a defensible practice: these people are paid to generate interest in (and, thus, more potential money for) their clients, and if a client is appearing in a city for only one day while on a promotional tour, the publicist is only doing his or her job by lining up as many interviews as a client will tolerate. Furthermore, meals and rest periods have to be penciled into the client's schedule. Time tables become very tight and an hour's time becomes precious. This is one of the reasons for press conferences' becoming so popular when a celebrity is on a promotional tour: by consolidating interviews, publicists are "cheating" on their hectic interview schedules.

Despite these pressures, a publicist will ask you how much time you need when you call to arrange an interview with a client, and you should have your response fixed in your mind before you call. If your interviewee is on a promotional tour, assume that, at best, you'll get an hour and a half—two hours if you're extremely lucky and happen to be writing your article for a major publication. Don't ask for more time than you'll need; yet, if you are given an inadequate amount of time in which to conduct your interview, don't hesitate to ask if you might be able to get a little more time. (Asking for an extra half hour is not considered to be an unreasonable request.)

One final point: rather than negotiate follow-up interviews with third parties such as publicists or agents, save these requests for your interviewee. In general, he or she will be more inclined to agree to a followup interview than will a representative.

TOPIC OR QUESTION APPROVAL

Any interviewee who insists upon approving topics of discussion or questions prior to an interview is flirting with a form of censorship. It's that simple, regardless of anything an interviewee may say to justify his or her demands, and you should be wary of consenting to such a demand. It's natural for an interviewee to be curious about the questions you intend to ask or the topics you hope to address in the interview—it's even natural for an interviewee to ask you about these things before the interview—but for the person to insist upon the right to approve them before he or she will talk to you is indicative of a person's implicit desire to control the interview and its content. It also should make you wonder how frank that person will be in answering those questions he or she chooses to address.

In general, warning signals should be sounding in your mind whenever:

- A potential interviewee informs you that specified topics are off limits in the interview;

- A third party (especially an agent or publicist) informs you that specified topics are off limits;
- A potential interviewee inquires, in a manner that's more than passing interest, about the nature of the interview and the questions you intend to ask;
- A third party requests a list of topics or questions before he consents to contact a potential interviewee on your behalf; or
- A third party offers to send *you* a list of questions or topics agreeable for discussion (or even offers them to you during the course of the conversation).

Sadly, none of the above listed requests/demands are uncommon, though the way they are presented to you can be quite creative. For example, a publicist of a large national publisher once sent me a press kit prior to an interview with one of the firm's authors. The kit was packed with photocopied reviews and interviews and, as far as background information is concerned, it was very useful. The package also included a list of questions that this publicist assured me would be great topics for discussion in my interview. Some of the questions were indeed compelling but, unfortunately, all of these questions, along with others, had been thoroughly addressed by the author in the interviews enclosed in the press kit. The cover letter accompanying the press kit made it clear — though it was never directly stated — that the interviewee would prefer to address these issues.

On other occasions, far more than I care to recall or list, I've been informed that a person would be delighted to talk to me, but that certain topics could not be addressed during the interview. It came as no surprise to me that, without exception, the off-limits topics were crucial to the interview and, in many cases, were the only reasons I had wanted to talk to the person in the first place.

Whenever you are confronted with the issue of topic or question approval, you should ask yourself a few questions. Why does the person insist upon avoiding certain topics? Are those topics essential elements to the article you're writing? Will a concession on your part damage your control of the interview? Would your refusal to concede the point cost you the interview? How important is the principle of the issue to you?

How you answer these questions will largely determine your position on question or topic approval, though a rule of thumb might be: If the forbidden topics or questions are truly matters of the legitimate protection of a person's privacy (such as an interviewee's asking you not to write about his or her family), a deal can be struck; if the forbidden topics involve issues that are newsworthy or already public knowledge, you should not agree to these conditions.

SCRIPT APPROVAL

It is not uncommon for interviewees to agree to talk to you only on the condition that they be allowed to review your manuscripts before they are submitted for publication. Others will want to see the quotes — in or out of context — that you intend to use.

More often than not, these people will assure you that all they intend to do is clean up the quotations in the interest of accuracy; they will insist that they aren't out to change your story itself, that they wouldn't dream of challenging your opinions or observations. They will appeal to your sense of fair play and your pursuit of the best, most accurate reportage possible. If all this fails, they may set their jaws and refuse to talk to you.

If possible, you should avoid granting script approval, not only because you are compromising your control, creative or otherwise, of the article you're writing, but also because the turnaround process may be time-consuming, thereby threatening the topicality of your story or an actual deadline. If the person disapproves of your article, you may have even bigger problems on your hands: it's not unusual for a person to call an editor or publisher in an attempt to block publication of a work that he or she doesn't agree with or approve of. People have even gone to court to block publication of what they consider to be unflattering profiles, biographies, and articles.

When a potential interviewee requests script approval as a condition for an interview, you can take either a direct or indirect approach in turning the person down. The direct approach is to tell the person that you don't give script approval to any of your interview subjects, that such approval creates too many problems with the story itself or your deadlines. When you say this, be firm but not too aggressive. Many interviewees request script approval with little hope of gaining it; to these people, agreement to this request is a "bonus," not unlike the feeling a car salesman experiences when he finds a customer willing to pay the sticker price without bargaining or negotiating. If you use tact in your refusal, you might find your interviewee willing to go along with you.

The indirect approach finds you citing outside forces as the reason for your refusal to grant script approval: you use an un-named third party's disapproval as the basis for your rejection. "I'll blame someone else," says Gary Provost. "I'll say, 'I'd like to let you see it, but my publisher really doesn't want me to show it to somebody else.' "

When using this tactic, you can cite editors, publisher's policy, rigid deadlines, and even other sources ("If I show it to you, I'd have to show it to So-and-So") as reasons for your refusal. Once again, it's important that you be firm and convincing when you do this: you don't want your interviewee to think you're weak or incapable of making decisions about your own w᷍rk.

How do you proceed if you fail in one of these approaches, if your interviewee still insists upon seeing a manuscript prior to the publication of your article? At this point, you will have to decide if the issue is worth taking a stand on. You'll have to ask yourself some hard questions. How important is this person to your story? Can you find an alternate source? If the person is insisting upon approval, can you be certain that you'll be getting honest, unlaundered answers to your other questions? Why is he or she standing firm? Can you write a good piece even if you grant the person this condition? Are you making a concession or admitting defeat?

You might try to buy some time before you reach your conclu-sion. Tell your potential interviewee that you will have to consult with your editor or project supervisor before you can make such a concession. Give yourself—and your interview subject—time to mull over the issue before a conclusion is reached. On occasion, the interviewee will reconsider his or her position and will back down on the demand.

If you don't have the time to stall, or if you feel that doing so will damage or terminate your chances of getting the interview, you will have to make a quick decision. Regardless of your choice, don't overemphasize the issue or dwell on it. Take a professional, businesslike approach to it and move on, either to the interview itself or to your next source.

A FEW EXCEPTIONS

There are occasions when an interviewee's request for script approval may be considered reasonable:

- When the interview is conducted over a long period of time;
- When an interview is conducted in several sessions, using more than one interviewing technique; or
- When the interview is intended to act as a "position statement" for historical or archival purposes.

In any of these cases, granting script approval may not be a matter of your making a concession; it may be best for the interview itself.

I've conducted a number of interviews that involved sessions that were spread out over a period of weeks, even months. Interviewees would be available only at certain times (for instance, they may be in the country one week, and abroad the next), and I would have to work the interview around their busy schedules. This is especially applicable to the long, Q/A format interviews I've conducted: at times, I've felt as if I were taking a guerrilla approach to getting a complete interview.

In cases like these, I've had no qualms about granting a person conditional approval, either of the quotes in the manuscript, or of a list of quotes submitted for their approval. By conditional, I mean that I tell an interviewee that he or she may *add* examples, anecdotes, or other types of color to the script, or they may clean up some of their statements, but they may not radically alter answers or change their original intentions or meanings. When I grant this conditional script approval, I remind the interviewees that the original interviews were spoken ones, and that their alterations must appear as if they, too, had been spoken. I also give the interviewees a date by which I need a response and the changes, if any.

The same can be said about granting script approval to people who have been interviewed in several different ways. Let's say that, to write a profile, you interview a person twice in person and twice over the telephone, and that those interviews are spread out over a period of a week or two. The interviewee may be apprehensive about using the mixed types of interviewing—especially if they occur over an extended period of time—and he or she may want to see the quotes, just so everything seems consistent. In cases like this, your article or interview may benefit from an interviewee's reviewing the manuscript. You may get better detail and more consistency by letting your interviewee take a look at what he or she said. Again: the spirit of the revision or change is not to alter, but to improve.

Archival interviews and oral histories are unique because they are intended to be lasting statements. Newspaper and magazine articles have limited shelf lives, but archival interviews and oral histories are intended to be "position statements" that could last for many years. Under those circumstances, an interviewee may rightfully expect to see the words as exact as he or she intends them to be.

I encountered this when I interviewed Raymond Carver, the late poet and short story writer. I was talking to Carver for a magazine piece to be published in the Q/A format. The interview went better than either of us had anticipated, lasting several sessions and covering more ground than we had expected. In every aspect, it was one of those almost magical interviews that moved and expanded as if it had a life of its own. After one of the sessions, Carver commented on how in-depth the interview was getting to be, and he asked if he could see a typescript before I submitted it for publication. Realizing that the interview might have some value to students of Carver's work, as well as to students of writing, I agreed. As it turned out, the interview wound up being one of the longest of Carver's life, and I was very pleased that he'd had the chance to see it published exactly as he wanted it to be.

DON'T MAKE PROMISES

When you are making preinterview arrangements with an interviewee, never make promises you cannot or do not intend to keep. Conducting your business this way is unethical and dishonest, and it could have legal implications as well.

The safe approach is to avoid *volunteering* anything that goes beyond the confines of the typical interview. Don't offer to show a transcript of the interview if the subject doesn't request it. Don't volunteer unnecessary cooperation, such as your submitting questions for approval or consideration prior to the interview. Most veteran interviewers take all this for granted—though veteran interviewers may be the worst offenders when it comes to breaking promises—but novices, in attempts to secure interviews they feel might be otherwise unavailable, sometimes volunteer more than they need to. This leads to problems that can affect the information you gather and ultimately, your article itself.

IF YOU'RE TURNED DOWN . . .

It would be unrealistic to expect that you are going to be successful every time you attempt to line up an interview. No matter how well you present yourself and your project, no matter how much you prepare before you contact the person, there will be times when a person will refuse to talk to you.

The reasons for this are as variable as the personalities, lives, and circumstances of the subjects you interview. People have their own policies about speaking to reporters and writers. Some feel an implicit distrust of the media, their feelings based upon the popular myth that the press places a low priority on truth and accuracy whenever there is a story they can bend to their wills, while other people are naturally shy and disinclined to speak for the record. Some people don't speak to the press at all. Other reasons for a person's refusal to be interviewed have been covered elsewhere in this book, but it's important to mention them again because you should prepare yourself for the unsettling reality of rejection.

You should also be prepared to interpret rejection because, while "no" ultimately carries the same immediate bottom line in all cases of interview-request rejection, it does not always mean the same thing in a larger sense. One person's "no" could mean "absolutely not — not now, not in the future, not under any circumstances," while another's "no" could be interpreted as "not right now, but maybe at another time." (Interviewees who may feel the latter don't always say as much, mainly because they're busy and don't want to encourage an interviewer to hound them or bombard them with frequent interview requests in the near future. It's easier to offer a flat refusal and let the interviewer make the next move.)

An interviewer's greatest asset is persistence, a quality not to be confused with thoughtless aggression. There is a huge difference between your saying "Why not?" and your asking "Do you think there's a chance that you'll be open to an interview in the future?" when your interview request is turned down; the former is the refusal to accept a person's right to reject your request, while the latter is a nod of acceptance with the voiced hope that attitudes or conditions may change.

Successful interviewers have an array of stories describing procedures they used in landing "impossible" interviews and, without exception, at the core of each success story you will find an interviewer's patient persistence.

In some cases, both patience and persistence were tested to the hilt and, on occasion, to unusual degrees. For his historic *Playboy* interview with John Lennon and Yoko Ono, interviewer David Sheff recalled talking to anyone who could put him in touch with the couple. Phone messages went unanswered. Finally Sheff sent a telegram to Ono, who agreed to a meeting *after* Sheff's horoscope was interpreted.

"I could imagine explaining to my *Playboy* editor, Barry Golsen, 'Sorry, but my moon is in Scorpio—the interview's off,' " Sheff later wrote, though one can only imagine what he would have done if indeed that had been the case.

Freelance writer Lawrence Grobel has his own set of stories describing his pursuit of celebrity interviewees. Among Grobel's "impossible" interviews are Marlon Brando, Barbra Streisand, and Robert DeNiro—all people who avoid the press as if their lives depend upon it. When he has finally landed difficult-to-obtain interviews, Grobel asks his reluctant subjects why they backed down and agreed to talk. Their answers, though not particularly earthshaking, are good examples of why you should be persistent when attempting to line up interviews.

"I sort of got tired of saying no, because it gets misread," Al Pacino told Grobel. "The reason I haven't before was that I just didn't think I would be able to do it. But after a while, you just start to feel like, why not? So I've been saying yes much more."

"I feel a need to let some information out," actor Bruce Willis explained, adding that he was bothered by interviews that focused on personal, rather than professional, issues. "I made a choice early in my career not to do a lot of press, not to open myself up to talking about my private life, which, when push comes to shove, is what people want to know." Despite these misgivings, Willis spoke candidly with Grobel of his private affairs.

Patricia Hearst offered Grobel still another reason for agreeing to be interviewed. "I just wanted to get on with my life," she said. "I just had to say what happened."

These examples are the commonplace, rather than the exceptional: reluctant interviewees change their minds all the time. An interviewer who takes a flat "no" at face value may be missing out on a rare or important interview opportunity.

If your request is turned down, do some quick analyzing. If you've been talking to the person (or third party representing a person) for any length of time, you've probably been given a good indication or reason for the rejection of your request. If you haven't, don't be afraid to ask for a reason, but be tactful. Perhaps a celebrity isn't interested in being the subject of an in-depth profile or interview at the moment, but might be agreeable in the future. Maybe a person needs more time to think about an interview. Or it could be that the circumstances make the prospects of an interview extremely uncomfortable. No matter what the reason might be, keep all doors open and make a note to check back in the future — provided, of course, that the person's public stock remains the same or rises in the future.

Some people, however, never back down. They'll remain adamant in their refusal to be interviewed. Neither passing time nor persuasive discussion will convince them that their words should be subject to public scrutiny.

George Plimpton has seen this happen on a number of occasions when *The Paris Review* has attempted to line up interviews with writers.

"There are some people you simply can't get," he explains. "Salinger has never agreed to one, although we've written him a couple of letters. Neither has Thomas Pynchon. Neither has Harper Lee. We've sent letters to her, and she's written back, very politely saying that she just does not give interviews. I've tried a couple of times with all of them, because they're such interesting writers that one hopes that they will partake of all this, but if they make up their minds not to, there's no way you can convince them. If they don't want to talk, they don't have to talk."

WHEN YOU SUCCEED . . .

In much of this chapter, we've addressed some of the hard-line aspects of obtaining an interview, and while this discussion makes the preparation for the interview appear to be only slightly less involved than contract negotiations between labor and management in a large corporation, it should be noted that the overwhelming majority of interviews are conducted without a hitch. Every day, reporters walk up to people on the street, secure interviews, and go about the business of reporting the news. Freelance writers call sources for support quotes that are readily and cheerfully provided. Celebrities—even the skittish ones—sit down with writers and pour out their feelings. Readers rarely hear about the behind-the-scenes aspects of interviewing, and writers only occasionally encounter the hard-line aspects detailed in this chapter. When agreements have to be struck, they're accomplished with minimal hardship to either interviewer or interviewee.

So it's good to remember that the odds are in your favor. Present yourself well and you will probably be taking notes or turning on your tape recorder before you've given the preparatory work a second thought.

When a person agrees to be interviewed, be sure to jot down any appropriate information. Don't count on your memory in matters such as the dates, places, and times of your interviews. If you're busy—and this is a status all writers hope to reach—dates, times, and places can become jumbled in your mind, and there's nothing worse than the sinking feeling of realizing that your Tuesday afternoon interview was really supposed to take place the morning before. Those things happen.

Finally, if you are to meet an interviewee at a location unfamiliar to you, ask for directions. It may appear to be an awkward question to ask, but it's not nearly as embarrassing as having to explain that you're tardy because you got lost. Write down the person's address and phone number, along with specific directions to the interview location, and take that information with you to the interview.

CREATIVE INTERVIEWING

Janet Kraegel, coauthor of *Just A Nurse*, a collection of conversations she and Mary Kachoyeanos conducted with nurses across the country, recalls the day she was scheduled to interview the director of a community health center. She was using the interview for research, and her interviewee was less than enthusiastic about the prospect of talking to her.

"He didn't want to do the interview," Kraegel remembers, "so he just sat there and wrote and conducted his daily business. He asked what I wanted, and I gave him my first question. In about five minutes, he could see that I was trying to understand him, and I think that's the secret to succeeding with interview subjects: they'll cooperate if they think you're trying to understand them. It just amazes you what people are willing to divulge—very sensitive things that could jeopardize them in many ways—if they think you're trying to understand where they're coming from and *why* they're coming from there."

Mary Kachoyeanos agrees. She recalls another project, a very difficult research study that found her interviewing the parents of children who had died suddenly. The interviews, she says, were emotionally draining and quite a test of her interviewing skills, but they offered surprising and telling results.

"I think my first interview subject was a bit leery," Kachoyeanos admits, "but I just couldn't hold back. She was in tears and I was in tears. After we finished talking, I asked her if there was anything else that she wanted to say, and she looked at me and asked if I believed in an afterlife. I told her I did, that though I don't consider myself formally religious, I felt I was very religious in another way. And she said, 'Well, I think I can tell you this. . . .' She told me about going to a medium to try to find out where her child was. But that didn't come out until she knew I was empathetic and sincerely felt for her. We had established that relationship."

From these two examples, you can see the rewarding results of employing good interviewing skills. Not all interviews, of course, are as emotionally demanding as the one just cited, nor will you necessarily have strong feelings, one way or another, for the person talking to you. You should, however, feel a commitment to what the person is telling you. It is not important to agree or disagree with an interviewee, but it is essential for you to connect with the person on a human level, to understand, as Kraegel suggested, the interviewee's perspective and how you can use that knowledge in the article, feature, or interview that you're writing.

Good interviewing skills make this possible. How you open your interview, pace your conversation, and follow up your questions will determine both the quality and quantity of the responses you receive. The way you pose difficult but necessary questions will determine the difference in your getting a complete, noteworthy response or no response at all. Your ability to listen and take notes will help you direct the interview into important areas that must be addressed. In short, creative interviewing is not the employment of the single skill of one's being able to talk; it is a package of skills that complement each other and lead the interviewee to *believe* that all you're doing is talking.

The trick is to make it look natural, even in the most difficult circumstances.

GREETINGS AT THE DOOR: THE FIRST MOMENTS WITH AN INTERVIEWEE

Over the years, I've talked to a number of interviewees who insist that interviews are "no big deal." These people would have you believe that they place no more weight on giving interviews than they do on tying their shoes or going for their nightly strolls. To them, the interview may as well be two old neighbors talking over a picket fence—it's that loose and easy.

I suspect that such a stated casual, if not cavalier, approach to being interviewed is so much bravado: I've never met any interviewees who didn't give an indication, at one point or another during the interview, that they were measuring words and were conscious of the fact that they were speaking for the record. Despite what these people tell you, they *care* about what they are saying and how they are saying it; they are fully conscious of the fact that you are going to use in your article whatever material or quotations they give you. They know they're being sized up, analyzed—they'd be disappointed if you were as casual in your approach to the interview as they claim to be in theirs.

I've also spoken to people who trembled in fear—literally—throughout the interview. The thought of being interviewed sickened some of my more reluctant or shy interviewees. Some displayed such great physical discomfort that I was uncomfortable myself. As an interviewer, you don't want to feel as if you are torturing the person you're talking to, even when the topics you're discussing are difficult to talk about.

One of the most urgent tasks in successful interviews occurs in the opening moments of the interview, when you must try to gauge your interviewee's state of mind and put your conversation in motion in accordance with what you learn. The first moments of the interview are a time of discovery, and you should devote this time to making mental notes of details that will be important to your interview or article.

Four areas to concern yourself with include:

■ *How is this person reacting to me?* You can read a lot into a greeting. Does the person smile? Is his or her handshake firm? Does he or she seem ready (if not happy) to see you? Does the person look you in the eye, go out of the way to make you feel comfortable? What tone of voice does the person use when greeting you? The answers to these questions will give you an indication of the person's predisposition to being interviewed, and that will signal the way you'll engage in small talk or open your interview.

■ *How am I reacting to this person?* Some reporters and writers, like some interviewees, like to entertain the little vanity that all interviews are alike. This attitude, they feel, helps keep them objective. In fact, there is a huge difference between being objective and recognizing your own feelings about an interviewee—and you *will* have feelings about the person you're interviewing. You, too, will have a predisposition about the person you're interviewing, and in the opening moments of the interview you will be matching that predisposition with the person you're actually meeting. By recognizing your initial feelings about the interviewee, you will be equipped to adjust your interview in a way that better assures the objectivity you need.

■ *What's going on around me?* The environment for the interview is important. In the moments directly following your meeting an interview subject, you will be seeing the environment in which the interview will take place. Are other people—friends, family, observers—present? If so, how will they affect the interview, if at all? Are you talking on neutral ground (such as in a restaurant or hotel room, on the street, or even in the person's living room or kitchen), or are you clearly on the person's turf (such as business office)? How has the person prepared for your arrival, if the interview has been prearranged? (Some people make a point of displaying—in what they consider to be a discreet manner, of course—certain personal effects, trinkets, books, magazines, etc. that *they* feel say something positive about them.) In your opening moments with an interviewee, you should take mental notes of all these factors.

■ *What kind of mood is the person in?* There may be a subtle difference between the way a person reacts to you and the mood he or she may be in. People mask their feelings, put up fronts. After you've met the person and have moved into the area in which the interview will be taking place, you may notice slight indications of the real face behind the mask; or you might notice this as the interview progresses, at a time when the person is comfortable with you and more apt to let down his or her guard. Be prepared for this reflection of your subject's true mood; it will tell you something about the quality of the responses you're receiving.

First impressions may not prove to have been entirely accurate by the end of your interview; nevertheless they are crucial considerations, because they will be the foundation upon which you build the opening of your interview. Equally important is the way you present yourself to your interviewee. A firm handshake, eye contact, a smile, good body carriage—all form an impression in your interviewee's mind. The way you're dressed and your professional demeanor will also help. In those first few moments of your encounter, your professionalism and humanity will establish you as a person who can be trusted and responded to, so you should know ahead of time — even rehearse — the way you hope to greet the person.

EQUIPMENT FOR AN INTERVIEW

For over a decade, I have been carrying around a large leather camera bag that acts as my portable office. My friends jokingly refer to it as my "Santa Claus bag," mainly because its many compartments are usually packed to the bursting point, making it seem to weigh only a pound or two less than my car.

All hyperbole aside, this work bag has been invaluable to me. I keep it where it is instantly accessible, packed with the gear that I'd take to any interview. I can't even begin to number the many times that this state of preparedness has helped me out, when interviews have popped up unexpectedly and I was ready to go.

In this bag, I carry an assortment of empty notebooks, an address book, pens, pencils, a tape recorder, blank cassettes, spare batteries, a set of headphones, and an AC adaptor, along with miscellaneous research notes and reading materials. Notes and reading materials may not help me much with unexpected interviews, but the other materials — items that I'd take along on most interviews, anyway — offer me a sense of security that can be quite comforting when I might otherwise be scrambling to get everything together for an interview.

By now, I take most of my equipment for granted. Through years of trial-and-error experimentation, I've learned which tools work best for me, and while I've also learned that equipment preference varies from writer to writer, there are a few points that should be made about the tools of the trade:

■ *Notebooks.* I prefer stenographer's notebooks, which seem to be a pragmatic compromise between the smaller reporter's notebooks and the larger composition notebooks used in schools, though I know writers who prefer the other styles. I also try to carry the smaller pocket notebooks for taking short, quick notes when I'd rather be inconspicuous in my notetaking.

For easy reference, I date all notebooks on the inside covers, and I always include a quick sketch or index of a notebook's contents. Notebooks should be filed and safely stored when completed and, depending upon the material in the notes, retained on file for at least five years. (Investigative reporters have had their notes impounded in libel and other court actions, and without the note-books, defense would be nearly impossible. Notebooks can also be useful as physical evidence in IRS tax audits, if you ever find your-self having to support your claims of the time and expense connected with an article.)

One last point: at the bottom of the inside cover of each notebook, you should include your name, address, and telephone number, along with a notation that you will provide postage, plus a reward, for the safe return of the notebook. I began this practice years ago when I saw another writer marking his notebooks, and it's a practice that paid off for me on one occasion, when I left a notebook behind in a restaurant. There were nearly a month's notes and research material in the notebook, and I hate to think of the work I would have had to redo if the notebook had been lost forever.

■ *Address book.* One bit of advice: never keep just one address book. Though it's never happened to me, I've heard horror stories from other writers who had lost or misplaced their address books. Keep a card file and an address book — or two address books — but don't have a single source with all-important numbers. Some writers (myself included) like to have an address book on hand at all times. I use initials for the names of the well-known entries as an insurance against what might happen if the book were ever lost or stolen.

■ *Pens/pencils.* I carry a healthy supply of both pens and pencils, a practice I adopted after I took only a couple of pens to a university library and learned that the library refused to allow pens in their rare books and manuscripts room. Since there were no pencils available, I had to leave the library and find a store that sold pencils. Use number two pencils with good erasers. As for pens, keep a stock of the type of pen you are most comfortable with. I was given this advice when I first started writing, and it seemed both obvious and nit-picky to me at the time, but as the years have rolled on, and I've worked with all kinds of writing utensils, I've found the advice to be sound. Your writing utensils should feel as good in your hands as a hammer or tool belt should feel to a carpenter. After all, you are working with your pens every day, and they are the source of your livelihood.

■ *Tape recorder.* The simpler the recorder, the better. Don't get hung up on expensive tape recorders with a lot of fancy built-in features or gadgets; they only offer more features to break down, and they can be distracting or disruptive when you are setting up for an interview. ("I don't use terribly expensive recorders, because I've found that if you buy an expensive recorder, as soon as you need it serviced it becomes a *terribly* expensive recorder," says Lawrence Linderman. "Tape recorders have become disposable to me: I have a bunch of them, and I will run through them.") A small, hand-held tape recorder using standard-sized cassettes is best. Microcassettes don't record for as long a period of time per tape, and you don't want to be changing cassettes every few minutes, especially if you're conducting a long interview. Built-in microphones are generally acceptable, though you may want to consider investing in an optional exterior, hand-held microphone for those occasions when sound quality is important, or when you're recording in places where the noises around you may be picked up by built-in microphones and blend in with the sound of your interviewee's voice. One essential is a built-in AUTO STOP device that stops the tape and gives an audible signal at the end of a tape; without such a device, you may wind up with a portion of unrecorded interview, resulting from a tape's winding down without your knowledge.

■ *Cassettes.* You don't need to spend a fortune on high-fidelity cassettes to be effective, but you shouldn't work with the budget types, either. Find midpriced cassettes manufactured by reputable firms, and you'll learn that these work well for voice recordings. Ninety-minute (forty-five minutes per side) are the best: the longer-running cassettes can be unreliable and will snap from time to time, and the shorter-running ones offer a sort of psychological disadvantage if your subject starts to look at his or her watch every time you have to stop an interview to turn over or change a tape. Keep a well-labeled and maintained tape file, the same as you would keep a notebook file, and for the same reasons.

■ *Batteries and AC adaptor.* Never scrimp on the quaility of the batteries that you use in your tape recorder. Most cassette tape recorders drain batteries at a pretty good clip, but the more expensive alkaline or nickel batteries last longer and will ultimately give you peace of mind when you are recording longer interviews. I always take an AC adaptor to interviews, but I never count on being able to use it. More often than not, the interview takes place either away from electrical sockets or at a time or location where it would be awkward to move the recorder to a socket. Assume that you will need batteries to power your tape recorder and you'll always be prepared.

SHOULD YOU USE A TAPE RECORDER?

Although the issue isn't debated as much today as it was at one time, there is still some disagreement over the best method to use in preserving an interviewee's words. Old Schoolers prefer to jot their interviewee's words into notebooks, while New Schoolers feel that a tape recorder is the only way to assure accuracy and safety at a time when litigation is a way of life in the publishing and newspaper businesses. Old Schoolers argue that tape recorders discourage candor, while New Schoolers contend that their not having to write down an interviewee's words affords them the opportunity to listen more carefully to what is being said.

There is merit in both arguments. Tape recorders have numerous built-in advantages and disadvantages, and each interviewer should consider them before deciding upon which method (recorder or notebook) seems best.

Among the advantages:

■ *Tape recorders capture the entire interview.* People who use notebooks rarely write out every word an interviewee says; in fact, some interviewers take down only those quotes or observations that they feel are essential to their article. ("It's distractive as hell," complains one frequently interviewed individual of the latter method of notetaking. "You'll be talking away, the guy who's interviewing you is nodding and listening, and all of a sudden he's writing like crazy. It makes you pretty self-conscious. First of all, you're wondering if you ought to slow down so he can write everything the way you're saying it, and then you start to wonder about why he's writing down some of the things you're saying and ignoring some of the other stuff.") When you're using a tape recorder, there is no issue of selective notetaking of the person's words, nor is there a concern of getting every word correct: the entire interview—your remarks and questions, along with the interviewee's responses and observations—is perfectly preserved.

■ *Tape recorders free you to devote your total attention to the interviewee.* By eliminating or drastically reducing the amount of notetaking you are obliged to do while your interviewee is speaking, a tape recorder offers you a better opportunity to listen to what the person is saying. You're also freed to observe and take mental notes on the interview subject's facial expressions, body language, and other telling forms of nonverbal comunication.

■ *Tape recorders assure you of accuracy when you quote your interviewee in your article, profile, or Q/A interview.* Accurate quoting is every good interviewer's goal, and by taking down every word an interviewee is saying, a tape recorder serves you the opportunity to do so. If you're writing an investigative report or dealing with sensitive or controversial topics, this accuracy may be crucial in the event that your article and its quotations are challenged in court.

At first glance, these advantages seem to offer you everything you could want in terms of interview mechanics. Not only can you engage your subject in lively conversation without having to worry about writing down everything he or she is saying, but you are also assured of total accuracy when you eventually write your piece.

The taped interview, however, is not without considerable disadvantages:

■ *Tape recorders can intimidate interviewees or encourage them to "perform."* The presence of a tape recorder is the presence of something official or formal, and people react to tape recorders in different ways. Some people freeze the moment a tape recorder is turned on; others may talk, but they become so self-conscious about what they are saying that their words are more of a discourse than honest discussion. Some will go so far as to look at the machine and dictate their responses to it, rather than to you. Rather than offer candid responses to your questions, the interviewee may perform for the benefit of your running machine.

■ *Tape recorders may encourage lazy interviewing habits.* Just as using a tape recorder can free you to turn your total attention to your interviewee, it conversely may lull you into the bad habit of relying too much on it. Your mind may wander or lose track of what the interviewee is telling you. It's easy to grow too dependent upon this mechanical device. "It tends to make me lazy," admits Tracy Kidder, an affirmed believer in the notebook method. "With a tape recorder, I sort of stop taking notes and miss a lot."

■ *Tape recorders can fail or break down during the interview.* Every interviewer who regularly uses a tape recorder can tell you at least one horror story about the way the machine betrayed him or her during an interview. Tape recorders break down or refuse to work; they will quit on you at the most inopportune times, often without your being aware of it until after you've returned home, turned on the machine, and heard a blank tape instead of your recorded interview. By placing your faith in a machine, you're also setting yourself up for being disappointed by it.

■ *Tape recorders create extra work after the interview.* If you've been taking notes and have written down everything an interviewee has told you, you have less work after the interview than the person who has to fully transcribe tapes or scan them for important details or quotes. If your deadlines are imposing, this extra work can be unnerving.

If you elect to use a tape recorder, how do you minimize its disadvantages? To make it seem less formal or imposing, you might try setting it off to the side — as opposed to the center of a table, between you and your interviewee — during the interview. Don't give the machine any more prominence than necessary. Use your small talk — or your basic closed questions — to warm up your interviewee, and once the person is talking, the tape recorder's presence will be less of a factor. During the interview, take occasional notes on what's being said. This will keep your attention focused on the interview. Jot down notes on possible follow-up questions; this will have the added effect of encouraging your interview subject to talk further, since it will look as if you are intensely interested in what is being said. If your recorder has a tape counter, and if you can station it in a position that lets you see the counter without its being obvious, make notes on where quotes may be located. After the interview, these notes will help you scan the tape for important quotes.

SMALL TALK
Turning on a tape recorder and beginning an interview immediately after introducing yourself is similar to starting a car in cold weather and racing its engine: without a brief warm-up period, you risk damaging your product.

As an interviewer, you should take a workmanlike, professional approach to your craft, but not at the risk of appearing cold, indifferent, or impersonal to the person you are interviewing. Rushing into an interview can produce those effects. It can leave an interviewee feeling used, as if you care little about the person and only about what he or she says. Or your interviewee might misinterpret your businesslike approach as arrogance, and the resulting tension or mistrust will affect the rapport you will need for a good interview.

The proper use of small talk is very effective in helping interviewer and interviewee ease into a conversation. People anticipate a certain amount of small talk at the onset of any social transaction — it's like "leader tape" to the business about to be conducted. Those same people expect very little to come out of small talk: they recognize it for what it is, and they treat it as a necessary part of the game.

Small talk, however, should not be a simple matter of your shooting the breeze; if it is, you are wasting your interviewee's time, as well as your own. Your small talk should have a sense of purpose. You may be warming up your subject, fishing for an opening to the interview, gauging your interviewee's mood, or putting yourself at ease — any of these can be accomplished by a few minutes of small talk.

The following is a fragment of the opening of an interview I conducted with a well-known author. From my research, I knew that the author was shy (which is why I do not now name her) and generally considered to be a tough interview; my research, however, did not give me any solid clues as to whether she was a tough interview as a result of shyness or as a result of impatience with interviewers who were prying into her life. Complicating matters was the fact that I was interviewing her while she was on a promotional tour for her latest book; I wondered if she would be comfortable in a strange environment, talking, perhaps begrudgingly, to strangers. After I introduced myself, and while I was setting up my tape recorder and taking out my notes, I engaged in the following small talk:

> Q. *Before we get going here, I want to congratulate you on your new book. I just finished it a couple of days ago and I thought it was wonderful.*

A. Thank you.

Q. *I've seen some reviews, and the criticism seems to be favorable.*

A. So far I can't complain, but I haven't seen that many reviews yet.

Q. *On top of everything else, the book's packaging was excellent. It has one of the prettiest covers I've seen so far this year.*

A. Isn't it wonderful? I was so pleased with the way it turned out. I picked out that cover painting myself.

Q. *Really? How did that happen?*

By this point, my notes were out and I had turned on the tape recorder. She didn't seem to notice. I was ready for the interview and so was she. In this case, the small talk netted an unexpected bonus: not only had I eased into the conversation and, in doing so, had become more comfortable with my interview subject, but I had also been given an important, unexpected piece of information that I could build upon in the interview itself. By the time we were finished talking about the book's artwork, it seemed quite logical to move into a discussion of the book. It is ironic that, considering the interviewee, this was one of the briefest and easiest small talk sessions I've ever had.

On the surface, there was nothing special about this brief exchange. I offered a genuine compliment, which was underscored by an observation based upon my research. I knew how writers fret about the artwork connected with their books, so my remark (again, a genuine compliment) was safe. Each of my first three remarks was innocuous and could not have damaged the opening of the conversation; and it was obvious, from the nature of those remarks, that I was trying to fill time and break the ice while I was setting up my tape recorder. I expected little, in terms of usable quotes, from the responses to those remarks, but I was fishing nevertheless. For all I knew, she might have had something to say about the critics' responses to her book and, as it turned out, she had plenty to say about the book's cover design. This was as much as I could have hoped for from a few brief remarks.

Studs Terkel has been known to use his setting up of equipment and small talk period as a means of breaking the ice and putting an interviewee at ease. Stories abound of Terkel's crawling around on all fours, searching for an electrical outlet, muttering about the inconveniences of the tape recorder. It's a maneuver, he claims, that offers its own peculiar benefits.

"Here's a tape recorder, which is my right arm," he explains. "I know how to push the right buttons now, but when I first started, I'd goof up. In some cases, that worked in my favor in a strange way. I'd be talking to somebody who had never been interviewed before, and as I goofed up, the person would say, 'Look, it's not turning,' and that person might help me with the tape recorder. If that person helps me, it knocks out the whole idea of somebody higher up coming down to interview him."

While the idea of loosening up an interviewee at your own expense may not be a recommended procedure for all interviewers, Terkel's story is an example of an effective way in which an interviewer can mix professionalism and humanity into the initial moments of an interview. There is no doubt that Terkel is a highly professional craftsman, yet by displaying his human side, he is inviting the interviewee to voluntarily *participate* in the business at hand. Interviewee participation is every interviewer's goal, and if it can be achieved early in the interview, the remainder of the interview will proceed much more smoothly.

Another effective way of engaging in small talk is to take a few moments to outline your plans for the article to the interviewee. Given your research and planning, you should have little difficulty in freely discussing the basics of your project, and your doing so gives your interviewee the opportunity to pose any questions he or she may have regarding your project.

When you're engaging in small talk, you should always try to stay on safe ground. Avoid controversial or gossipy topics, and don't come on too strong; familiarity may cause your interviewee to withdraw into himself. Above all, know when to stop. Too much small talk makes you look phony or unprofessional; it also eats into the time you have for your interview. Take a few minutes and move on.

OPENING THE INTERVIEW

The opening of your interview—your opening remarks and the first few questions you ask—will largely determine the procedure for the rest of the interview. Your interviewee will have formed first impressions based, for better or worse, upon those few moments in which you introduced yourself and engaged in small talk; the opening of the interview will either strengthen or alter these impressions, depending upon how you fare in starting off your questioning. Although it may not be fair, an interviewee *expects* something from you. He may be a cynical veteran of numerous bad interviews, and therefore he expects very little from you. She may be frightened or anxious, and therefore she may expect you to guide her along, acting as part interviewer, part counselor. If he has information he's eager to get off his chest, he may expect you to show empathy and intelligence in the way you conduct the interview. Whatever the expectations, their formation is out of your control. Your duty is to open the interview in such a way as to make those expectations secondary or immaterial to the interview itself.

OPENING QUESTIONS

To a large degree, there is a contradictory element in the first formal question of an interview: while the first question is enormously important for its ability to set the tone for the conversation to follow, it should never be the most important question that you ask. Unless you're cramped for time or limited in the number of questions you can ask, your first question is usually a formal sense of transition, a determined movement from small talk to the interview itself. It has to say, "Yes, we're conducting serious business now" without being threatening or intimidating to the interviewee.

If you have been successful in the small talk segment of your conversation, your interviewee will have warmed up to you, at least to a certain extent, but that doesn't mean that he will be ready to bare his soul to you in response to your first question. Trust operates on many levels, and you have just attained the first one. Other levels will be developed as you move along.

Your first question should be designed to serve five basic functions. It should:

- Be a recognizable signal that the interview is beginning;

- Further establish the degree of trust the interviewee is beginning to place in you;
- Be challenging in the sense that it addresses an issue or topic that the interviewee either has not addressed in the past or has not addressed at this angle in the past;
- Encourage the interviewee to talk (or lead to a question that requires an expansive answer); and
- Be strong enough to build the first portion of your interview upon.

You may have formed your first question when you were planning your interview questions, but you should always be prepared to improvise. During your small talk, an interviewee may offer you a better opening than the one you had anticipated, or the person's mood might discourage the practicality of the first question you had prepared. One surefire method of opening an interview is to address your interviewee's most current interest—an approach that is especially attractive if you're interviewing a celebrity. If the person is on tour to promote a product such as a new book, movie, record, etc., talk about that product. Your interviewee expects to discuss it, and he or she will be prepared to answer questions about it. Once you have the conversation flowing, you can easily move to other areas of interest. If you're dealing with newsmakers, your opening question should focus on the event that placed that person in the news, though you should save the tougher questions for later in the interview. Take a circling approach: start on the outside, a reasonable distance from the core of your story, and move in.

TOUGH OPENERS
Not all interviews afford you a breaking-in period for small talk, or opening questions that lead up to the main points you want to address in the interview and your resulting article. There may be severe limitations on the time you have with an interviewee, or the nature of the conversation itself may dictate a no-nonsense approach. There will be no time for chit-chat if you are interviewing a politician in the time it takes for him to walk from his office to his car. There is no easy way to lead into the main subject of your conversation if you are a reporter interviewing a witness to a shooting. In either case, the point of your interview *becomes* the interview.

Nevertheless, you will need to use some tact when you open your conversation. You should not bludgeon your interviewee with an insensitive opening question, nor should you make the person feel as if he or she is being ambushed. Unfortunately, this kind of insensitive approach occurs too often, especially in daily news reportage, and it has bruised the reputation of journalists in general.

"I call it shallow crap-journalism," Studs Terkel asserts. "Paparazzi journalism has always been popular. There's always been a yellow journalism in which the person is nothing. You've seen it on TV: There's a fire and a woman carries a kid out—the kid has died—and the reporter says, 'How do you feel?' *How do you feel?* The woman has lost her baby!"

In his remarks, Terkel points directly to the one major factor missing in the opening question: interviewer empathy. "How do you feel" may be precisely what the interviewer wishes to address in his or her story—though, in cases such as these, the person's feelings are obvious—but the wording of the question makes the interviewer look insensitive or callous to the interviewee's situation or feelings. Reporters and journalists have (deservedly, in some cases) gained the reputation of blocking out everything but the business at hand, and such a prejudicial reputation is an obstacle an interviewer often has to overcome.

Genuine empathy, shown simply or subtly when it is appropriate, works wonders in opening difficult interviews. Showing that you care is neither a sign of weakness nor a concession of professionalism; it is a display of common humanity, a sign that you don't regard your interview subject as ten column inches of newsprint or just another assignment.

It can be difficult to interview people who are grieving or depressed. It leaves you with the helpless feeling of not knowing where to begin. How do you deal with people who are crying or in emotional distress? Can you retain your sense of objectivity without presenting yourself as being emotionally cold?

In some cases, displaying empathy may not be a compromise of objectivity. "For our study of parents whose kids died suddenly, we did twenty-seven interviews," Mary Kachoyeanos says. "The parents were together, and there wasn't one interview I didn't cry in. Before we started, we talked to a person from Compassionate Friends. I asked her what would happen if I started crying, and she said it would be a wonderful thing because the parents would know that I cared. The interviews were very emotional, and they sort of allowed the freedom to cry."

Another tough opener is the one with a person who is angry with someone other than you. This person is seeking a catharsis, a means to ease tension or frustration; a vehicle for rage. You, the interviewer, are a convenience.

These interviews are difficult for two reasons. First, all of the person's responses will be tempered by anger because, as we all know, people say things they don't really mean, or they exaggerate what they're saying, when they are angry. The second problem is logistic: to obtain the responses you need, you will have to somehow get beyond the person's anger.

When opening an interview with such a person, the best policy is to allow the person to speak his or her mind. Maybe the anger will burn itself out and, once it's spent, the rest of the interview will go along more smoothly, on a more even keel. Hang tough: don't argue with the person or display impatience or annoyance. If it becomes apparent that the anger isn't going to dissipate, or if the attacks begin to involve you personally (and this has been known to happen), then you may need a change of procedure. One approach is to remind the interviewee that you are neither the enemy nor the person or situation that has angered him. ("Hold on a second. We're on the same side, remember?") Another approach is to suggest the postponement of the interview for another time. In either instance, the interviewee will be reminded that you aren't accomplishing what you set out to accomplish in the interview, and, more often than not, will settle down.

No matter what the circumstance, you must address the tough openers with a level head. The interviews are difficult to begin for good reason, and a lack of understanding on your part will only jeopardize the interview. If you cannot show empathy for the person, at least stay neutral. Stand your ground, but be gentle.

PUTTING AN INTERVIEWEE AT EASE

Putting a person at ease and gaining his or her trust are not one and the same; in fact, one usually leads to the other. At the onset of an interview, an interviewee may trust you on the most basic level, but only after you have made your subject feel comfortable will that trust develop to the point where he or she will give you information or opinions that might otherwise be held back.

To put an interviewee at ease, you must first show the person that *you* are relaxed. If you are sitting stock straight across from your interviewee, a grim expression on your face, your pen poised, your eyes boring holes into your interviewee, the person is going to be more self-conscious than if you are businesslike but relaxed. Your mood, attitude, and presentation can be infectious: if you look loose, informed, ready to empathize, appropriately attired and professionally poised, serious but not severe, and prepared to conduct a formal conversation (as opposed to a formal *interview*, though that's what you're doing, of course), your interviewee will probably relax. Keep your tough questions hidden until you secure the person's trust in you. Show the person that you've done your homework by bringing parts of your research into the early conversation.

Some subjects will never loosen up; they will be on edge from the time you begin to the time you leave, no matter what you do to try to relax them. When you run into such interviewees, the temptation is to become more serious and formal, to adjust your approach to match their mood or attitude, but doing so can be a big mistake. If a person is nervous about the interview and you suddenly become very rigid or formal, the atmosphere of the interview can be intimidating to the person. Rather than make adjustments in your interviewing style, you should proceed according to your plan. Comport yourself as you would with an open, friendly interviewee. Display enthusiasm for the topic of discussion, even if the interviewee does not. Try to persuade the person, through your attitude and line of questioning, that you are not an opponent but, in fact, an interested individual seeking information or opinions. The interviewee may not ever loosen up, but he or she may grow to trust you enough to provide you with the information you are seeking.

PACING THE INTERVIEW

The way you pace your interview will depend upon how much time you have to conduct it. If you have ten minutes, pacing the interview will not be an issue to consider; you will ask the most important questions on your list and hope they will be answered in that short period of time. For longer interviews, or for interviews that will be conducted in more than one session, pacing becomes an important issue.

If you were to graph the pacing of a lengthy interview, you would wind up with a chart depicting a series of peaks and valleys. Those peaks and valleys represent the *momentum* of your conversation. At the low end of each valley would be the point at which one topic was exhausting itself and another was beginning; at the peak would be the point at which the topic was receiving its most detailed and important discussion. The key to pacing is to control the momentum of the interview, to work the various upswings and downswings in a manner that picks up and exhausts topics of discussion to the ultimate benefit of your readers. Going from beginning to peak to end may only require a handful of questions or, in a multisession interview, it may take dozens of questions, but the overall effect you're looking for is the completely exhausted topic.

Good pacing is not difficult to achieve; in fact, it is the most natural way of carrying on a conversation. Think about a recent conversation you have had with a friend or family member: chances are excellent that, if you were to graph the pacing of that conversation, it would be a series of peaks and valleys. The transitions from one topic of discussion to the next occurred when one person picked up a thread of discussion and built a new topic of conversation from it.

The formal interview works the same way, except you, the interviewer, are required to direct the pacing of the conversation. To pace an interview is to *manage* it, to guide it. You must see that all important topics are covered, while at the same time you allow the interviewee the opportunity to put his or her own mark on those topics. You must be alert about the pacing of the conversation and make decisions on whether to move an interview along or let a topic of conversation play itself out. If you're too rigid, you might miss out on interesting anecdotes (which are usually the result of your using open-ended questions and letting the interviewee talk), but if you're too loose, you risk letting the interviewee ramble on at the cost of your covering other crucial topics of discussion.

Here is where your planning will help you. If you have blocked out the interview's topics ahead of time, you will know how many major topics you need to cover, and you will be able to place that loose interview outline into the context of your interview's pacing. For example, if you know that you have to cover five topics in a one-hour interview, you are allotting an average of twelve minutes to a topic, and you will be able to pace the interview accordingly. Obviously, you cannot put a stopwatch on the interviewee, but having an overall, preconceived notion of the interview's pacing will help you when you get into the interview itself.

Your interviewee's availability will also be a deciding factor in the way you pace your conversation. If your interview is a "one-shot deal" with little or no chance of your later contacting the person with follow-up questions, you will have to guide the pacing of the interview much more than you would if you had greater future access. If you know, going into the interview, that you would be able to meet or call the interviewee if you were to have follow-up questions or needed further information, you would be in a much better position to allow the interviewee to go off on tangents, be more expansive with his or her answers, and, in general, have a greater influence on the pacing of the interview.

If you don't know whether the interviewee is open to a follow-up interview or further questioning, you should ask. Find an opening, early in the interview, to inquire about these possibilities. Most interviewees are open to the idea. After all, they want as complete and accurate a representation as possible.

Your planning, however, will only give you a vague idea of how to pace your interview. You will have to be prepared to improvise, to use your instincts and judgment as the final determining factor. You will need to have a *feel* for the direction the interview is taking, especially if your interviewee is off on a tangent and the clock is ticking away.

"Part of the process is looking at your questions and your watch," explains Gary Provost. "I'll let people go on for a while, and then I'll try to get them back to the point in a way that doesn't sound as if I'm saying 'shut up and let's get back to the point.' I try to make a question sound as if it's related to what they're talking about. For example, let's say I wanted to talk to Dan Wakefield about writing fiction, and he's telling me about a time when he was in Cuba, writing a nonfiction piece for *The New York Times*. I might say something like 'Did you ever think of writing a novel about Cuba?' I'm really trying to get him back to a discussion about whether he prefers writing novels over nonficton, but it sounds as if we're discussing Cuba."

Experienced interviewers like Provost are adept at guiding their interviewees through conversations; they prefer interviews that have a smooth, undulating—as opposed to straight or choppy—feeling to them.

To achieve this undulating effect, you have to know how to work with your transitions. Hard breaks between topics—an effect gained by one's reading questions off a list—disrupts the motion and flow of the interview. Provost's example is an excellent indication of how skilled interviewers move from one topic to another. When possible, you should wait for the right signals that indicate your ability to move on without interrupting the movement of the conversation. An interviewee will almost always provide you with an opening, no matter how small, which allows you to switch topics smoothly.

When you recognize such an opening, don't jump on it. Let your interviewee finish his or her thoughts, and then double back. Never interrupt an interviewee unless there is no other way to get back on track. You can always return to a point or opening in a manner that doesn't intrude upon the interview ("A few minutes ago, you were mentioning . . . .").

Each topic you'll be discussing has a beginning, middle, and ending. You begin when you (or your interviewee) brings the topic into play. From that point on, your pacing will involve your guiding the discussion to the point that has the most use for your article or interview (middle), and you'll wind down as the topic is exhausted. Your priorities will indicate the topics that need the longest discussion, while your instincts will guide you to others. For less important topics, move the conversation more quickly than for focus topics, and try not to bunch all of your main questions at any one point during the interview. This helps establish the undulating effect that you're aiming for.

DURING THE INTERVIEW . . .

While you are interviewing a person, you will want to keep the following in mind:

■ *Make each question count.* As an interviewer, your job is not to simply fill time; anybody can do that. Your job is to use the time you have, whether it be ten minutes or ten hours, to its fullest advantage. The sign of a terrific interview is your leaving with the knowledge that you have gathered more material than you need, that the most difficult part of the writing itself will involve a process of elimination. To increase your odds of achieving this effect, you should make each question work for you. Every word you utter during the course of the interview should have a purpose, each question should move the interview along.

■ *Try to get complete statements.* There are two important aspects to obtaining complete statements. First is getting a complete idea: be sure the idea has a beginning, middle, and ending, and take nothing for granted. You're always better off in having your *interviewee* provide a complete idea than you are in filling in the blanks in the article you're writing. The second aspect of obtaining complete statements focuses on getting a complete sentence: interviewees will often assume that you know what they mean when they're talking about certain issues and, as a result, they will fail to complete their thoughts in full sentences. Half-sentences, phrases, and partial statements make poor quotations, so you should attempt to get your interviewee to supply you with complete sentences. Press for further details or information. Rephrase the person's answer in the form of a question. These tactics encourage an interviewee to repeat him- or herself, and you will probably wind up with the complete statements you need.

■ *Prod the interviewee when it is called for.* Interviewees will often make statements hinting of strong anecdotal background ("I didn't learn a thing about politics until my last year of college. . . ."), without readily volunteering anecdotes or examples. In most cases, their failure to supply the anecdotes or examples is more a case of oversight than their withholding information. When this happens, nudge your interviewee into telling you more. "Oh?" "Really?" "How so?"—these are all examples of a nudge that should prod the interviewee into expanding a statement into the *complete* story.

■ *If you need examples, ask for them.* I recently watched a television talk show in which the interviewer was talking to a rock musician who has recorded his first album. The interviewer asked the musician if his making of the record was everything he had hoped it would be, and the musician responded by saying that, while it had been a generally positive experience, there were many negative experiences to the creation of the album. The musician had been very frank throughout the interview to that point, and he showed no sign of being unwilling to discuss the downside of the recording business. The interviewer tried to prod the interviewee with an "Oh?" but the musician missed the cue. ("Yeah," he answered.) Since there was plenty of time remaining in the program, I was surprised when the interviewer nodded and proceeded to ask a question totally unrelated to the one he'd just posed. Why, I wondered, had he not asked specifically for examples of the disappointing aspects of the business? He may have had his reasons, but this example illustrates one crucial aspect to interviewing: if an interviewee makes a statement that cries out for examples to support it, don't hesitate to ask for specifics. Examples fortify statements and add dimension to your interview. You should ask for them whenever possible.

■ *Let your ignorance work in your favor.* You cannot know everything there is to know about every topic under the sun, and no one, including your interviewee, expects you to. You're interviewing the person for insights or information, and you would be foolish to leave the interview without a clear picture, simply because you were afraid of showing your ignorance. When you don't understand something an interviewee is telling you, ask for a clarification or further explanation. This is also an effective way to gather anecdotes or pin down generalizations—you're encouraging the person to talk, to give you information. Don't be shy about admitting that you're not an authority in the field, that you just aren't catching everything the person is telling you. Most interviewees will be more than willing to comply. After all, supplying you with the explanation or information makes them look good.

■ *Let your knowledge work in your favor.* What you already know can be very useful if the interviewee is slow to provide information, or if he or she is giving general, rather than specific answers to your questions. Interviewees may assume that you know what they're talking about—and these assumptions are well-founded if you've proven that you've done your research—but the two of you should never assume that your *readers* will be well-versed in the topic of discussion. If the important details are being skipped or skimmed over, you might find it easier to obtain the information or anecdotes you need if you assert your own knowledge. ("Wasn't there a time when you marched in a protest against apartheid? How did that happen?") Your knowledge is also very useful if you suspect that your interviewee is not telling you the truth, but you'll need to use discretion if you believe this is the case. A challenging or argumentative tone may produce negative results. However, by dropping well-timed hints about what you know, you will be showing your interviewee that you've done your own thorough job of researching—a fact that might give him pause if he is considering the notion of giving you a fabricated or less than totally honest story.

■ *Don't interrupt your interviewee.* You might be tempted to interrupt when your interviewee says something that jogs a memory or leads into an area of discussion that you had planned to explore, or you might impatiently feel like interrupting the person if he or she is off on a tangent that seems intentionally designed to avoid an answer to your question. Resist these temptations. Not only are interruptions rude or irritating to the speaker, but they tend to break the person's train of thought and discourage the completion of a thought or idea. Rather than interrupt your interviewee by injecting your comments into the conversation, make a note to bring them up later in the interview, when a better opening occurs. If the person is avoiding your question, you are well within your rights to restate the question or point out that it hasn't been answered, but try to find the right time to do so. Evasive answers tell you something about the interviewee, and by hearing out such responses—at least to a reasonable extent—you may learn something about your interviewee that otherwise might have been hidden from you.

■ *Use pauses or silence as a tool.* Silence is occasionally necessary and often useful. Novice interviewers often mistake silent moments for wasted moments and, in an effort to keep the conversation moving, they will jump in the second an interviewee pauses for any time longer than it takes to draw a breath. This policy may fill a cassette with sound, but it doesn't necessarily assure you of the best interview. Experienced interviewers have learned that there are skills associated with the ways they deal with silence. "Sometimes it's listening for the pause," says Studs Terkel. "There's a silence, and the person is *changing*. Maybe he doesn't finish a sentence because he said something painful and is going on to another subject. I might not pursue it *then*, but I might come back to it later on, at a better moment for that person." By allowing the silence to play out its course — as long as the pause doesn't become awkward — the interviewer gives the interviewee the option of filling the silence. It affords the person the time to consider a response, as well as encouraging more complete responses.

■ *Hate the sound of your own voice.* Simply stated, if you are talking, your interview subject is not. If you are dominating the conversation with a lot of your own remarks, you are cutting into the amount of time your interviewee has to give you strong, quotable material. You may want your interview to seem like more of a conversation than an inquisition — and you should strive for that — but in a formal conversation meant for publication, the other person should be the one dominating the discussion. You are the *guide*, the one who moves things along. When you're transcribing tapes, you should hate the sound of your own voice. (In fact, there's an exercise you can practice that will help you in this area: when you're transcribing your tapes, write or type *every word* that you utter; obviously, this is not necessary for the final product, and it will cut into your time, but it will also give you a hard lesson in how much you are talking. You'll grow to resent the way you may ramble on, or you may wince at the verbose way in which you get around to asking some of your questions, but after typing out a few interviews' worth of your comments and questions, you'll start to get the point. You'll get a very clear picture of how much of the interview's time you are eating up.) Hating the sound of your own voice will only lead to your full appreciation of the sound of your interviewee's.

■ *Keep a straight face.* Any emotional signal that you send off, no matter how subtle, will affect the way a person addresses a question. A nod, a slightly raised eyebrow, a shrug, a shake of the head — these and other responsive signals indicate that your interviewee is reaching you. Some of this interaction is healthy for the continuation of the conversation; no one wants to talk to an emotional zombie. On the other hand, there are times when your response, however honest, to what a person says can damage or even shut down an important part of the conversation. This is especially true if you are working on an investigative or hard news piece. Let's say you are working on an investigative piece and your subject has just made a startling revelation. If you show surprise, or worse yet, disapproval, your source might just clam up on you, figuring that your reaction may be proof that he or she won't be treated fairly in the published article. Or it may cause your subject to wonder if too much has been divulged. The same principle applies when you are interviewing a person for a profile or feature. If you indicate surprise at something that's said, your interviewee may panic, wondering if too much has been revealed, and then you've lost some important material for your piece. The best policy is to stay neutral — keep a poker face — when your subject is delving into touchy or surprising areas. Or, if you react, do so in a way that encourages the person to go on. ("Oh?" "Really?" These two questions have spurred on many a discussion.)

■ *Take note of all forms of nonverbal communication.* Tape recorders don't capture the telling glance, the shrug, the smile or frown, and other forms of nonverbal communication. Gestures and body language mean nothing to a rolling tape. However, they do mean something to you and your readers, and you should make notations of all forms of nonverbal communication displayed during an interview. Ask yourself what a certain expression or gesture might mean. The interviewee is telling you something, even if not intentionally or directly, and the signals you pick up might lead you to a deeper area of discussion.

■ *Put yourself in your reader's place.* "Sometimes you can visualize how something a person tells you will look on the page," says Lawrence Linderman. "You will see answers working because the way you react as an interviewer is really the way an audience is going to react. Your job is to see that what affects you will affect the audience in the same way." Linderman's point is a crucial one: as an interviewer, you are not simply an individual; you are a representative of the reader. You must trust your instincts. If you have a strong reaction to something an interviewee is telling you, you should pursue the topic. Chances are, your readers will agree with your interest.

■ *If it's helpful, bring yourself into the conversation.* As a general rule, interviewees are not interested in your experiences or opinions, no matter how related these things are to the topic of discussion. Interviewees consider the conversation to be *their* moment in the spotlight, and they tend to resent or grow impatient with interviewers who continually bring their own experiences into the conversation. As a result, you should be very cautious about inserting yourself into the interview. Still, there are times when this tactic works. An interviewee might be hesitant to talk about a topic, or he or she might be genuinely shy. In cases like these, you might nudge the conversation along by bringing up a shared experience. "I'll say things to lead the person on, something like 'Oh, yeah, that happened to me,' " says Studs Terkel. "If I bring some of my own stuff in, maybe that person will feel more akin to it."

■ *During the interview, keep secondary markets in mind.* When you enter an interview, you will have a strong notion of the ground that needs to be covered to satisfy your article's angle, but that doesn't mean that all discussion that fails to fall into that preconception is valueless. Quite the contrary; an interviewee might go off on a tangent that would be an interesting article unto itself. Be on the alert for this kind of tangent. If it seems unique, contains interesting anecdotal and quotable material, and if the idea seems complete, with its own built-in angle, consider the tangent valuable. Rather than steer the interviewee back on course, allow him or her to finish these thoughts. After you have written your assigned article, you will have the material for another separate article.

■ *Honor your time agreements.* A time agreement can be a difficult discipline if your interview is going very well and you notice that you're running out of time. In this circumstance, the temptation is to proceed as if you lost track of time, to wait until the interviewee mentions the time and halts the interview. This tactic works, but it is neither fair to the interviewee nor necessarily beneficial to the interview. You have no way of knowing how your interviewee's time has been scheduled and, by not honoring time agreements, you may be disrupting the person's schedule. If your interviewee is watching the clock, the responses to your questions will be less complete or useful than they might be if they were being offered with little concern about time. If your interview is going well and you would like to continue, you should take one of two approaches: you can either ask if you can continue, or you can request a follow-up interview. Your interviewee will appreciate your concern about the time factor, and will probably help you in any way possible.

OFF-THE-RECORD REMARKS

Many an interviewer's heart has sunk when an interviewee has offered a surprising, informative, intriguing, or otherwise crucial piece of information, only to frame the statement by saying, "This is off the record." In fact, it has almost become a journalistic standard that any information offered "off the record"—that is, information or statements not to be published or attributed to the speaker—will be every bit as interesting or important as anything offered for publication. As soon as you hear the words "off the record," you can almost bet that you will be hearing something that you, your editor, and your readers would pay hard-earned dollars to read.

Unfortunately, there is little you can do but listen to the person's secret; legally and ethically, you are obliged to honor off-record requests. A person has a right to privacy, even when sharing secrets unintended for publication. Clever interviewees will even offer off-the-record remarks as a defense mechanism: if you, the interviewer, are aware that certain topics or pieces of information are considered off limits by the interviewee, you not only will back away from publishing the remarks, but you might avoid publishing the information if it's given to you by someone else. Or so the interviewee reasons. It's a longshot bet, but some interviewees are willing to gamble on it.

For example, let's say that you live in a midsized city and your local school board is looking for a new Superintendent of Schools to replace the one who is retiring. In talking to members of the school board, as well as the other officials in the school system, you learn that an out-of-state candidate is being given serious consideration for the job—much to the probable dissatisfaction of the local community and business leaders, who have stated that they would prefer to see a hometown candidate fill the position. Furthermore, you learn that one of the board members has visited the candidate for an extensive interview in his own town. When the board member returns, you call and request an interview, but before you've even begun, the board member tries to cut you off at the pass.

"This is very sensitive material," he tells you in his most confiding manner, "and I'm not sure it's really information that should be public knowledge just yet. In fact, I'll tell you—and this is off the record—that it looks as if we'll be hiring the man sometime next week. We don't want to make a formal announcement until we've worked out the final details of the contract and have had the opportunity to come up with a public statement that will at least keep the public disapproval to a minimum, but I assure you that a statement is forthcoming. When the time is right, I'll be happy to talk to you, but until then, I want all this information strictly off the record."

In talking to you in this manner, the board member is hoping that your sense of civic obligation and humanity will quell your journalistic ambitions. He realizes that your editor would want you to write about this information and, perhaps suspecting the possibility of a "leak" from another board member, he is trying to discourage you from publishing the information he's giving you, with the silent understanding that it wouldn't be wise to publish the information if it were given to you by someone else. By tempering his off-the-record demands with the promise to talk to you as soon as "the time is right," he is hoping to persuade you to back away from the story until that time.

Such a ploy is probably a futile one, since most journalists, citing the fact that the public has a right to know what's going on, would dig around until they found someone willing to go on the record with the information, but the board member is taking a long-shot gamble. He's making you consider the implications of his off-the-record statements.

In general, as an interviewer, you do have options to consider when you are given off-the-record information. First, you can take the idea at face value and simply ignore the remarks. This is usually the course of action taken when the off-record statements have little or no bearing on the main thrust of the article being written. If you're off on a tangent and are given off-record remarks, and those remarks mean little to your article, you might honor, without protest or comment, your interviewee's request.

If, however, the remarks *are* valuable to the article you're writing, you should take one of two approaches. The first involves your putting your interviewee on the defensive: "*Why* should these remarks be off the record?" In most cases, the answer to this question will be obvious, both to you and your interviewee, but a subsequent discussion of the reasons may convince the interviewee that the information is publishable. Even if the person remains adamant, you'll be learning more about the person's attitudes.

Some interviewers prefer to take a circling, as opposed to a more direct, approach to addressing the issue. Rather than challenge the interviewee the moment the person declares certain comments or statements to be not-for-publication, the interviewer will agree to the request, only to address it later in the conversation, when the interviewee is less passionate or defensive about the remarks. When taking this approach, you should guide your interview to safer ground immediately after off-record remarks are spoken, but don't stray too far from the topic. Interviewees have reasons for giving you the information they don't want published: maybe they're looking for an audience or sounding board, someone to listen to thoughts they've kept to themselves for too long; maybe they're afraid to go on record themselves, but they want to provide you with hints of important topics you should pursue somewhere else; maybe they simply want to be convinced that they *need* to go on record with their remarks. In any event, and despite their insistence that they don't wish to speak for the record, these interviewees wish to speak. If you cut the conversation short and return to it later, you might have more success in persuading the person to speak for the record.

Another question you will need to ask yourself — as well as your interviewee — involves the fine line that separates "not-for-publication" and "not-for-attribution." "Would the interviewee be willing to speak for publication, on the condition that his or her name not be associated with the quotation, or on the condition that the information be used solely for background?" In cases such as the school board member example, where the speaker is easily identifiable, this approach may not work. But quite often, interviewees will inform you that certain statements are off the record when they really mean that they don't want to be named as the source of the statement in the published article. In instances such as this, the speakers want the information to be published, but for personal or professional reasons they don't want to be directly connected with the quote. We've all seen articles that quote "a source close to the President" or "an insider." The quotations given are direct, but the source isn't named.

There are legal and ethical ramifications connected to your using unattributed or off-the-record sources, many of which will be addressed in Chapter Eight. No matter how you look at it, you are in the wrong if you print and attribute off-the-record material. In the worst scenario, such as an instance where the quote invades another person's privacy or slanders another person, you might wind up in court; at the very least, even if the person says nothing about the statement and lets it pass, you are guilty of untruthful, unethical behavior that could damage your reputation, as well as hinder other journalists dealing with the interviewee in the future. In general, editors frown upon — or flatly refuse to consider — quotations from unattributed sources. Nevertheless, some off-record material can be used as background, and you should consider this when a person asks not to be identified with information given to you during an interview. If you feel as if you might be able to find corroboration for the information elsewhere, and if the information is important to your article, you should ask the interviewee if you can use it as deep background or in an unattributed quote. These usages are not as effective as the direct, attributed quotation, but they are preferable to your keeping critical information entirely off the record.

LISTENING

Studs Terkel, an intellectual Renaissance Man who can speak on a large variety of topics — and who has used this knowledge to his benefit in the thousands of interviews he has conducted over the years — believes that one of an interviewer's most useful interviewing tools is not so much what he or she can bring to or discuss during an interview as the ability to listen. In far too many cases, Terkel asserts, an interviewer is so locked into his or her own agenda that important points are either missed or dismissed. To illustrate his point, Terkel acts out a quick parody of an interviewer and an interview subject:

> *Interviewer: "So what happened?"*
> Interviewee: "My father was killed in an auto crash."
>
> *Interviewer: "Oh, that's good. Then what happened?"*

"That's a caricature of the horrendous stuff that we hear on occasion," Terkel concludes, shaking his head.

Successful interviewers agree that a person's listening skills lead to strong interviews and solid, quotable material. Gary Provost may have put it most succinctly when he noted, "When I'm speaking, I'm not getting anything."

By being a good listener, you are accomplishing several important tasks:

■ *You are paying respect to your interviewee.* Whether it be an everyday conversation or a formal interview, speakers want to be listened to; they want to feel as if you care about what they are saying. When you show a person that you're listening to what's being said, you are complimenting that person. You are indicating that the person's statements *matter*, even if you don't agree with them. By paying an interviewee this kind of respect, you are encouraging the person to talk, to provide you with more information. You're also building your trust level, which will help you when you ask your tough or difficult questions.

■ *You are putting your skills of perception to work.* When you listen to a person, you should be aware of *what* is being said and *how* it is being said; the former can be picked up in an interview transcript, but the latter is only accomplished through careful listening. Tone of voice, inflection, emphasis placed on key words — all are important indicators that you should listen for. Diligent listening will give you an indication of how your interviewee's mind works. How does the person choose to reveal information or tell a story? What points does he or she emphasize? How does the person look at the world? If you listen for details and signals, you will hear more than words; you will hear the heartbeat of a human being behind the words.

■ *You are discriminating between words and ideas.* Poor listeners hear words and assume that they are ideas; in fact, there can be a vast difference between a string of words and one simple, complete idea. This will become apparent after the interview when you're going over your notes or transcribing your tapes. If you haven't listened carefully or asked appropriate follow-up questions, you will find "holes" in your interviewee's statements. Ideas will be touched upon but not completed. Anecdotes will be missing important details. You'll wonder how you could possibly have missed asking for the needed information, only to realize that you weren't listening as intently as you should have been, that you were taking everything you heard at face value. It's an easy trap to fall into, especially if you are recording the interview, or if your interviewee is telling a long story. With the former, you are placing too much confidence in the recording capacity of a machine at the expense of your own listening capacity; with the latter, you are assuming that your interviewee is providing you with all the information you will need. In both cases, you'll tend to relax and let your interviewee talk, only to later regret your lack of careful listening.

As we'll see later in this chapter, your listening skills are crucial in telephone interviews, but they can be just as important when you are interviewing a subject in person. Good listening skills are your surest passageways to a better understanding and perception of your interviewee. Or, as the saying goes, it's sometimes best to keep your ears open and your mouth closed.

HOW TO LISTEN

Listening, however, is not the simple matter of not speaking, nor is it a passive undertaking. To be an effective listener, you must discipline your mind to grasp, absorb, and interpret what your interviewee is telling you; you must be both inquisitive and analytical. You must be open to the unexpected and willing to use what you hear to further direct the interview. You must be capable of recognizing an interviewee's signals that indicate emphasis or transition. You must be as alert as you can possibly be, both to what the interviewee is saying and how you intend to react to what that person is saying.

Listening requires patience and self-control. In everyday conversations, the pace of the exchange is quicker than in a formal interview; we tend to jump in when we receive cues from the people we are talking to. Unless one person is clearly dominating the conversation, our everyday conversations tend to offer equal time to all speakers involved. Ideas, opinions, and statements are exchanged, built upon, embellished, debated, and bandied about until the speakers have had their say. In everyday conversations, we don't look for a *reason* to speak; in fact, our speaking is expected if we're to take seriously the cliché of one's holding up his or her end of a conversation.

When you are interviewing someone, you are expected to hold up your end of the conversation, but in an entirely different manner. You are the conversation's guide, whether that entails your choosing topics of discussion or moving the interview along. Interviewees expect you to listen, so, in a sense, you *do* need reasons to speak. Those reasons include your asking questions, prodding the interviewee, and moving the conversation from one topic to another. All are linked to your ability to listen.

To listen effectively, you should:

■ *Determine the way a person answers a question or tells a story.* This can be accomplished early in an interview. Some people are succinct while others ramble; some have minds for details while others present bare-bones facts; some are quick to offer examples while others deal in generalizations. By recognizing the manner in which questions are addressed or stories are told, you will be able to make the adjustments necessary for complete answers and stories. For example, if a person tends to offer generalizations, you should be cautious about asking open-ended questions and pepper your conversation with closed questions that invite more specific responses. Or, if you determine that the person is a natural storyteller, you might want to solicit colorful anecdotes or examples by playing into the interviewee's strength. Your course of action will be determined by what you perceive early in the interview.

■ *Determine the way a person emphasizes his or her points.* We all have ways of underscoring the important points we make during a conversation. A shy person might emphasize a point by presenting a declarative sentence in the form of a question ("I like to jog first thing in the morning as a way of getting my mind untracked?"), while an aggressive speaker might challenge you to agree with him or her. People who avoid eye contact will often look directly at you when they emphasize a statement. Some people place emphasis on a point by returning to the topic repeatedly throughout the interview. Voice inflection and volume are two of the most common methods of accenting a point. These emphatic points are building blocks of strong interviews; they invite follow-up questions, expansion, and colorful examples. Once you have determined the way a person emphasizes his or her points of interest, you'll be ready to direct your conversation into areas that produce passionate or compelling discussion.

■ *Determine how a person completes a thought.* If you are aware of the way a person finishes a thought and yields the floor to someone else in a conversation, you will be less inclined to unintentionally interrupt your interviewee. Does the person simply stop talking when he or she has finished addressing a question? Does this subject look at you expectantly, as if waiting for the next question? Does a person seem to be grasping for something to say? Patient listening will help you determine the way a person completes a thought, and from this determination you will be able to make smoother transitions in your interview.

■ *Determine when a person is actually answering your question and when he or she is "performing."* Even the most relaxed interviewees are aware of the fact that what they're telling you is being used for publication. As a result, there is a "performance" element — telling you what the person thinks you want to hear, as opposed to what he or she really thinks — in many interviews. People will speak out of character, exaggerate, or occasionally lie if they believe it is to their benefit to do so. By listening carefully, you will be able to make character assessments that will help you recognize the "performance" factor in an interview. This recognition is crucial because it tells you something about the quality of the answers you're being given.

■ *Determine when a person is on familiar ground and when he or she is in unfamiliar territory.* Staying with the familiar is the easy road for both interviewer and interviewee. It's comfortable and it requires less work. It also produces the least desirable responses. It's not difficult for you to avoid what you know is familiar turf for your interviewee. Your research will have acquainted you with some of the territory that's familiar to your subject, and if you've been thoughtful when you were developing your questions, you will be challenging your interviewee even when you're in that territory. However, you won't have seen all of the person's interviews, and you won't know what he or she talks about when not being interviewed, so you should be on the alert for statements that sound "pat" or "prepared," as if they've been offered on countless occasions. Your listening habits will help you here. When addressing the familiar, people exude more confidence (and, occasionally, indifference), and they tend to speak more rapidly than when they are in uncharted areas. They'll rattle off their examples, anecdotes, and statistics as if they are reading off a teleprompter. Their answers will generally be longer, with fewer pauses. Their thoughts are more organized. If you suspect an interviewee of giving you prepared answers, you should try to devise follow-up questions that might lead into unfamiliar offshoots of the topic being discussed. Doing this will challenge your interviewee and please your readers.

■ *Determine how a person's attitudes are reflected in his or her answers.* Often-interviewed people are adept at disguising their real attitudes when they're responding to questions. Think of the interviews you've read with politicians, entertainers, athletes, or corporate officials. These types of interviewees will address questions, but they have a way of staying detached, as if they have no emotional connection to or attitude about the topics they're discussing. Or they will disguise their emotions in an offering of clichés. ("Hitting three home runs today was no big deal. What really matters is that the team won.") This is another way in which a person "performs" during an interview, and your job is to move beyond these barriers and into the person's true feelings and attitudes. Thoughtful listening will give you clues as to how to accomplish this.

People will offer you subtle, unintentional hints about their feelings and attitudes. They'll contradict themselves. They'll stumble on their words or fail to finish a thought. They'll pause to collect their thoughts when they're getting too close to revealing feelings they wish to hide. An interview has little value if you wind up depicting a fabricated personality in your article or profile. Listen for signs of a person's actual feelings or attitudes, and use this information to gently challenge your interviewee. Once confronted, the person may drop his or her guard and give you the truth.

When you're listening, present yourself as an interested party. Maintain eye contact and a relaxed pose. When taking notes, avoid looking away from your interviewee for too long a time; doing so implies disinterest or diverted attention. Your mind may be working as fast as the words coming at you, but you should never look as if you are devoting your attention to anything but what the person is telling you. The more you interview, the more you will realize that listening involves as much craft and discipline as asking good questions.

THE DIFFICULT QUESTION

It is likely that the most important question of your interview will also be the most difficult to ask. Your interviewee's response to that question will be the heart of your article — or, if it is not the focus of your story, it will be an integral part of it. It is one of the main reasons you were assigned to write the article, as it is one of the primary areas of interest for your readers. The questions may address a controversy, it may be one that elicits a great emotional response from your interviewee, or it may be one that deals with sensitive or delicate issues. No matter what its specific nature, it will be a question that you are as uncomfortable in asking as your interviewee is in answering. Ironically, it is also the question your interviewee most expects you to pose.

In comedy, timing and delivery are everything, and so it is with asking the difficult question in an interview: your success will depend upon when and how you pose your question.

Let's say, for example, that you are writing a profile of a popular entertainer who, a year earlier, had a run-in with the police at a demonstration against the use of nuclear energy. Chances are the entertainer will be more than willing to discuss his opposition to the use of nuclear energy, but he might be less than happy about discussing the particular details of his arrest at the demonstration. You will want this information — after all, the entertainer is attaching his name to this cause, using his public standing to give it more publicity — but you will also need to find a way to ask the tough questions about the arrest.

How and when do you pose such questions? Most interviewers agree that tough questions should be saved for the latter part of the interview, for a time when the highest level of trust has been established. Asking a difficult question at the onset of the interview might turn your subject off, or in the worse scenario, end the interview. Although your interviewee anticipates your asking the question, he or she will be more open to answering it after a sense of rapport has been established.

The way you word your question is crucial. Taking an inquisitorial, "Perry Mason" approach will net you much less than finding a softer approach to posing the question, especially when you are dealing with controversial or sensitive areas. A bluntly worded question can appear confrontational to the interviewee.

"For print, these types of questions aren't asked in the same way as they're asked on television," says Lawrence Linderman, pointing out that the way a Mike Wallace or Sam Donaldson asks a tough question in front of rolling cameras and millions of viewers is entirely different from the way a journalist, armed only with a tape recorder and sitting in private with an interviewee, might pose a question. "You're not a prosecutor and nobody's watching you," Linderman asserts. "You're not nailing him with the question. I know that if I don't phrase those questions in the right way, I can turn somebody off—and by that I don't mean that I'll be getting him annoyed. He's not going to *talk* about it."

Gary Provost agrees. "I generally take a soft touch and try to make people feel as if I'm on their side. I don't like to take the adversarial approach. Sometimes I can't avoid it, but even then I usually take a point of view that says 'You already look bad, and I'm just trying to balance the story and get your side of it.' "

Experienced interviewers can be quite cagey in the way they phrase a difficult question. The question may say essentially the same thing as a bluntly worded one, but by removing some of the confrontational element from it—by softening it—the interviewer can ask the most pointed question and still receive an answer.

For example, television journalist Sam Donaldson, when talking to John Tower, a former senator and, at the time of the interview, presidential appointee for Secretary of State, used great skill in coaxing Tower to address the controversial issue of Tower's drinking habits. At the time, the news media had been pressing Tower to address the issue, but the most complete response came as a result of the following question:

> *As you know, many of the allegations have to do with, to put it rather inelegantly, the charge that you're a common, or uncommon drunk, that you admitted that, in the seventies, you had a drinking problem. But the allegations are that it has persisted. Now, what can you tell us to reassure on that point?*

Although the question looks to be as pointed as you'll ever hear, Donaldson, as tough a questioner as television journalism has seen, used caution and discretion in the way he worded his tough question. He made a point of mentioning the fact that his question was based on public allegations—allegations that the interviewee was already aware of—and while he didn't back away from the "common drunk" allegation, he restated it with a half-apology, calling his own phrasing "inelegant." Finally, by asking for "reassurance," Donaldson displayed a sense of objectivity and fair play that encouraged his interviewee to respond. In essence, Donaldson was asking the tough question, but he was doing so in a way that said, "We want to believe you, so tell us these reports are false, and why."

When you ask the tough question, which you should have prepared and rehearsed before the interview, put yourself in the interviewee's place. How would you react if you were that person and were asked the same question? Would you react in anger? Would you refuse to answer the question? Would you consider the interviewer to be pushy or demanding? Would you give an honest answer?

Interviewees want to feel as if they are being treated fairly. The tough questions are, to them, indications of how objective an interviewer will be when writing the article or profile. If the tough questions are presented as challenges, interviewees may feel as if they will be treated poorly in the resulting article; if those questions are presented as genuine inquiries, posed in the spirit of gaining information or objective opinion, interviewees may be more willing to offer the sought-after information.

THE MOMENT OF TRUTH: THE SELLING QUOTE

"A lot of times when I'm doing an interview, a person will say something and I'll suddenly realize that *that* is the lead to my story or article. It's an instinctive thing for me."

A long-time freelancer, Gary Provost has learned to trust those instincts. These quotes may not wind up as leads, Provost admits, but they usually end up in the article. When viewed as potential leads, they also encourage the interviewer to a more fervent pursuit of what the interviewee is saying. "The lead is like having a ball of string in your hand, and you're trying to find the end of it," Provost says. "Once you find the end, you've got it all."

Good interviewers recognize the "moment of truth" quotation: Almost as soon as the words are spoken, you see them as if they were appearing bold and lighted up on a marquee sign, and you realize that your editor and readers will react to these quotes, which are so powerful that they virtually guarantee you a sale, in the same way. "Selling quotes" are passionate but unforced, and they seem to frame everything an interviewee is saying. They are the foundation upon which you build your article or interview. Listen for these quotes and expand upon them as soon as you hear them.

EMOTIONAL REACTIONS TO INTERVIEWEES

No matter how objective you try to remain during an interview, there will be moments when you are emotionally affected by something you are told. Mary Kachoyeanos, coauthor of *Just A Nurse*, recalls numerous occasions when the stories she was hearing left her *and* her interviewees in tears. Lawrence Linderman notes that, on a number of occasions, his *Playboy* interview subjects left him feeling as if he were a psychologist guiding them through rough remembrances of their lives; so often, Linderman says, the interview was a catharsis for his subjects and he couldn't help but be affected by the emotions they were experiencing.

For interviewers, this is a good news/bad news proposition. The good news is that an emotionally charged conversation will help create an excellent story. After all, the interviewer is a single representative—a symbol—of a readership, and if you're experiencing a strong emotional reaction to what someone is telling you, chances are good that your readers will respond in the same way. The bad news is that your response *can* affect your objectivity in a story. You want to grasp the human level in every story that you write, but never at the cost of clouding the bigger picture.

Even more dangerous than empathy is a strong negative reaction to an interviewee. You might find yourself talking to someone you despise, or to someone whose lifestyle is so loathsome that your objectivity is threatened. The idea, of course, is to retain your composure. In the print media, interviewers aren't performers in the mode of television's Morton Downey, Jr. or Geraldo Rivera; readers expect you to frame a subject's words, not be the focus of them.

Studs Terkel, who has been interviewing people for nearly four decades, has interviewed people he didn't like or agree with on numerous occasions. Many of these conversations found places in his best-selling books. Terkel believes the best policy is to put your emotions aside and let the interviewee talk. If the person is outrageous or contemptible in your eyes, he or she will probably be the same in the eyes of your readers.

"I've talked to a number of people I don't like," Terkel says. "For instance, I painted a picture of Gerald L.K. Smith in *Hard*

Times. He was a very celebrated American fascist, active in the thirties and a friend of Huey Long. I talked to him in the sixties, and I let him contradict himself. He said, 'You don't call me *Reverend* Smith — it's *Mister* Smith. These young preachers and priests should take off their collars like me. Don't be hidden by the collar.' A few minutes later, he's saying, 'Down in Georgia, a bunch of Roosevelt people came at me as though to lynch me, and I hopped up on a rock and said, "Whoever dares attack me attacks a man of God!" ' I just left that in, that's all. I didn't have to say anything."

The best rule is to never let yourself be governed by your own emotions. You're responsible for bringing in the story, and losing your cool may jeopardize that task. Keep in mind that there's a great difference between empathy, sympathy, and anger; chances are, you'll get away with the first two emotions but not the last.

GENERAL INTERVIEW ETIQUETTE

Discussions of etiquette, I've come to believe, are necessary only because so many writers have proven themselves to be lacking in good common sense. Let's face it: unless you're interviewing a Head of State or some other individual whose position or standing requires special protocol, conversation etiquette should be composed of equal parts of professionalism and common sense. You wouldn't apply for a stockbroker's position if you were wearing torn, faded blue jeans, nor would you light a cigarette in church. Common sense, as well as a sense of respect, dictate the proper behavior in these instances. Most interview etiquette is dictated by the same.

You should approach an interview the same way you would approach a job interview and, to a certain extent, you should respect a person's home the way you might respect the environment of a church. Show up on time, dress with the knowledge that an interviewee's first impressions of you could dictate the tone and effectiveness of the conversation, and conduct yourself as you might under the searching eye of a potential boss.

Let the situation, as well as the person you're interviewing, serve as a barometer for your behavior and general etiquette. For example, you don't need to dress the same for an interview with a rock star or athlete as you would for an interview with a senator — though torn jeans are still out with conversations with rock stars, even if they wear them. Dress well, but comfortably; present yourself as well-groomed and professional. Smoking and gum-chewing are usually taboo, though you can follow your interviewee's lead on these, as you can on the matter of drinking. (If you're in a restaurant or bar, and your subject orders a drink, it's acceptable to order a drink for yourself, but you should be practical in this matter.) You should avoid any kind of cursing during the course of your conversation, even if your interviewee sounds like a busload of Marines; cursing implies a familiarity that can jeopardize the interviewer/interviewee relationship, since people expect you to follow certain professional standards, even if they wouldn't otherwise object to this kind of language from others.

On occasion, you will find yourself conducting an interview over lunch or dinner, or you may go out to lunch or dinner before or after an interview. This can create a "who's got the check?" scenario. In these situations, the rules of etiquette are usually governed by common sense. If your interviewee suggests that you go out to dinner, assume that either he will be picking up the check or that you'll each pay separately; if you suggest the dining, you should be prepared to foot the bill.

When you are in an interviewee's home or office, remember that you are a guest—a stranger, actually. Don't snoop or wander around, even if your interviewee has left the room and you find yourself tempted to explore. You will want to take notes on the person's intimate surroundings, but never at the expense of literally or figuratively invading his or her privacy. Imagine how you would feel if you invited a salesperson into your home, only to find him wandering around and making himself all-too-comfortable in your private domain. You would be less than pleased. Nor would you be happy if you left your office for a few moments, only to find a person flipping through your card files when you returned. The same principles apply to the way you should behave in an interviewee's home or office.

CLOSING THE INTERVIEW

The conclusion of an interview, like the beginning, should not be abrupt, nor should your conversation end while you are discussing one of the major topics of your interview. Our everyday conversations often end in silence, when both participants quietly acknowledge that everything has been said; formal interviews should not end on a note of silence, but they should have that general feeling.

That's the ideal. In reality, an interview never appears to reach the point of completion. There always seems to be a question unanswered, a topic untouched. Some interviews end very abruptly, with the interviewee informing you that he or she has no more to say. Time runs out, deadlines approach, other appointments must be honored. Interviewer/interviewee fatigue may also be a factor.

It's always best if you are the one who initiates the closing of the interview. If time is running out, allow your interviewee to finish his or her thoughts on the question being addressed, and then mention the fact that you are reaching the end of the agreed-upon time limit. If there is no time limit, continue the interview until it becomes obvious that the person is either growing tired or has nothing else to say; when you've reached that point, look for an opening in the conversation, a lull that allows you to initiate the closing of the interview ("Well, you've given me a lot of information. . . ." or something similar). While you're winding down the interview, be sure to ask if you can call with any further questions, and don't forget to ask for the interviewee's address and phone number if you do not already have them.

Closing an interview is not unlike knowing when to leave a party: you don't want to wear out your welcome. In fact, if you know that you will be conducting a follow-up interview, or if you know that a follow-up interview is possible, it's a good idea to leave a little early. If you leave while you and your interviewee are still "hungry"—that is, while you both know that there is material yet to be covered—you will both be ready and willing to pick up the conversation in the near future, at a time when your thoughts are clear and fresh.

WHEN TO TURN OFF THE TAPE RECORDER

Although it might seem logical, the end of the interview is not necessarily a signal for you to turn off your tape recorder—nor should *you* signal the end of the interview by turning off your tape recorder. Veteran interviewers will regale you with stories of the good quotable and anecdotal material they failed to record simply because they'd put their tape recorders away while the interviewee was still talking.

Interviews don't end in total silence; they end only when you have said goodbye and are walking away from the interviewee. The *formal* conversation may have concluded fifteen minutes or even a half-hour before you leave, but in many cases, you both will be talking — unwinding — for a brief period between the time you ask your last formal question and the time you leave.

For the most part, your winding down period will be similar to your small talk period; instead of easing into the interview, you will be easing out of it. It's not advisable to use this period to ask important questions, but you shouldn't waste this time, either. You never know what your interviewee will say.

I learned this lesson the hard way, years ago, when I interviewed author Norman Mailer. As soon as we had concluded the formal questioning in the interview, I packed my tape recorder and notebook into my shoulder bag, while Mailer signed the books I'd brought to the interview. At one point, he asked me if I'd ever worked on a book-length project, and I told him I was working on a novel. While he inscribed my books, Mailer talked about the problems he had had in finishing some of his books; he spoke of how tough it was to write novels and gave me a few words of encouragement. While he was talking, I couldn't help but think about my packed-away tape recorder. Some of Mailer's observations were as good as anything he'd given me during the interview itself.

To prevent this scenario from occurring, turn off your tape recorder only when 1) it's awkward to leave it on any longer; or 2) you're literally getting up to leave. While you're winding down, keep the conversation lighter, more informal, than it was during the interview. Chances are your interviewee won't notice that the tape recorder is still running, and even if he or she does, it probably won't make any difference.

And if your tape recorder isn't running when an interviewee says something interesting or valuable after the interview?

"When I make that mistake, I get in the car, turn on my tape recorder, and start repeating what he said," says Gary Provost. On occasion, he adds, when the interviewee is talking about an important topic after the interview, he will reopen the formal discussion. "I'll turn the tape recorder back on if it's still handy," he says.

PHOTOGRAPHING THE INTERVIEWEE

A well-written article with good photographs always has an edge over a well-written article without photographs. It's that simple. If, in a query letter to an editor, you are able to mention that you can provide high-quality photographs with your article or profile, you will have given yourself a real boost toward selling your idea. Not only do editors (and readers) like to see pictures of the principal speakers or characters in an article, but they prefer original, candid photographs. Public relations firms and publicists can provide editors with photographs, but those pictures are usually stock shots that have appeared in every article written about a person during a given period of time. Furthermore, since obtaining photographs from other sources can be time-consuming and on occasion frustrating, editors are always relieved to hear that a writer can supply photographs with an article.

However, you should never assume that anyone, famous or unknown, will be happy to be photographed. People aren't as eager to be photographed for publication as you might suspect, and you should advise an interviewee that you'll be bringing along a photographer—or taking pictures yourself—when you call to line up the interview. That way, the person will be prepared when you arrive.

Choose your photographer carefully. Be familiar not only with a photographer's work, but with his on-the-job style. You don't want the unpleasant surprise of learning that you have a photographer who moves an interviewee around or "poses" him or her while you're trying to conduct your interview, any more than you want to discover that the photographer cannot take good pictures. When you contact a photographer, make certain that he or she understands that the publication—not you—will be paying for any pictures that are published, and never, *ever* agree or offer to pay for a photographer's developing expenses. Unless you are writing a book (and are therefore personally responsible for the expense of procuring photographs), reimbursement and payment to photographers is your publisher's responsibility.

Reach all agreements (between you and your interviewee about his being photographed, between you and your photographer) *before* the interview. The last thing you need when you're beginning an interview is confusion or distraction.

When is the best time to photograph a person? This varies from individual to individual, although generally speaking, two rules can be made:
  ■ With an often-photographed interviewee (such as a celebrity,

public figure, etc.), you may photograph during or after an interview. These people are accustomed to being photographed under all kinds of conditions and circumstances, and they are not likely to be distracted if they're being photographed while they're talking or answering a question. Some celebrities, however, are more temperamental than others; if you have serious doubts about a person's attitudes toward being photographed, refrain from photographing until the end of the interview session.

■ With people unaccustomed to being photographed (private citizens, people whose work is generally accomplished out of the public eye, etc.), you should wait until the interview is finished. These people might be nervous about being interviewed in the first place, and a photographer could distract them or disrupt their line of thinking. When you interview such people, tactfully remind them that they have agreed to be photographed, and tell them that you will be taking pictures after you've finished talking. Have your photographer keep a low profile during the interviews themselves; you don't want your interviewees feeling as if they're talking to an audience, or that they're being ganged up on. You want the feeling of a one-on-one conversation, not a feeling of performance.

MULTISESSION INTERVIEWS

If you are working on an in-depth magazine profile or a long interview to be published in the Q/A format, you will probably require more than one interview session with your interviewee. Such multiple-session interviews are preferable to a single-interview session, not only because they allow you to ask more questions in sessions that are less taxing of your endurance, but also because they give you more than one look at the person you are interviewing or profiling. People's moods vary from day to day, and multiple sessions are the best way to gain (and, therefore, report) a well-rounded perspective of the person you're talking to.

Conducting multisession interviews is similar to conducting the single-session interview, with the exception of scale and pacing. For multisession interviews, you will require much more background information and you will have many more questions to ask. Because you have more time in which to ask your questions, you'll also have greater opportunity to focus on those areas that you might otherwise ignore in a single-session interview. You can allow a topic of conversation to run its own course, even if that involves your venturing up more blind alleys than you might in a short, single encounter.

In multisession interviews, much of the control of the conversation's pacing belongs to the interviewee. Since you aren't as rushed to get to the main points of the interview, you can allow the interviewee, within reasonable limits, to determine the direction of the conversation.

Many of Lawrence Linderman's *Playboy* and *Penthouse* interviews have required many sessions to accomplish, with a single published Q/A often requiring 10-15 hours to accomplish. These sessions, Linderman points out, involved the usual array of peaks and valleys in the conversations, but he has learned to let the conversations set their own pace.

"All my questions are contained on one sheet of legal paper," he says, "and I've often had long sessions where I may have asked *one* question from the list and didn't get back to any of them. You know that you can always go back to the questions, so you relax and listen to what somebody is saying and bounce off of that. I know, mathematically, that I'm going to ask all those questions before we're finished talking."

However, this is not to imply that such sessions lack a sense of direction, that the conversations are dominated by aimless chitchat or table talk. As with single-session interviews, your duty as interviewer is to align the topics you intend to address with the time in which you have to cover them, and you must pace the interview accordingly. For example, if you know that you are going to have three sessions to cover seven or eight major topics, you'll want to designate several topics to each session. Since you'll have plenty of time in each session to cover these few topics, you'll have more time to let your interviewee provide you with examples, anecdotes, and possibly an unforeseen topic of discussion.

"SEAT OF THE PANTS" INTERVIEWING

I once was asked to interview jazz trumpeter Maynard Ferguson for an area entertainment magazine. Ferguson, one of the music business' genuine nice guys, was playing a benefit concert at a local high school and, besides myself, there were two other reporters present to interview him. His scheduling was tight, so all three of us were going to interview him together.

Shortly after the concert ended, as the three of us were standing backstage, talking and waiting for Ferguson to come out for the interview, one of the reporters turned to me and mentioned that she knew absolutely nothing about Ferguson or jazz. Although she had just seen him perform, she had no idea of what questions to ask him. She complained that the hardest part of her job was the "seat of the pants" interview.

For reporters covering different news events or writing feature stories every day, this kind of interviewing is especially challenging. There is little or no time for preparation or research — and even if such time were available, there's quite often little or nothing on file to look up. The interviewer is expected to use common sense in coming up with the angle to the story and the appropriate questions to ask.

This is also a concern for interviewers who conduct daily radio or television shows. The bigger "names" in the business have research staffs that do much of the preparation for them, but there's still a difference between being briefed on a person and digging up the information yourself, just as there's a difference between reading a book and reading a plot synopsis of the same book.

In her book *How to Talk to Anybody About Just About Anything*, Barbara Walters recalled her hectic days on "The Today Show," where she often found herself talking to five different authors in a week's time. Because she didn't have the time to read the authors' books, she developed a type of shortcut that helped her through the interviews.

"If the book is non-fiction," she wrote, "I read the first chapter and the last, and a few in-between. If there isn't time, or I can't get a copy in a hurry, I try to find a review of the book. It is no substitute for having digested the entire book, but it's better than no preparation at all. Sometimes the subject matter can be a springboard for a discussion. If you know the author has written about urban decay, for instance, ask his opinion of what is happening in your city."

From this brief passage, you can see why Walters is one of the best interviewers in the business; you also can see how using one's common sense and creative touch can turn a potentially embarrassing or disastrous situation ("I haven't had time to read your book, but. . . .") into a successful one ("What do you think of Mayor So-and-So's model city program?").

Studs Terkel, another acclaimed interviewer with a regular interview program, agrees that common sense is the key to success in the "seat of the pants" interview. For Terkel, success is determined by concentration on what you know, rather than fear of what you don't know.

"When I interview a person, I may not know him as I might know, say, the author of a book, but I know *something* about him," Terkel says. "Maybe he's a guy who was a prisoner of war in Germany during the bombings of Dresden. He was being bombed by an American plane, like in Kurt Vonnegut's *Slaughterhouse-Five*. There's a guy like that in *'The Good War'*. I know that much about him and I take off from there."

In "seat of the pants" interviewing, listening becomes one of your most important tools. The more your interviewee talks, the more you're going to learn. Listen carefully to everything he or she says, and take occasional notes when you hear something that could lead to further questioning or discussion. Show plenty of enthusiasm for or interest in what you're told; this encourages your interviewee to continue talking. Pursue any lead that looks as if it may pan out into something valuable. Always try to have a question or two ready to ask.

In this way, there is very little distinction between the "seat of the pants" interview and the one you have prepared for.

There are, however, four "don'ts" you should try to keep in mind whenever you find yourself conducting this kind of interview:

■ *Don't pretend to know more than you do.* It's one thing to try to conceal your ignorance by keeping quiet, but it is quite another matter to try to conceal your ignorance by "spreading it on thick." The former tells your interviewee absolutely nothing about what you do or don't know (unless the interview is plagued by too many moments of awkward silence), while the latter will give you away every time, especially if you're talking to an authority on a given topic. Even if an interviewee doesn't call your bluff, it will affect the way he or she perceives you and, as a result, the way he answers your questions.

■ *Don't apologize for your ignorance.* As we've already seen, your lack of knowledge can be a blessing when it is used to keep a person talking or clarifying answers. The same principle applies in the "seat of the pants" interview, even if it involves your applying it more often. Apologizing for not being prepared or for ignorance can have a negative effect on the interview, with one of the biggest effects being the doubts it casts upon your professionalism in the mind of your interviewee. If you find yourself in a situation where you *must* admit that you're unprepared, such as in the instance when an author asks you how you liked her latest book (which you haven't read), try to find a humorous, perhaps slightly self-deprecating way to admit the truth, or tell it straightforward, but never make grand apologies.

■ *Don't use eloquence to mask ignorance.* This point is related to the first entry on this list. People see through flowery or obtuse verbiage, as well as overblown intellectualism, and the resulting effect is the same as you find when someone approaches you with a lot of flowery, bombastic verbiage, only to hit you up for two bits. Keep your questions simple and to the point. The more embellishment you add, the more unprepared you look.

■ *Don't let them see you sweat.* This sounds like the slogan for a popular deodorant commercial, but the same principle applies: no matter how nervous or unprepared you are, never let your interviewee sense it. Exude confidence in your ability to hold up your end of the interview; don't be tentative in either the questions you ask or in the way you pose them. It's amazing how far your attitude can carry you in these kinds of interviews. If you present yourself in the light of a professional, you'll probably be treated as such; if you're tentative, nervous, or uncertain, you risk looking like a "rookie" or "hobbyist," and you'll be treated accordingly.

THE "NONINTERVIEW"

Over the course of your writing career, there will be a number of occasions when you will conduct what can be best termed a "noninterview." You will carefully research your subject, devise good, compelling questions, set up the interview, and generally play ball the way it's supposed to be played, only to find, for one reason or another, that your interviewee is unwilling to impart the wisdom you've come to gain. Your interviewee is like liquid mercury: no matter what you do as an interviewer, you won't be able to grasp anything meaningful in the conversation. You have a sinking feeling, even as you're packing away your tape recorder and notes at the conclusion of the conversation, that your tapes and notes are a veritable scrapyard of worthless verbiage.

Near the beginning of my career, a magazine asked me to profile Mike Royko, the Pulitzer Prize winning columnist with the reputation of being one of journalism's bona fide tough guys. To prepare for the interview, I'd read all of Royko's books and spent Lord-only-knows how many hours at a nearby university library, rummaging through his newspaper columns of the previous year. I checked out all the available biographical information. I labored over every question I wanted to ask him. I interviewed a number of his friends.

Despite my preparations, the early part of the interview went nowhere. Royko was having some problems with a tooth and was feeling subpar, and his answers were clipped and occasionally impatient. My attempts at follow-up questions were all but brushed aside. At one point during the interview, my photographer gave me a little shrug, indicating that he recognized and sympathized with my plight.

When the time came for Royko to go to his dentist, he told me that I could accompany him to the dentist's office or remain at the newspaper offices. "We can continue later," he told me, which indicated to me that it was his discomfort, more than my method of questioning, that was affecting the interview. I decided to stay at the newspaper office and try to regroup—a decision that was later criticized by some of my colleagues, who envisioned what it would have been like to go to the dentist's office with one of the Windy City's best-known curmudgeons. For me, the anecdote wasn't worth the price of the interview. At that point, I was stuck with a potential noninterview, and I was more than a little intimidated by my interviewee.

While Royko was away, I went back over my notes and reformed my sequence of questioning. By the time he returned, we were both ready for another round. Royko, now feeling better, was more than gracious in his responses. In fact, he invited me back for a follow-up session.

Not all of my failing interviews worked out so well. I've talked to people who fought me every inch of the way. Others had nothing to say. Some offered me information that could be used as background information, but little that could be quoted. These experiences were frustrating, to say the least—nobody wants to spend time researching and conducting interviews that go nowhere—but the experiences were valuable in terms of their helping me hone my interviewing skills.

From these experiences I've drawn the following conclusions:

■ *Never take the failures personally.* If you're prepared and holding up your end of the interview, the failure is not necessarily a reflection of your lack of skill. It may instead be an indication that something is misfiring with your interviewee. Some people, for instance, agree to be interviewed only out of sheer sense of obligation, due to pressure from external sources such as their employers, agents, publicists, or others. These interviewees show up for the interview as promised, but they're impatient, rude, or indifferent. They don't dislike *you*; they're angry with the situation. Their refusal to address questions is a manifestation of their anger. Or, in cases such as my Royko example, other human factors may be distracting them to such a degree that they cannot entertain your questions adequately.

■ *Analyze your position and form alternatives.* In most noninterview cases, it doesn't take long for an interviewer to see that the conversation is going nowhere. When you see this happening, what do you do? This is where your skills at quick improvisation might save your story. Look for the tiniest sparks, the emotional signals (smiles, frowns, certain body language) that may indicate a direction you might take. ("Very often, you will hear a laugh at a certain moment," says Studs Terkel. "A black man, for instance, might laugh at a moment when he recounts his humiliation. . . . Well, that laugh is a bitter laugh, but it's also a safety valve.") Don't be afraid to follow any lead, even if it's into an unanticipated or unneeded area of discussion. Noninterviews occasionally turn into good interviews if the person being interviewed changes attitude or stance. Just keeping the conversation going can help.

■ *Know when to quit.* If all of your best efforts are failing, and it's apparent that you're not going to get any useful information from a person, terminate the interview at the first convenient moment. Terminate the conversation with grace. Don't show anger or irritation. Be diplomatic. You might find the person willing to talk at another date, and even if this is not the case, you don't want to sacrifice your sense of professionalism to a hopeless cause. On the other hand, you don't want to devote a lot of your time to an interview that leads you down a dead-end road.

■ *Don't confuse the "noninterview" with a "nonstory."* I may believe in the noninterview, but I don't subscribe to the idea of the nonstory. With a little creativity, any experience, including the noninterview, can be written into a compelling, salable article. Perhaps the angle to your story is why your interviewee *won't* address your questions. With further research, along with a couple of interviews with the person's acquaintances, relatives, business associates, and so on, you may find that a couple of the quotes you considered useless in your noninterview are quite fertile indeed. If you look hard enough when you're reading newspaper or magazine articles, you'll see countless examples of times when noninterviews were converted into very successful articles, in which profile subjects may only be quoted once or twice in an entire story.

■ *Learn from the experience.* Rather than sulk about your being the victim of a noninterview, try to learn as much as you can from the experience. When reviewing your tapes or transcripts, question every moment of the interview. What do the person's responses tell you about his or her psychological makeup? How can you apply that knowledge to further your skills as an interviewer? If the person was putting you on or avoiding your questions, why was it happening and what might you do if it happens to you in the future? It could well be that there's nothing you can do. If that's the case, you've learned an obvious, yet very important lesson: human beings are unpredictable, and because of this, all the preparation and interviewing skills in the world won't guarantee you a great conversation. A noninterview could, however, inspire an interesting story.

TELEPHONE INTERVIEWS

Telephone interviews are never preferable to in-person interviews, but they have become a necessity, a fact of life in every type of nonfiction writing. Telephone interviews save time and bridge distance barriers; they are effective ways of gathering quotes or conducting surveys. They are a major means of conducting short follow-up interviews. Telephone interviews are godsends to reporters who must piece together a front-page story in a matter of hours; for freelance writers working on articles for large magazines, they've come to replace the extravagant traveling expenses once necessary for pieces with a national scope.

Nevertheless, there are disadvantages to telephone interviews as well. You cannot see the person you're talking to or observe his or her facial expressions, gestures, or body language. In telephone interviews, people tend to be more formal and guarded than in face-to-face encounters. In telephone interviews, it's more difficult for you, the interviewer, to use your interviewing style to put the interviewee at ease. Long distance tolls can be expensive.

To diminish the negative elements in the telephone interview, conduct your interview as you would in person, bearing in mind the following considerations:

■ *Keep the "table chat" or small talk to a minimum.* Small talk doesn't play as well in telephone interviews as it does in the in-person interview, where your interviewee can see you and become relaxed by his or her interpretation of your facial expressions, body language, and other nonverbal forms of communication. However, you shouldn't just dive into the interview, either. Use the first few minutes of the phone call to give your subject a *little* information about yourself and your project, and devote a few minutes at the end of the interview to wrap things up, arrange for a follow-up interview (if necessary), and thank your interviewee. Your call should be warm but businesslike. Remember: the meter's running on your telephone bill and your interviewee's attention span.

■ *Word your questions carefully.* Tough or pointed questions can be very tricky in telephone interviews — much more so than in face-to-face encounters. Consider it a matter of depth perception. In face-to-face encounters, your conversation is three-dimensional, whereas the telephone conversation is flattened out or one-dimensional. An interviewee will be more at ease when he or she can see the interviewer react, gesture, emote, and inquire, and a tough question will be addressed in accordance with the interviewee's perception of the questioner. During in-person interviews, questions may be perceived as tough but fair, asked in the spirit of gaining information. In telephone interviews, tough questions, even if posed with the same wording as for in-person interviews, can be perceived as confrontational.

An interviewee who hasn't met you, and therefore knows you only by your voice, is much less inclined to give you the same consideration as an in-person interviewer. It's also much easier to avoid a question or terminate an interview when the interviewer is on the phone. Wording becomes crucial. You'll want your interviewees to feel as if they are volunteering information, not being grilled under a hot light or cornered into answering questions they'd prefer not to answer. You don't want to appear as if you're out to provoke or brow-beat them. On the other hand, the telephone interview offers you the chance to ask the tough question in a more precise way than you might ask it in the in-person encounter. Since the person cannot see you, it's easy to have the exact wording of your question written down; you can then read the question, posing it without the sense of awkwardness you'd experience if you were to read a written question to a person sitting across the table from you.

■ *Be aware of the effect of the tone of your voice.* In telephone conversations, your tone of voice is the single most important element that gives your speech its depth and, to a large degree, personality. Tone of voice can work in your favor, or it can be a disadvantage. If it contains warmth, compassion, or understanding at the right moments, it bonds you to your interviewee; if it's edgy, monotonous, or vague, it may send the wrong signals to the person you're talking to. Ideally, your tone should be similar to the type you'd use with a good business associate: neither too familiar nor too distant, professional with a sense of purpose, authoritative but not arrogant, tinged with the human elements that create trust.

■ *Be aware of the volume of your voice.* As with tone of voice, volume of voice sends signals to an interviewee. The person who shouts or speaks too loudly might seem aggressive to an interviewee, while the person who talks too softly could appear timid or unsure of himself. Stay on an even keel, using the same volume as you would if the person were sitting across the table from you. Speak slowly and clearly, with the realization that words can blur if the person isn't there to "see" them spoken.

■ *Be on the alert for extraneous problems or distractions.* Just because an interviewee is talking to you does not necessarily mean that you can be assured that the person is giving you full consideration and attention. Other things may be going on even as the person is speaking to you. He or she might be rearranging office files or putting a signature on a pile of papers; almost anything could be going on while you're talking. Worse yet, there may be someone in the room with your interviewee, so some of the responses may be laundered or modified to protect the interviewee from other "ears." Outside of asking a person about such distractions — or actually hearing the sounds of someone else in the interviewee's room — there is no definite way to know what is occurring. There are, however, signals that may indicate that your interviewee isn't entirely focused on the conversation. For example, is your interviewee rambling on in such a way as to suggest that he or she is talking but not totally paying attention to what's being said? Does the person's mind seem to be elsewhere? Does he or she seem rushed or out of sorts, or talking in a hushed tone, as if to avoid being overheard? If you sense that the person's attention is elsewhere, you might suggest another time for the interview ("Is this a bad time to call? Should I call back at another time?"). If your interviewee is genuinely distracted, he or she may be willing to reschedule the interview for a better time; if the person is simply not paying attention, the suggestion will have the effect of gently steering your subject back to the interview.

■ *Listen for signals that indicate interviewee fatigue.* In face-to-face encounters, people can talk much longer without tiring than they can on the telephone. Keep an eye on the clock. If the conversation lasts more than an hour, look for signs that indicate that your interviewee may be fatigued. Are your answers less complete than the ones you were getting earlier? Does your interviewee's mind seem to be elsewhere? Is the person growing impatient with your questioning? Are you getting subtle signals that the interviewee would like to terminate the call and is only being polite in not doing so? If it's apparent that your interviewee is tiring or losing interest in the conversation, find a way to close out the interview. Mention that you might have to call back with another question or two. It's always better to obtain good answers in two conversations than weak or so-so answers in one.

TAPING TELEPHONE INTERVIEWS

Whenever possible, you should tape your telephone interviews, not only because a taped conversation will afford you accuracy in quoting, but also because it will act as a kind of insurance policy in the event that your interviewee disputes any of the quoted material in your article — or even disputes that the call occurred in the first place. Busy people take dozens of calls per day, and it's possible that no record of your call will be made by your interviewee. Memories fade, and people tend to remember less the people they speak to on the telephone than the people they meet. A person may deny having made certain statements or claim that you fabricated your notes, but a taped conversation is impossible to refute.

State laws vary in regard to the taping of telephone conversations. Some laws require you to advise an interviewee that you're taping the call, while others have no such provisions. The safest policy is to always inform your interviewee that you are taping the conversation. Do it formally and at the onset of your interview. When you've completed your small talk and are beginning the formal interview, turn on your tape recorder and say something like, "This is John Smith, talking to Jane Doe, on such-and-such a date." That way, the record of the call, the taping, and the interviewee's knowledge of the taping, has been recorded.

Some journalists or writers tape all of their phone interviews, with or without a person's consent. The issue of obtaining formal consent is a debatable one. "People get nervous when you tell them you're recording the interview," one reporter says. "More often than not, they don't know you and they're not all that comfortable about talking for the record. If you tell them you're recording the interview, they can get scared and freeze up on you."

That reporter assumes that, in consenting to the interview, the interviewee automatically consents to the taping of the interview. ("He's got to figure that I'm taking down what he says, and he's got to hope that I'm going to quote him accurately, so what's the difference between writing everything down and taping it?") This attitude would probably work in the case where you call ahead and arrange the telephone interview, but this idea changes dramatically if the person doesn't expect your call and is suddenly confronted with questions that put him or her on the defensive. In this latter instance, taping without consent borders on unethical or ambush journalism. Furthermore, it may be illegal.

Find a light-handed way to get an interviewee's consent to the taping. Mention that it's just a formality that has to be taken care of—this makes it look as if the matter of consent is someone else's rule, not yours. A few people may pause at this mention, but they'll almost always agree to the taping.

To tape the conversation, you will need a device that connects your tape recorder to the telephone. The most popular device is the telephone jack which, at one end, plugs into the microphone jack of your tape recorder and at the other end attaches itself to your telephone via suction cup. The jacks are very inexpensive and can be purchased at most electronics stores. Test all recording equipment prior to your call. You don't want to tape an important interview, only to discover afterward that your taping equipment wasn't working properly.

BEFORE YOU CALL . . .

Don't underestimate the value of personal comfort during the interview. You're going to be sitting in one place for a while, and you'll have a piece of hard plastic pressed to your ear. Once you begin, you don't want to be interrupted, and you won't want to be uncomfortable, so the best policy is to be certain that you're comfortable and fully prepared for the interview before you call your interviewee.

Find a chair you can sit in for an hour or so without growing restless or uncomfortable. Gather all notes and research materials, along with your taping equipment, and have them on hand before you call. Some interviewers like to keep a glass of water nearby.

Whenever possible, eliminate (or at least diminish) outside noises that might distract you. During the warm months, noises from the street—passing or honking cars, people's voices, the sound of construction work, etc.—can be annoying; in the winter months, the sound of a furnace blower kicking on can wind up on your tape and compete with the sound of an interviewee's voice. Find a way to diminish the effects of these and other noises. Shut off the television and any separate phone lines that you may have. Move your kids to another area of the house.

All this, of course, is the ideal. Some of your calls may originate from phone booths or in newsrooms, where it will be impossible to eliminate distractions or outside noises, or to set up the most comfortable environment for your conversation. Work with whatever circumstances you have, but remember that interruptions or distractions, especially those that might require your leaving the phone for any reason, can ruin an interview.

One final word: If your telephone interview is long distance and you haven't previously called the person to arrange the interview, keep the country's time zones in mind. Know the time at your *interviewee's* end of the line, and call at the best time for that person.

THE WRITTEN INTERVIEW

Some interviewees want more time to consider your questions and prepare their responses than an in-person or telephone interview will allow. These interviewees suggest that you submit a list of questions that they'll consider, answer, and return at their own leisure.

The written interview is problematic for a number of reasons. It is anything but spontaneous. You don't actually see or hear your interviewee talking. Written interviews tend to take a great deal of time, due more to a person's procrastination than an overwhelming interest in giving complete answers to your questions. Follow-up questions are impossible unless you have a wide-open deadline, and even if you do, the answer you're following up will have been stated weeks before you propose the follow-up, and the interviewee will have to think back to recall the original response. Written interviews tend to sound less like conversations and more like prepared statements — or, more likely, more like encyclopedic recitations and less like human speech. Written interviews generally lack warmth.

Despite these flaws, there are times when the written interview is suitable for the type of piece that you're writing. Written interviews or questionnaires are often employed in roundups — articles in which several interviewees answer the same questions on the same topics — and in which only a couple of questions are asked. Written interviews can be useful for research or background, as well as for a support quote or two. More lengthy written interviews work well for the archival interview.

George Plimpton, who has conducted and published a number of written interviews with authors in his *Paris Review Interviews* series, is satisfied with using this format in his publication.

"Some people don't feel that they're very good talking to machines or being interviewed by reporters," he explains. "It's interesting: very often, what you say seems very fraught with meaning and intelligence, but it isn't that way on the printed page. The idea (for *Paris Review* interviews) is to get these people to talk about their writing, and it doesn't make much difference to us whether the interview is typed out or spoken."

One of the magazine's most unusual interviews, he points out, was its interview with Cynthia Ozick. "She was asked questions with the questioner right there in the room, and she typed out her answers on the typewriter. That was probaby the most mysterious way of getting information."

Most written interviews follow a more standard procedure. Once you have contacted an interviewee and this format has been agreed upon, you should conduct your research in the same manner as you would if you were preparing for an in-person encounter. Be thorough. Don't assume that ignorance or lack of preparation will not show through in the written questions you submit; if anything, your written words will be considered more carefully and given greater weight than if you were speaking the same words over the course of a long conversation. When you have finished your research and have prepared your questions, type them on one or two sheets of paper — or, better yet, type them one question to a page, leaving the rest of the page blank for the interviewee's response. (By doing the latter, you eliminate the chance of an interviewee's accidentally passing over a question, and you're supplying your interviewee the paper, a slight professional courtesy that will be appreciated.)

When you're working on your questions:

■ *Be specific in the way you word your questions.* A vague question will draw a vague response — if the question is answered at all. Remember, you won't be in the room to clarify your question to the interviewee. If you must, frame your questions in contexts ("In an article published in the June 15 issue of the *Washington Post*, you said that the most difficult aspects. . . .").

■ *Do not submit too many questions per mailing.* In a two-hour, face-to-face interview, you would probably ask scores of questions that your interviewee would have little trouble answering adequately. In the written interview, responses take more time. People spend more time considering a question if they don't feel pushed into an immediate answer, and the answers themselves take more time to type than if they were spoken. A packet of forty or fifty questions could be too intimidating for your interviewee to answer them all, or if he or she did, it might be with brief one- or two-sentence answers. Limit the number of questions you submit. Twenty questions should be your maximum per mailing, the optimum being ten to fifteen questions.

■ *Make each question count.* Since you are limited in the number of questions you'll be asking, make sure each question deals with an important aspect of the piece you're writing. Stay to the point. If you've come up with a lot of questions as a result of your research, set a list of priority questions and submit those questions with the highest priority, with the hope that your interviewee will agree to answer another batch of questions if the need should arise.

■ *Don't ask for too much.* Since, as noted above, responses take more time with written interviews than with in-person conversations, don't pose questions that might take pages and pages to answer. This idea is in keeping with the first notation on this list, but even specific questions can demand long answers. People have better things to do with their time than write entire books in response to a handful of questions. Asking them to do as much is an imposition they're apt to resent. This applies to multipart questions as well: if you suspect that a question, by its nature, will demand a lengthy response, break it down into several more specific questions.

■ *Ask for examples or anecdotes.* Don't assume that a person will supply you with colorful anecdotes or examples that illustrate the major points of an answer. When you are asking a question that has anecdotal possibilities, mention, in parentheses, that you would appreciate the interviewee's including anecdotes or examples in the answer. Better yet, you may solicit these illustrations by asking a number of "how" or "why" questions; anecdotes and examples spring naturally from such open-ended questions.

When you have completed your preparation and typing of your questions, package them neatly, as you would if you were submitting a manuscript for an editor's consideration. Send a neat typescript (questions maybe single-spaced), void of any strikeovers and smudges. Paper-clip the sheets together and put them in a large manila envelope, along with a brief cover letter reminding your interviewee of your agreement, deadline, and the basic details of the article you're writing. Don't forget to enclose a return envelope with sufficient return postage affixed.

Allow your interviewee four to six weeks to respond. (If your deadline demands a quicker turnaround, mention as much in your cover letter.) If you haven't heard from the person in that period of time, send a postcard reminder—but be diplomatic. The interviewee owes you nothing, and the written interview can be demanding of his or her time. Any impatience displayed on your part may result in the termination of the project.

THE TAPED MAIL INTERVIEW

An alternative to the written interview is the taped, through-the-mail interview, which involves an interviewer's sending an interviewee a list of questions and a blank cassette for the responses. This practice has become more and more popular as people have become accustomed to dictating their notes, thoughts, and ideas into tape recorders. If a potential interviewee mentions a preference for a mail interview rather than in-person or telephone conversations, you might suggest that the answers be taped, rather than written.

The taped approach offers advantages over the written interview. First of all, you're hearing the person's voice, and even if that voice is flat or monotonous, as dictated words can often be, this is always preferable to the written word. Since taping answers is easier and less time-consuming than writing them, the person's responses tend to be longer and more complete, which affords you the luxury of asking more questions. Finally, since the process of answering questions is less time-consuming, the turnaround time may be reduced. Keep in mind, however, that you will have to transcribe the tapes, and this procedure takes time—time that might affect your honoring deadlines.

To prepare questions for a taped interview, follow the same procedure as you would for the written interview—though you should type all questions on one or two sheets of paper. Don't shortchange yourself in the number of questions that you ask. Because you have no idea of how long the interviewee will talk, you will want to use a bit of strategy in the way you sequence your typed questions. Assume that the person will feel awkward or self-conscious about speaking into the tape recorder at the onset of the interview, and keep your opening questions simple. The best bet is to ask a general question, something that will get the ball rolling. Questions about the person's life, or those asking for specific information about his or her job, are good icebreakers, though you should not ask questions that could have been answered by good research. Many people enjoy talking about themselves, and opening the interview in this manner will put them more at ease. In this regard, the taped mail interview is not that much different from the in-person interview.

However, you shouldn't spend *too* much time away from the main thrust of the interview. Without another person in the room to interact with, a person can grow bored or lose interest in the taping. Get to the point fairly quickly—a few questions into your typed-out sequence—so you receive your most complete answers to the most important questions while your interviewee is still fresh, interested in the interview, and willing to talk. Many interviewees will answer the questions at their own leisure, over a period of several recording sessions, but it's never wise for you to count on their doing so. To be safe, assume that they're going to sit down and answer all questions at one sitting.

Send a new, high-quality, 90-minute cassette for the person's responses. Don't send a tape that you have recorded on previously; it will only make your interviewee wonder when you will be having someone else recording answers over his or her responses. Ninety minutes is a good cassette length because anything less encourages short responses, while longer cassettes (or more than one cassette) can make the interview look like an intrusion. In the event that your interviewee becomes inspired and wishes to speak more than 90 minutes, chances are excellent that he or she will supply another tape.

For mailing, use a strong cassette box or package (available at most office supply stores), and be sure to enclose a self-addressed return label and sufficient first-class postage.

THE INTERVIEWER AS CONDUIT

As we've seen, there are numerous ways to conduct interviews. How you choose to conduct your interviews will depend upon the nature of the piece you're writing, the disposition of your interviewee, the time at your disposal, the circumstances of the interview, and other factors discussed in this chapter. The most vital role you can maintain is that of a conduit between your interviewee and your eventual readers. If you are able to transfer a clear understanding of what your interview meant to your readers, you will have accomplished your task as an interviewer and writer.

It's important to remember that raw quotes no more make an article than a tape full of conversation constitutes an interview. To be an effective conduit between interviewee and reader, you must use as much skill and thought in applying your interviewee's words to your written piece as you used in applying your preparation and interviewing craftsmanship in filling your tape or notebook.

Your interview may be finished, but you haven't finished listening yet. You will now be listening with the ears of your readers. What you "hear" will determine what you write.

USING YOUR INTERVIEWEE'S WORDS

The most challenging moment of any interview occurs the moment you have finished the conversation and turned off the tape recorder or closed your notebook. At this instant you begin to redefine who you are as a writer and craftsperson. So far, you have relied on others for much of the work. You've looked to other sources when you were compiling your research, and the person you interviewed did the yeoman's share of the work in the interview itself. From this point on — from the moment you thank your subject and say goodbye to the moment you file your story — the success of your article will rely solely on the choices you make while transcribing your tapes, editing the transcript, and writing the article. It's a challenge — and sometimes it can be an intimidating one.

On the other hand, you should also feel very good at this point. You no longer have external factors influencing the direction of your article, profile, or interview. An interviewee can't delay or back out of the conversation and you no longer have to think about what you are going to ask or how you are going to ask it. Chances are good that you have a fairly accurate idea of where your story is going and how it will get there. You should even have a strong idea about how difficult it will be to write the story. If you're lucky, between your research and taped conversations and notes, you will have more than enough material for your article. You'll need to perform a kind of triage in order to assure that what you serve to the public represents the best fruits of your efforts.

It all comes down to the choices you make.

POSTINTERVIEW ETIQUETTE

Once an interview has been concluded, there is usually no reason for you to further contact your interview subject, unless you have promised to send a transcript of the interview or list of quotes to be used in your article.

You would also be justified in contacting your interviewee if you were sending:

■ *A letter of acknowledgement.* As a general rule, whenever I've taken two or more hours for an interview, I send a brief note of thanks for the person's time, and reaffirm that person's importance to my story. It's a minor courtesy that takes only a few minutes to accomplish, and I believe it adds a touch of professionalism that most people appreciate. Keep such letters brief, warm, and genuine. Don't fill your interviewee in on all the events that have taken place in your life since you talked, but don't be so formal that the letter appears to have been written only out of a sense of obligation.

■ *Clippings of the published article.* "I'll send you a copy of the article when it's published" is one of the biggest lies in the writing business. This is a sad statement, but it's true enough; writers have a bad habit of making promises they don't keep. Some agencies and public relations firms have clipping services that provide them with clippings of published articles about their clients, but you should not depend upon this happening with your article, especially if it is being published in a regional or local publication. Send a couple of tear sheets or photocopies of the published article to your interviewee, either directly or through his or her agent. It's the kind of professional courtesy that may pay off for you in the future, in terms of the person's putting in a good word for you at an opportune time, or remembering the courtesy when the time comes for you to interview that person again for another article.

Some interviewers make the mistake of trying to be "buddies" with the people they interview, and while you occasionally hear stories about friendships that have developed as a result of an initial professional encounter, it is best to really mean it when you say goodbye at the end of an interview. Your interviewee is busy doing all the things that made you want to interview him or her in the first place, and any further contact is likely to be seen as an intrusion, even if your interviewee is too kind to tell you as much.

Uninvited familiarity can also lead to embarrassing or awkward moments for both of you. Television critic Monica Collins, who has interviewed such high-profile celebrities as Larry Hagman, Dan Rather, and Barbara Walters, shared such a moment with *Mademoiselle* readers when she recalled approaching Don Johnson at a party shortly after she had interviewed him. Hoping to strike up a conversation with the actor, she was instead greeted with a blank stare. He had no idea who she was.

"Never expect celebrities to remember your name," Collins advises. "In fact, never expect celebrities to remember what you look like, who you are, or the fact that they ever met you. You may have been thrilled to meet them—but to them, interviews are nothing more than a crass encounter. You're using them to help sell newspapers. They're using you to promote their careers. It's a commercial transaction, masquerading as a human exchange."

IMMEDIATELY FOLLOWING THE INTERVIEW

If you did not tape your interview, the hour or so immediately following your conversation is crucial. In your notebook you will have page after page of shorthand or phraseology, and in the time directly following the interview, while your subject's words are still fresh in your mind, it's best to translate your shorthand to full, completed quotes. You should not trust your memory. In a day or two, your shorthand will start to look like a foreign language, and you won't be as certain of *exactly* what your interviewee said. You may remember the gist of what a person told you, but you should not approximate direct quotes if you can avoid doing so.

As soon as possible after the interview, find a quiet place and write out or type the person's quotations—or at least the quotations you're certain you are going to use. Be exact. Don't hurry through the task. Keep in mind that one misplaced or "misremembered" word can change what a person said or meant.

If you tape-recorded the interview, you're in much better shape: you can begin transcribing at a time of your choosing. However, in the time directly following an interview, you should sit down and flesh out the notes you took during the conversation. Jot down your impressions of the interview, of your interviewee, and the environment of the conversation, using as much sensory detail as possible; all this information will help you bring your interviewee and article alive for your eventual reader. Create a vivid sketch of the person's attitudes, demeanor, body language, and way of speaking. Try to remember every little detail.

Then, unless you are up against a tight deadline, kick up your feet and relax. Let everything steep in your head overnight.

In the morning, when you are rested and your mind is fresh and capable of a solid perspective on the conversation, the hard work begins again.

TRANSCRIBING YOUR TAPES

There is no absolutely correct way to transcribe taped interviews, but there is a *best* way: a word-for-word transcription, containing every utterance, including incomplete sentences, poor grammar usage, meandering thoughts — the whole works.

However, a word-for-word record is not always necessary or even possible. If you are using the interview only for information or research — if you don't intend to directly quote your interviewee — you might find that listening to the tapes and taking notes is preferable to the tedious task of transcribing your interviewee's words verbatim. Or, if you're gathering only several select quotes from an interview that lasted an hour or two, you might scan the tapes and make exact transcriptions only of those important quotes. Time is also a major factor in your decision: if you're on a tight deadline, you won't have time for a total transcription. In this case, you would again be selecting only the appropriate quotes.

Some interviewers like to "index" their tapes for quick access to particular quotes. Gary Provost, who has interviewed hundreds of people in his fifteen-year freelance career, has a method that works well for him, especially when he is tackling the small mountain of taped interviews that he uses for his nonfiction books.

"I know what I'm going to need and what I'm not going to need," he says, noting that during the early stages of a series of conversations with a person, everything sounds as if it could be used; but as the sessions wear on, an interviewer gets a feeling for what will make the final cut. "I listen to the tapes and make notes on where things are, because I don't want to spend time transcribing a lot of material I'm not going to need. I give each tape a name so I'll know what's on it."

Provost uses his tape counter for reference to where certain topics are discussed on a tape. He notates the counter numbers in a notebook and thus has his own subject index when it comes time to find the appropriate quotes or information for a book passage or magazine article.

It's easy to understand why writers are constantly looking for a less time-consuming method of transcribing tapes. I have yet to meet a writer who relishes the transcribing process. It eats into the time one could be spending on writing or interviewing and, as the saying goes, time is money. Count on spending about two hours in transcribing each hour of taped conversation. If you're interviewing someone for a Q/A format interview, the task of transcribing ten or fifteen hours of tape-recorded interview can be prodigious or downright daunting.

Lawrence Linderman, a regular "Playboy Interview" contributor for over a decade, hires reliable transcribers to work on tapes of his longer interviews. Some publications, he points out, consider this a reasonable expense and will reimburse him for the costs of transcribing services; so hiring out the transcription work doesn't cost him a cent, and it frees him to pursue other, more pressing writing tasks.

"I've had nineteen 45-minute sides on people for *Playboy*," he explains. "I wouldn't try transcribing that."

When hiring someone to transcribe, Linderman suggests, it's important to find a person who can be trusted to transcribe accurately everything an interviewee is saying. Sometimes the words will be unintelligible or garbled—in which case, Linderman says, he goes back over that part of the tape and tries to fill in the gaps himself—but you can't fudge on the words. Linderman doesn't regard a literal transcription of his *own* talking as important, as long as the transcriber types the essence of what he said. The questions will be typed in later, when the Q/A interview is being pieced together.

ADVANTAGES OF A VERBATIM TRANSCRIPT

If transcribing tapes is such a tedious, time-consuming process, why would anyone go to the trouble of preparing a complete transcription of an interview? If shortcuts are available, why take the long route home?

As we've seen, some interviewers avoid complete transcriptions or hire someone to do the work for them, but for those interviewers who transcribe their own tapes, there are five basic advantages to taking the time to do a verbatim transcription of an interview:

■ *The process of transcribing the tapes refreshes your memory.* No one's memory is perfect, and verbatim transcriptions will jog your recollection of the interview. You'll remember not only what was said, but the sequence in which points were made and how a person addressed a question. You may be reminded of the way a person began to talk about something but drew up short. You'll hear the person laugh. You'll relive the conversation in its entirety.

■ *To actually see a person's words in print may give you a new perspective on the conversation or offer you a new angle for your article or interview.* During the course of an interview, your mind is working on a number of levels. You're hearing and absorbing what a person is saying. You're thinking of follow-up questions. You're trying to maintain the flow of the conversation. Depending on the length of the interview and the person you're talking to, an interview can be a draining experience. When you're transcribing a tape, you're hearing everything for a second time, but your attention will be more focused on what's actually being said. A person's words have a way of being very naked in print, and you may find that this stark quality leads you to another possible angle to your story.

■ *A close study of a verbatim transcript will show you where there are "holes" in your interview, where follow-up questions are necessary.* Quite often a person appears to have answered a question during an interview, but after you've looked at a transcript you see that the answer is incomplete or needs further elaboration or clarification. More information may be necessary before you (and your readers) fully understand what your interviewee is saying. By studying the transcript, you're more capable of seeing exactly what you need than you might be if you were looking over notes, approximated speech, or even a partial transcript.

■ *A total transcription is accurate, assuring you of the best opportunity to quote your interviewee correctly and in context of the discussion.* Accurately quoting someone involves more than getting each word correct; it involves putting those words into the exact context in which they were spoken. A verbatim transcript supplies you with that context.

■ *By studying your transcripts with a critical eye, you can improve your own skills as an interviewer.* If studied carefully, a transcript is a graph of your skills as an interviewer. By going over a verbatim transcript, you'll see how you asked and sequenced your questions, how you worked your transitions into the conversation, when you may have talked too much or listened too little. You may not like what you see, but if you analyze the interview and consider the positive future measures you might take to be a better interviewer, a transcript can be one of the most effective learning tools that you have at your disposal.

Transcripts have become an important part of my filing system. For each of my published articles, I keep a file folder containing the transcript, a photocopy of the manuscript, and tear sheets of the published article, along with any correspondence that comes up as a result of the article.

Keeping the transcript is useful if there's ever a question about a quotation or the context of the interviewee's response to a question: instead of having to run through a tape for the quotation or context in question, you will have an instant reference to the interview—a reference that is easy to use, since all of the conversation will be in writing.

WORKING UP THE TRANSCRIPT

A transcript "workup" is designed to answer the questions: "What exactly do I have in this interview?" and "What am I going to do with it?" It is an optional step that will make the organization and writing of your article much easier.

Let's say you have the transcript of a two-hour interview in front of you. The single-spaced transcript will probably run about thirty pages. Chances are good that the conversation meanders and moves around, with your source jumping from an important point to another topic of no significance to your piece, then back to the point, and so on. Your transcript is a conglomeration of valuable and valueless material.

The purpose of the workup is to create an accessible reference guide to your interview and transcript, to break the transcript down into needed topic areas and isolate the quotes that best address those topics. It's a process that involves three basic steps.

First, go through your transcript and number each question (or answer, if you prefer). These numerals can be used in reference or cross-reference. (You can see how this works by looking at the example on page 229.) After you have assigned a number to each question or answer, go back over the interview and make topic notations in the margins of the transcript; this will allow you to scan a transcript for a specific topic of discussion, rather than having to reread it. While you're notating your topic areas, underline any important quotations that appear to be usable in your article or Q/A format interview. These three steps offer an instant reference to any subject discussed during the interview, along with important quotes on the topic, and you'll find that the short time that it takes you to accomplish this workup will pay huge dividends when it's time for you to write your article.

FINDING THE BEST QUOTES

Direct quotations are the spice of nonfiction writing; they give your article, feature, or profile flavor and character, they bring a flat piece of narrative to life. They help pace an article; they make good transitions. Yet, like spices, direct quotations can be misused, overused, and underused. If not used thoughtfully, they can ruin an otherwise fine work of nonfiction.

When you directly quote someone, you are allowing another voice into your writing. In effect, you are yielding the floor to a speaker who will say something more eloquently, more authoritative, or more colorfully than you might say it yourself, and because this is the case, you should take care in the selection of quotes for your writing.

The best quotations serve one of the following functions:

■ *They represent the voice of authority.* Readers will more willingly believe an expert than they will take the word of a "layman," especially if the statements or opinions concern controversial or unusual issues. Rather than state a crucial point yourself, allow one or more authorities to consider it, debate it, and put it in perspective.

■ *They present the voice of the eyewitness.* Nothing will bring more drama and credibility to your nonfiction than the direct account of an eyewitness or participant. You could devote 2,000 words to the effects of a hurricane and its aftermath on a small coastal city, and those words would carry only a fraction of the impact of an eyewitness account.

■ *They underscore the major points you're making in your nar-*

rative. Besides looking for voices of authority, you should also be on the lookout for voices of *agreement,* for those quotations that back up the statements you're making in the narrative of your text.

■ *They offer anecdotes and examples.* A story or example offered directly from an interviewee carries much more clout than an anecdote or example simply incorporated into the narrative. These quotes humanize the interviewee for readers.

■ *They tell you something important about the speaker.* People reveal their true colors when they are speaking. In one or two brief remarks, they can uncover more about their attitudes and emotions than you could describe in much longer passages of narrative. Because you are quoting the interviewee, the revealed aspects of their personality are more vivid and direct in the minds of your readers than they would be if you stated them yourself.

■ *They make statements you could not or should not make yourself.* Investigative reporters understand the fine line that separates the truth from the stated truth. You may know for a fact that Senator Joe Blowhard is guilty of accepting kickbacks from firms awarded defense contracts as a result of his subcommittee's endorsements, but you would be ill-advised to state as much unless you had sources who were willing to go on the record, say it for you, and supply you with reasonably solid evidence to back their claims. (As we'll see in Chapter Eight, you can still be sued for libel if you repeat someone else's libelous statements.) The same principle applies to strongly stated opinions. You wouldn't dare state, as if it were fact, that Senator Blowhard is an arrogant jerk, but such strongly worded opinions, when backed by solid evidence, may be voiced by your sources.

If you have conducted a thorough, thoughtful interview, you will find in your transcript an abundance of quotes that fulfill the above-listed functions. You will find statements that either address an issue or reveal important facets of the speaker's personality. When you're selecting direct quotations for your article, profile, or feature, avoid using quotes that state the obvious ("I hate when I get hurt"); aim for remarks that are offered in a unique way, with their own built-in color. Chances are you recognized the best quotations when you heard them during the interview. Your job now is to put them to their best use.

HOW TO EDIT YOUR INTERVIEWEE'S WORDS

Very few people speak with perfect grammar, and most people are not well organized when they are stating their thoughts. In conversation, people tend to focus more on *what's* being said than on *how* it's being said, and as a result, the transcripts for the overwhelming majority of your interviews will feature a hodgepodge of incomplete sentences and uncompleted thoughts, fractured grammar and word usage, disjointed or vague statements, and gobbledygook.

Generally speaking, you would be irresponsible if you were to publish unedited an interviewee's words—and it would be a rare editor who would allow you to do so. Interviewees expect to be presented in the best possible light, and readers tend to become distracted by or annoyed with quotations that aren't clear and grammatically correct. You should strive for a natural feeling to the direct quotes included in your work, but never at the expense of diminishing the value of your narrative.

"I remember having a debate about this once," says Lawrence Linderman. "I was on a panel that was discussing the art of the interview, and somebody was talking about 'how dare you touch the person's words.' And I said, 'I'll tell you what. I'll run an unedited transcript and I'll bet you that 95 percent of the people who are interested in the person talking won't even be able to read the damn thing.' No, you don't want to put ideas or words into anybody's mouth, or use words that the guy or woman doesn't use. It's important not to change any of the emotional content or meaning of what someone says, but you are polishing words and bridging certain things when you edit. Sometimes you will be boiling down paragraphs into sentences. But I never polish anything to a luster that it doesn't already have."

When you're editing, you aren't *changing* anything, nor are you destroying the spontaneity of the interview. To put this into perspective, think of your own writing: no matter how much or how little revision you ordinarily apply to your work, you never turn in work in the *exact* manner in which it spilled out of your head. You rearrange, tighten and compact, and improve your copy—all because you want your work to represent your best efforts. The same idea applies to your editing of an interviewee's words.

Editing quotes is a two-part procedure: first, you deal with the person's thoughts, and then you deal with the individual words within those thoughts. It is a process that moves from the general to the specific.

When you're dealing with a person's thoughts, your main concerns are organizational. You want the interviewee to say something in its most organized, precise, and interesting way. An interviewee might have spent, say, fifteen minutes in a detailed discussion of a topic with you, or might have addressed a topic on several occasions during an interview. Since you won't be able to include everything the person told you in your article, profile, or feature, you will be looking for the best-selected quotes available. You will be breaking down longer thoughts (and passages) and combining shorter ones.

To break down longer passages in your transcript, you should look for the main theme of the passage, as it is stated best or most concisely, and build off of that. As Lawrence Linderman pointed out, the editing is a boiling-down procedure.

For example, when I interviewed author David Leavitt for my book, *Reasons to Believe*, we had a fairly lengthy discussion about the nation's obsession with youthful writers. This interest had resulted in the categorizing of young authors that Leavitt found appalling. The following is a direct, verbatim transcription of a portion of that discussion:

> *I think it's over, basically. It was a fad. It was a media invention. It happened even more strongly in Europe than it did over here. But it just wasn't very interesting. I mean, it seemed to me that what it was, was an outcropping of the whole sort of fascination with Yuppies—you know, with these sort of young, unbelievably ambitious, well-dressed, rich bankers and things, so . . . . Clearly, youth sold magazines.*

Then, in another quote, he said:

> *Well, what happened was there were a few books published that actually had a lot of success and then, the next thing was, you know, the media vipers sort of jumped on it. But the articles were stupid. They aren't written by people who*

care about literature; they're written by people who care about gossip, who care about selling. It's created problems because it's annoyed the writers so intensely.

In the published form, these passages, as well as numerous others, were substantially compacted. I didn't want to make this discussion the angle of my profile, nor did I want to assign it an inordinately long section of the book. However, it was important, not only for its commentary, but for what it said about Leavitt's intentionally isolating himself from the spotlight. In the book, I used the above passages in this manner:

> *He labels the national interest in young writers a "media invention, a fad."*
>
> *"It was an outcropping of the fascination with Yuppies, with these young, unbelievably ambitious, well-dressed bankers and things. Clearly, youth sold magazines; articles about young achievers sold magazines. There were a few books published that actually had a lot of success, and the next thing you knew, the media vipers sort of jumped on it. The stories weren't written by people who cared about literature; they were written by people who cared about gossip and selling. It's created problems because it's annoyed the writers so intensely."*

The "hook" for the discussion was Leavitt's labeling the national interest "a media invention, a fad," and even though Leavitt didn't use those five words in that precise manner, the tightening of his quotation was fair and reasonable. I wasn't putting words in Leavitt's mouth, nor was I changing the meaning of what he was saying or taking it out of context. As you can see from the rest of the passage, a certain amount of organization and tightening of prose was necessary to make Leavitt's statement as succinct as it could be. By keeping the passage short and to the point, I wasn't giving the discussion too much significance in the overall body of the text.

In the same book, I took a different approach in my profile of short-story writer Amy Hempel. Unlike Leavitt, who gave lengthy answers to my questions, Hempel gave short, more direct responses. Instead of asking two or three questions to cover a topic, as I did with Leavitt, I would ask Hempel a lot more questions before a topic had been exhausted. There were occasions when I took a "circling" approach to gathering my information and quotes: we'd talk about a topic, move to another, then return later.

Editing Hempel's words was a "stitching together" process: I would pull all the quotes that addressed one topic from my transcript and stitch them together into one longer, more organized, and easier-to-read passage. For example, I gathered biographical information from Hempel during three separate interview sessions—two sessions taking place months apart in New York, and a third interview conducted over the telephone. When I wrote my biographical passage in the profile, I combined the three sessions, making it look as if we had discussed this topic during one sitting. I placed the discussion in a sequence that put her life in chronological order. In the book it looked as if we started at the beginning of her life and worked our way to the present, when in fact we hadn't discussed these events in sequence.

Working in this fashion was both fair to Hempel and good for the profile. Nothing was taken out of context, and the topic was consistent throughout the discussion. If I had presented the important events in her life in the order in which they had been discussed, the reader might have become confused or impatient. By combining quotations, I was able to achieve a better sense of organization in the passage.

You can combine quotations as long as you are addressing the same topics in the same context in two or more quotes. You are well within your rights to combine the answer to a follow-up question with the answer to the question that inspired the follow-up question. By doing this, you will be establishing a continuity that makes the quotation easier to read. You are making the interviewee's thought process more organized and complete.

The second part of the editing process—dealing with the individual words—is a matter of fine tuning. You have worked on selecting the best thoughts to include in your nonfiction piece, and now you want to be certain that those thoughts are appropriately stated. Instead of content editing, you will now be line editing, making sure that the person's statements are grammatically correct. To accomplish this, look at each line of each quotation or passage. Are all pronouns consistent with the nouns they represent? Does a singular verb follow a singular noun? Are your adjectives and adverbs correctly placed? You should be conscious of these and other points of grammar, though you shouldn't edit to the point of flattening out an interviewee's words. Most of this type of editing involves judgment on your part: if the grammar is blatantly misused and makes your interviewee look unintelligent or fatuous, you should correct the mistakes; if the grammar misusage is slight, and if your correcting it might result in your disrupting the rhythm and flow of the quotation, you should leave the statement intact.

While editing your interviewee's words, remember that clarity is the main objective of the task. If the purpose and meaning of the quote are clear to your reader, you have fulfilled your editing job.

WHEN YOU SHOULDN'T EDIT A PERSON'S WORDS

When you are editing a person's words, you should draw a distinction between poor grammar or word usage, and colorful language. All people do not speak alike, and one of the hazards of the editing process is your making them sound as if they do.

Colorful language and phrasing are personality signatures, so when you are working with your interviewee's words, you should avoid editing:

■ *Important colloquial or rhythmic language.* Fiction writers go to great lengths to preserve the colloquial flavor of their regional characters. You should do the same, as long as it doesn't interfere with or distract the reader from your narrative. "She ain't what you'd call the world's smartest person" may not be grammatically correct, but it tells you something about the speaker's attitudes — not to mention the irony in the statement about the person's intelligence — just as the occasional inclusion of the expression "y'all" preserves the regional speech characteristics of the person quoted. The way people talk — the rhythms and sounds and arrangements of language — is important to preserve. It makes your speakers more credible, more interesting to your readers.

■ *Unusual phrasing that seems to be a part of your interviewee's personality.* Yogi Berra's "It ain't over 'til it's over" — one of baseball's delightful clichés — is an example of how unusual phrasing is inextricably connected to the speaker's personality. Even if it were possible, you wouldn't dare edit such a statement. To correct the grammar would be a washing out of the speaker's personality.

■ *Any type of statement consciously designed to be out of the ordinary.* For some people, it's natural to speak in metaphor, simile, or hyperbole, especially when they are speaking passionately about a topic or issue. When you are editing your interviewee's quotes, you should be more concerned with maintaining the flavor of such statements than with making everything consistent and grammatically correct. Quotes with mixed metaphors, offbeat similes, and outrageous hyperbole add, rather than detract from, your nonfiction writing.

Other verbalizations should be approached on an individual basis. "Ums" and "Ahs" are useless and should be excised from quotes, but other throwaway expressions ("You know," "I mean," "See," "Look") help give a quote conversational feeling and should occasionally be used to keep that flavor. Once again, the decision concerning inclusion or exclusion of such expressions is a matter of judgment on your part, but you shouldn't include so many as to depreciate the value of what the interviewee is saying. Include such sayings when they add emphasis to a statement; otherwise, keep them out of your quotes.

APPROXIMATING SPEECH

"If you're going to misquote someone, make sure you flatter the person when you do it."

This idea, long accepted as an informal maxim among reporters and writers who "approximate" the words of the people they quote, is little more than the lazy way out. It is so wrong-headed that it manages to harm everyone connected to the quote: it shows contempt or disregard for the facts on the part of the interviewer; it insults the interviewee, who may have carefully chosen his or her words; and it assumes that the general reader is more concerned with an idea than with the accuracy in which the idea is stated. It perpetuates the acceptance of the harmless "little white lie" and, in doing so, it further encourages a writer to choose the convenient over the hard-earned. Finally, it assumes that people are willing to be misquoted as long as they don't look bad in the process.

The maxim originated before the era of the tape recorder, at a time when reporters were writing their interviewee's words in their notebooks as quickly as the person was saying them. Some reporters developed a kind of shorthand that enabled them to accurately note virtually each word a person spoke; others copied only the important phrases and filled in the blanks through recall. Approximating speech was neither wrong-headed nor lazy at that time—it was necessary.

People were bound to be misquoted. Try as they might, reporters weren't able to quote *each word* the way one can with today's electronic devices, and no one had total recall. Reporters did the best they could under their circumstances. The statement that heads this section is the by-product of good intentions tempered with the full knowledge of the realities of the day.

Today, however, things are different, even though many writers and reporters continue to shun tape recorders in favor of notebooks. For the person who is always pressed by daily deadlines, using a notebook eliminates the process of transcription, but he or she must still be concerned with the issue of being accurate when quoting from notes.

By definition, to "approximate" does not mean to "duplicate," so there will always be a problem of accuracy in approximating a direct quotation. You'll always be misquoting the person, at least to a small degree. As a general rule, it's never wise to approximate a person's words if you are going to be quoting him or her extensively in your article; the more you approximate, the more you are going to be misquoting. When you are planning your interview, if you feel that you will be directly quoting someone more than two or three times in an article, or if you anticipate that the direct quotations you'll be using will run more than a couple of lines, you would be better off using a tape recorder when you conduct your interview.

HOW TO APPROXIMATE A PERSON'S WORDS

If you are not taping your interview, it is essential that you follow the postinterview procedure outlined earlier in this chapter: As soon as possible after your interview, while a person's words are still fresh in your mind, go over your notes and write out the direct quotes you anticipate using in your article. You should never let your notes sit for more than 24 hours before you do this.

Even so, you are not guaranteed total accuracy, a point I discovered when I was interviewed by a reporter who was writing a profile for a newspaper. The reporter was asking me about my early interests in writing, and I told him of a terrific high school creative-writing teacher who had taught me a great deal. "I didn't get my best grades from her," I told the reporter, "but I probably learned more from her than I've learned from anyone else."

Although the reporter wasn't using a tape recorder—a fact that made me very self-conscious, resulting in my giving him my responses at a very slow pace—he did a reasonably fair job of approximating my responses to his questions. The above-cited quote, however, was approximated to: "I didn't get *good* grades from her ...." As soon as I read the quote, I knew I'd be hearing from the teacher, who still lives in my city, and who was certain to have seen the article. I'd never received a grade below a "B" from her—a fact she remembered and cheerfully reminded me of when I heard from her.

Not that this minor misquotation mattered that much—if anything, it served me well, since I had the chance to talk to the teacher, whom I hadn't spoken to for years—but this example does illustrate the way that even a tiny turn of word or phrase can alter meaning.

Nobody wants to be misquoted, in a flattering sense or otherwise, and you must be especially cautious when those quotes are using names, dates, places, and other specific references. The best time to nail down the accuracy of such remarks is during the interview itself—stop your interviewee for clarification, if necessary—but if you did not, and if you find yourself pausing and struggling to remember the actual context (or even the spelling) of this kind of detail, you should never guess. Call the person and get the exact information, or better yet, if the quotation seems crucial to your story, get the person to restate the quote. (Telling the interviewee that you're fuzzy on that point affords you the opportunity for such restatement without your embarrassing yourself or your subject.)

Quantitative statements are also important, as is evident by my earlier example. Just as there's a difference between "best" and "good," there is also a great difference between "some" and "many," "often" and "sometimes." If you know that you are approximating someone's speech, you should jot these types of words in your notes during the interview; if, for some reason, you did not, it is always best to consult with your interviewee before you place quantitative statements in a direct quotation.

PARAPHRASING

When you paraphrase, you are choosing your own words over those offered by the interviewee. Rather than directly quoting your subject, you are offering a summary of what the person said. You attribute to your source, as you would if you were using a direct quotation:

> *Six years after being wrongfully convicted of armed robbery, John Doe claims he feels no malice toward the people who put him in prison. Instead, he says, he is happy to be home with his family and back at his job at the local factory.*

Such passages make you wonder why the person didn't directly quote John Doe. Why summarize the man's feelings when he could give them to you himself?

There are many reasons for paraphrasing. The example just cited, though fictitious, could have been the result of an exchange such as the following:

Q. Six years is a long time to pay for a crime you didn't commit–
A. You're telling me . . .

Q. Are you bitter? Angry?
A. I don't feel much of anything. I'm just trying to put that time behind me.

Q. What about all the people who put you in prison — the district attorney, the witnesses —
A. Man, I just don't want to talk about it. They did what they felt they had to do. I'm not holding any grudges.

Q. You're just looking ahead.
A. Right . . . that's right. I'm just glad to see my wife and kids again. I'm back at the plant, working second shift. I'm not doing anything special. I'm just trying to get back in the swing of things.

As you can see, there is very little quotable material in the exchange. John Doe seems less than thrilled about being interviewed, and while his responses tell you something about his state of mind, no single statement stands out as a strong, usable quote. Rather than use a weak quotation that states the obvious or repeats a cliché

("I'm just trying to get back in the swing of things") or even a weak quote that makes a surprising statement ("I don't feel much of anything"), a writer might choose to paraphrase those statements that indicate the interviewee's feelings.

Paraphrasing is also useful when you are breaking down long quotes or anecdotes. Lengthy direct quotations should be avoided, unless you're writing oral history (in which case, virtually the entire passage is a direct quotation) or have an anecdote or statement that absolutely sizzles. Generally speaking, a direct quotation should never run longer than 200-300 words in magazine articles, or 50-75 words in newspaper pieces. Anything longer can be confusing to today's readers who, for better or worse, are accustomed to short paragraphs and quick quotations.

If you are breaking down a long quotation into a combination of directly quoted material and paraphrasing, you should incorporate a kind of rotation system into your writing, alternating strong quotable material with your paraphrased material. The following is a passage, quoted verbatim, from an interview I conducted with author Bobbie Ann Mason. We had been discussing the ways a writer could use common, everyday language in fiction when Mason offered this observation:

> *I think I am generally trying to pick the words that convey a certain kind of attitude that's hard and blunt and practical and no-nonsense — an attitude that comes without frills. I mean, this idea is divorced entirely from that whole discussion about minimalism. This is about how people use language to say what they think. My characters, my writing, and myself — I, as a writer — don't use pretentious language because it's not true. When my mother says she's 'going to shell a big mess of butter beans,' that's exactly what she means: she's using plain, direct Anglo-Saxon words. I'm always drawn to that style of speech, not just because it's documenting but because it's not romantic. It cuts illusion down to size. It's not prettied up. It cuts through the superfluous while it maintains some kind of soul and dignity in one's connection with the world, with one's turf . . .*

In a Q/A format interview, in the context of a lengthy discussion about the use of everyday language in fiction, this passage would work wonderfully; but in a profile or article, the quotation is too long and, without frames of reference, a little too esoteric. In cases like this, paraphrasing simplifies the long quotation and, when combined with material from other parts of the interview, Mason's meaning becomes clearer to the reader. For example, here is one way that one could use paraphrasing to break down the quote and clarify some of the points the speaker is making:

> *Bobbie Ann Mason's stories are written in a spare, direct style that pays careful attention and tribute to the way people sound when they speak. Critics have characterized her style as "minimalist," but Mason insists that the label has nothing to do with her interest in language and how it is used by her characters.*
>
> *"This is about how people use language to say what they think," she says, adding that, like her characters, she disdains the use of language that she feels is pretentious. For Mason and her stories' characters, an "attitude that's hard and blunt and practical and no-nonsense — an attitude that comes without frills" expresses what's on one's mind better than flowery language. When her mother tells her she's "going to shell a big mess of butter beans," Mason explains, "she's using plain, direct Anglo-Saxon words.*
>
> *"I'm always drawn to that style of speech," she continues, "not just because it's documenting but because it's not romantic. It cuts illusion down to size. It cuts through the superfluous and maintains some kind of soul and dignity in one's connection with the world, with one's turf."*

In this revision of the transcribed interview passage, every one of Bobbie Ann Mason's points is addressed but, in paraphrasing, the long quote is broken down into several shorter quotes. There is a mixture of quotation and explanatory narrative. The second passage is longer than the first, but the meaning of the passage is also clearer to the reader who may not be familiar with Mason's work.

Besides the two examples already addressed, there are other occasions when you should paraphrase instead of directly quoting your interviewee. In each of the instances listed below, you are strengthening your text by *not* quoting your interviewee directly.

You should paraphrase if:

■ *Your interviewee has stated the obvious.* Never use a direct quote when it states what a reader can assume or already knows ("I'm very excited," Mrs. Smith said, after winning $50,000,000 in the lottery), even if the person's statement is needed in your article. Paraphrase the obvious statement and then, if you have the material in the interview, directly quote any supportive statement. This same principle applies to those occasions when an interviewee gives you information that is already part of the public knowledge.

■ *Your interviewee has given you only a partial statement or an incomplete sentence.* You should use paraphrasing to bridge gaps if you are *certain* of the content of the missing material. You may have been involved in an extensive discussion on a topic, only to find your interviewee giving you a phrase or half-sentence for a pay-off line. When you are writing, you can either paraphrase the entire statement, or you can paraphrase the missing portion of the statement.

■ *Your interviewee has provided you with dates, numbers, locations, or statistics.* It's not necessary to directly quote a person who has given you information you can get elsewhere. ("I was born in 1926, in Newark, New Jersey," said poet Allen Ginsberg.) Work all figures, dates, locations, and other such information into the body of your narrative, or if you wish to connect statistics to a speaker, do so by paraphrasing. (A Department of Transportation official pointed out that 68 percent of the fatal accidents that occurred over the Labor Day holiday weekend were the result of drunk driving.)

When you are paraphrasing your interviewee, you should stay as close in your wording to the original quotation as possible. You must always paraphrase in the context of the interviewee's words, the same as you would if you were directly quoting your interviewee, and you should identify the source of your information. Above all, be responsible. Don't put words into your interviewee's mouth, even if you're paraphrasing. Stick close to the intent and spirit of the original quotation.

STAYING IN CONTEXT

One of the main characteristics of shoddy or "yellow" journalism is the out-of-context quotation. News-hungry writers, eager to beat their competition in the constant race for the BIG story, will present only a portion of the real story — that portion being the segment or quote that is bound to grab a reader's attention. Fortunately, this kind of journalism is not a major issue: despite protestations from interviewees who are angered or embarrassed when they read their words in print, this type of out-of-context quoting is not a standard — or even common — occurrence in the writing business.

Of more concern is another out-of-context issue, this one finding the writer giving complete, accurate quotes that are not properly framed. There is a huge difference, for example, between a convicted killer's saying "I'm so mad I could kill him" and an angry or frustrated actress's saying the same thing. Part of the difference can be found in the character of the speaker, and part in the context of the remark.

Interviewees make outrageous or provocative remarks all the time. Interviewers, always quick to notice a pay-off line when it's delivered, will not only take note of these remarks, but they will encourage the expansion of them. They'll egg the person on, encourage further discussion, fake empathy in an effort to keep the conversation going. Then, when the conversation is finished, they will rush to their typewriters or word processors and build a story around the comments.

There is some debate as to whether these words should be reprinted at all. Should hundreds, thousands, or even millions of readers hold an interviewee accountable for remarks made in the heat of the moment? Is this fair play — even if the person knows he or she is being interviewed? What is the value of words spoken during a crisis situation? Should interviewers quote or not quote as a result of judgments based on context? Should journalists even act as such judges?

There are no easy answers to these questions. It is important, however, that you be fair in whatever action you choose to take. You cannot isolate quotes from their contexts, nor can you bend or reshape the context to suit the purpose of your article. You must properly frame the quotes you intend to use.

Unscrupulous writers like to hide behind the truth. "He said it, not me," they'll tell you as a defense of their publishing quotes out of context. The fact is, accurately quoting someone, word for word, is not necessarily the *truth*; it is a representation of a percentage of the truth, and it could be a fortification of the cliché that insists that things are never as they seem.

If you don't believe it, think back to the last time you really blew your top. Would you want your character and credibility based on what you said during those moments of anger? Even if you were to be judged as a result of the words you spoke or shouted, you would be quick to mention that everything had been said in the heat of anger or frustration. You'd want to provide a context.

Give your interviewee the same benefits.

USING YOUR QUOTES: SUPPORT QUOTES

Support quotes strengthen your narrative, either by supplying it with information you can build upon, or by corroborating what you're saying in the narrative itself. Support quotes have secondary usages, such as assisting in the pacing or transitions in your article, but they must always be used to strenghten your material. If their purpose is not clear to the reader, they lose their credibility and effect.

Support quotes weaken your narrative if:

■ *They merely repeat a point previously raised in the narrative.* Indeed, you need authoritative corroboration, a quotation from an expert that reassures the reader that what you're saying in your narrative is correct and important, but the quote should never just repeat what you've said. Look for quotes that not only support, but also elaborate or expand upon what you're saying.

■ *They are vague or poorly stated.* When you're talking to an interviewee and have plenty of time to reach an understanding of what the person is saying, you have little difficulty in grasping the meaning of the person's words. A short quote, inserted into the article with only minimal framing to put the quote in a proper context, is another matter. What made perfect sense in the interview suddenly looks vague or poorly stated in print. Ambiguity ruins a quote. When you're choosing your quotes, be sure that each one is self-contained, clear, and well-stated.

■ *They state the obvious.* We addressed this issue earlier in this chapter, when we dealt with the topic of paraphrasing an interviewee's words, but it bears repeating. Far too often, you will read quotations that state what every reader can take for granted. The only time such quotations have any value is when they represent an official response. The President's response to the death of a foreign minister — no matter how hackneyed or obvious — is always quotable, as would be any other official response to questions of national importance.

■ *They serve no apparent purpose in the article.* Writers will sometimes include quotes simply for their "name value." Names sell papers and magazines — that's true enough — but the person you're quoting must have something to say; otherwise, he or she serves no purpose in your article. When you are choosing your support quotes, ask yourself *why* you're selecting those words. The best quotes need no defense for their inclusion in an article — their purpose is apparent.

The best support quotes are the reverse of the types just mentioned. The best support quotes are unique, corroborative, well- or cleverly stated, informative, clear, and useful to your narrative. They will make your text better than it would be without them.

Choosing strong support quotes is not difficult — they will be apparent when you go over your notes or read through your interview transcript. You will see statements that, for their information or by the way they are worded, will command attention. How you use the quotes is an issue that demands the application of your organizational and writing skills. You may want to open or close your article with a strong quotation. You might decide to group several quotations from different sources to give the appearance of consensus or argument. You will certainly use much of your quotable material to support the statements you make in your narrative.

No matter how you decide to use your quotes, when you directly quote a person, you should:

■ *Attribute sources.* Never assume that your readers know the source of a direct quotation. Even if your source does not wish to be identified, you must characterize the speaker ("a source close to the Pentagon," "a company spokesman," etc.). Be as specific as possible. Don't attribute one person's statement to a group ("the Army said," "the Yankees claim"). Your readers need a specific sense of who's speaking in any given quotation, and only precise attribution will give them that sense.

■ *Use complete sentences.* A direct quotation, like any sentence in your narrative, should be a complete sentence. People don't always speak in complete, grammatically correct sentences, and it is easy to overlook this point when you're inserting quotes into your article. Check each quote that you use. If it is not a complete sentence, you will have to either strike it from your text or complete it by paraphrasing (leading in — or out — of the quote with your own words) or the use of brackets ("[It] cost me $250 [to fix]").

■ *Remove yourself from the quotation.* Writers will make the mistake of unintentionally inserting themselves into their quotes by poor or excessive use of adjectives and adverbs. Report only what you know to be true, and be specific in the way you report it. To write that a person said something "dutifully" is an intrusion upon the quotation. How do you *know* that the person felt duty-bound to give you the information? Did he or she say as much, in so many words? To characterize a quote as being "announced with great regret" is ambiguous. What does *great* regret mean to your readers? Chances are the adjective will mean different things to different readers. After you have written your article, check all of the adjectives and adverbs in your narrative. If they don't say something specific, strike them from your text or replace them.

■ *Be certain that the person's words say exactly what you want them to say.* Sometimes you can become so close to the writing of an article that you make assumptions that aren't necessarily true. Some quotes look and sound good, even when you see them on the printed page, but, upon full examination, you realize that they fail to serve the function you've given them. In a way, it's an "apples and oranges" idea: you and your interviewee may be talking about fruit, but you're seeing apples while your interviewee is seeing oranges. For example, in your article you might be writing about the need to establish a "911" emergency code in your area. To support your article's claim, an ambulance driver says, "We're not getting to some of the calls quickly enough to save lives. We're losing people we could be saving." This is a dramatic quote with a lot of impact, but it is still too general. The driver could have been talking about a shortage in ambulance attendants, vehicles, or poor communications, in general. To be effective, you must get specifics:

get the driver to say a "911" number would save lives. A direct quote shouldn't "approximate" the statement it is supporting—it should be a complete match. A direct quote should maintain the meaning and integrity of the speaker while it boosts your narrative.

USING QUOTES IN PROFILES

When you are writing a profile, you should use your quotes, in the same way that you use quotes in your articles or features, with one major exception: in your profile, the quotes from your subject should reveal the person's inner self.

You are wasting your reader's time if your profile subject's words give information that could be found elsewhere. Readers want thoughts, opinions, emotions, and ideas—anything that tells them something they don't already know about the true person. Public figures are selective about what they reveal to the public. Their images are carefully calculated, their actions measured against an anticipated response from the public. Readers are familiar with the *public* person; what they are looking for in a profile is an accounting of the private self.

Your profile subject's quotes should reveal that private self. If you must address the part of your subject that is already public knowledge, do so through the voices of the person's friends, family, enemies, acquaintances, and professional associates. Their quotes will add credibility and support to what's already known. But when you are selecting quotes from your profile subject, look for quotes that only that person could have given you. Let your reader in on that person's inner self. The result will be a well-rounded, fully developed profile.

THE QUESTION/ANSWER INTERVIEW

The Q/A format interview is designed to look as if it is a direct transcription of a conversation but, in actuality, that's about the last thing it is. In reality, the Q/A format is as calculated, polished, and finely executed as an article, feature, or profile. The interviewee's words have been carefully chosen, edited, and placed in a logical sequence that gives the interview a sense of clarity and order. Like any other nonfiction piece, the Q/A has a structure that makes it logical and easy to read.

"A lot of organization goes into our interviews," George Plimpton says of his *Paris Review* interviews, all of which are published in the Q/A format. "They're put together so they have a beginning, a middle, and an end. We put a scene at the beginning, to give it a sense of theatre, and we try to end them climactically, with a good curtain line. We try to develop a particular theme for each interview."

The trick, of course, is to accomplish all this while maintaining a feeling of spontaneity in the interview. The interview may be tightly organized, but it still must give the appearance of being a transcription of the conversation.

To accomplish this, you must first come to regard the interview as you would an article, except that in the case of the Q/A you have been given the words to form into the article. Read your transcription carefully. What was the main focus or theme of your conversation? How can you build around that theme? What statements could you use to begin or end your conversation?

Organize your Q/A in the same manner as you would organize an article, piecing together the various components until the Q/A has its own solid structure.

For the best results, you must:

■ *Begin with compelling leads.* A Q/A, like an article, has to hook a reader into continuing to read. If you must build a mood or tone for the interview, do so in your introduction. Don't waste the opening of the actual interview with a lengthy buildup. "It's important to get the interview off and running," says Lawrence Linderman. "You want to engage an audience quickly. You want to give your reader a look—a taste—of what's coming in that first question. You want to suck the reader into the interview."

■ *Use logic in the way you sequence your interview.* In the written Q/A, you should use as much logic in sequencing questions as you used before you actually conducted the interview itself, when you were preparing the questions you wanted to ask the interviewee. Scattershot questioning and sequencing gives the appearance of disorganization, even if you wind up posing all the questions you intended to ask. When you're sequencing your Q/A, establish the conversation with a strong opening, move quickly into the theme of the conversation, and build off of that. This will give your Q/A its sense of purpose and direction.

■ *Make smooth transitions from topic to topic.* When you are sequencing the questions and answers in your interview, you should aim for smooth transitions as you move from topic to topic. Rough transitions make the interview seem awkward and unnatural. If the transitions didn't occur naturally during the interview, you may create them in your write-up, as long as you don't change the context of the questions being addressed. For example, you might write in a reaction to a response — a reaction which you didn't vocalize during the conversation — if it helps create a transition to another topic of discussion: "I see. That reminds me of another matter I wanted to discuss . . . " Smooth transitions maintain the Q/A's conversational flavor.

■ *Maintain a fast pace throughout the written interview.* Readers are not patient with interviews that take a long time to develop, nor are they interested in a lot of discussion that has no direct bearing on the main topics being addressed. The Q/A, even if it is a long one, must move along quickly. The interviewee's answers may vary in length, but each answer must stick to the point of the question, and it must move the interview further along. When you are editing your Q/A, eliminate incidental talk. Tighten each answer until it has the appearance of being spring-loaded. Maintain as quick a pace as you can.

■ *Conclude the interview on a high note.* There should be an air of finality to the conclusion of your interview. It should neither dwindle down to a slow, agonizing fade-out nor end in the middle of a hot or animated exchange. When you are organizing your Q/A, look for a sequence of questions that summarizes either the interview or an important characteristic of your interviewee. A passage with a summarizing effect is a good way to end a Q/A. Ideally, the ending should make an important statement or raise a question that will keep the reader thinking after he or she has finished the interview.

The best way to see how all this works is to carefully study successfully executed Q/A's. Read the Q/A interviews in *Playboy, The Paris Review,* and other publications, with a critical eye. Take notes on how questions are posed and sequenced. Try to determine the way the interviewer established transitions in the finished product. Follow the way the interviewer developed the theme. Ask yourself how the writer maintained the conversational flow in the printed interview.

Chances are you'll find that the trick of the trade, as mentioned earlier, is the application of your skills in a way that makes the conversation look easy, spontaneous, and natural.

OTHER WAYS TO CONDUCT AND USE INTERVIEWS

To this point, this book has primarily dealt with the one-on-one, privately conducted interview. We've been addressing the uses for the interview as they apply to the gathering of support quotes or background information for magazine or newspaper articles, features, profiles, and Q/A interviews. These are the most common uses for the interview, but they are far from being the only ways in which interviews are employed by writers. In this chapter, we'll look briefly at other applications for the interview, as well as other ways in which they are conducted.

PRESS CONFERENCES

The press conference is an interviewer's nightmare. In theory, it allows the interviewee the opportunity to address a lot of interviewers at one time; in reality, the press conference is little more than a staged performance.

In press conferences, the interviewee is in complete control. He or she decides when and where the session will take place, what topics will be discussed or ignored, and who will ask the questions. Spontaneity is discouraged, probing questions dismissed with prepared responses. The responses to questions not only tend to be generic, but they tend to result in generic stories, since every response belongs to every reporter in the room.

Unfortunately, the press conference may be the only chance you have to "meet" an interviewee. Busy people have neither the time nor the inclination to sit for one-on-one interviews if they can be avoided, especially if the interviewees are in the news and are being besieged with interview requests. To these people, the chance to meet the press on their own terms is a convenience that is too good to pass up.

Whenever possible, you should try to avoid the press conference scenario, but if you must attend a press conference to gather information or quotes for a story, keep the following in mind:

■ *Arrive early.* If you are standing off to the side or in the back of the room, you will not only find it difficult to see or hear the speaker, but your chances of being called upon to ask a question will be greatly diminished. Arrive early and locate a position or seat as close to the front and center as possible.

■ *Be skeptical of any statements or handouts issued by the speaker.* Opening statements at press conferences, as well as any materials distributed to journalists present, are prepared position papers representing an official stance on a given topic. You should pay attention to these statements, but at the same time you should be aware of the manipulative element in them. Look for inconsistencies between the person's statements and his or her past actions. Examine each declarative sentence for possible questioning. Approach the offered statistics with a jaded eye. This is not to imply that the person will be lying to you in these statements; it is instead a caution, a warning that you should realize that you are being manipulated. To take a statement solely at face value and structure an article around it is to ask for trouble.

■ *Record or take notes on other reporters' questions.* Listen carefully to all of the questions and answers. Everything said during a press conference is fair game for all reporters present. Furthermore, by listening and taking note of the questions asked by others, you will get an indication of some of the angles that might be taken by the competition—angles that you will want to avoid when you're writing your own article.

■ *Don't pose your top-priority questions in public if there is any chance you will be able to ask them in private.* If you're lucky, you might be able to persuade a person to answer a few of your questions, one-on-one, in a short interview session either before or after the press conference. If you have made such arrangements—or have strong reason to believe that such arrangements are possible—either remain silent or ask a lower-priority question during the press conference itself. There is no payoff for sharing your best information with your competition.

■ *If you have a follow-up question to the one you're asking, say as much before you pose your initial question.* Press conferences are free-for-all events: as soon as a question is answered, reporters raise hands, shout questions, jockey for position, and generally do their level best to see that the speaker's attention is turned to them. If you don't specifically mention that you have a follow-up question, you probably won't be heard in the noise that erupts after your first question is answered.

■ *Ask open-ended questions.* At a press conference, the main goal of all in attendance is to get the speaker to talk for as long as possible. The more a person talks, the greater your chances of getting surprising or spontaneous responses. Closed questions are quickly answered or brushed aside. Prepare the wording for your question — or, better yet, write it down — before you ask it. Be specific in the wording of your question, and avoid asking anything that will prompt a prepared response.

Press conferences may be far from the ideal interviewing scenario, but good articles resulting from them are constantly being published. When the president holds a press conference, it makes the front page of the next day's newspapers. When an actor or actress assembles a press conference as a means of promoting a new movie, features and news stories pop up all over the place.

If you carefully examine the best of these articles and features, you will notice that the press conference is only the springboard for these pieces. The press conference may have been the occasion for the person's surfacing in public, but it is hardly the only point of an article.

Instead, good writers use the information gleaned from a press conference as the starting point for articles that examine the implications of what was said or explain new angles that cropped up during the press conference. When you attend a press conference, do so with the intention of using only a few quotes in your piece. Devote the rest of what you hear to background for your article. Interview experts to gain reaction or perspective to the person's statements. Dig into the person's background for inconsistencies. Try to obtain a supplemental, one-on-one interview with the person. If you take a creative approach in the way you enter and react to a press conference, you'll be minimizing the control aspects of the meeting and defining the direction you want to take.

INTERVIEWS CONDUCTED IN FRONT OF AUDIENCES

A form of interview that has gained popularity in recent years is the interview that is conducted in front of an audience that has paid for the opportunity to eavesdrop on a conversation. In this format, interviewer and interviewee sit on a stage, converse, and when the formal interview is completed, take questions from the audience. Its structure is a cross between the television talk show and live radio call-in shows.

At its best, this type of interview is informative and entertaining. Because there will be no editing of the questions and answers, and because there is a live audience ready to pose questions to the interviewee, there is an almost palpable feeling of spontaneity to these interviews. To succeed, an interviewer has to be at his or her best.

"It puts you on your mettle a little bit because you have to perform," says George Plimpton, who has conducted a number of these public interviews. "People are looking at you as much as they are at the person who is being interviewed. You become a moderator as well as an interviewer."

The main difference between the private and public interview, Plimpton says, focuses on the element of entertainment present in interviews conducted before live audiences. Not only must an interviewer pose strong provocative questions, but he or she must also do so in a way that is entertaining to the audience.

"You have to consider it a theatrical production," Plimpton points out. "You like to play for laughs or for some sort of response. It may not be the best way to do an interview, because the one disqualifying element might be that you and the interviewee have to entertain, but on the other hand there are people who flourish in this situation because it puts them on their mettle, too."

To hold an audience's interest, the public interview must be quicker-paced than a private interview. Transitions have to be sharp and pauses avoided. The interviewer must be ready with a question at all times.

The key to success is in the way you prepare for such interviews. Your research must be thorough, since there will be people in the audience who are well-versed on your interviewee—people who will notice any lack of preparation or knowledge on your part. You will need more written questions addressing a wider variety of topics. You will be expected to improvise more, to follow the direction of the conversation without disregarding your interviewee's or audience's interests.

This type of interview is not recommended for novices. Personalities like Johnny Carson and Larry King make interviewing before an audience look easy and relaxed, but their styles have been honed by many years of interviewing. For most interviewers, just coming up with the right questions and obtaining the most useful answers is difficult enough; to be required to entertain in front of a critical audience is a tall order indeed.

SURVEYS AND QUESTIONNAIRES

Although they are interviews only in the most technical sense, surveys and questionnaires are very effective means of gathering information for articles or of asking a few brief questions for roundup articles. By using surveys and questionnaires, you can compile your own statistics and form conclusions based upon what you learn. Both methods of getting answers are less expensive and time-consuming than the formal interview.

Surveys and questionnaires are generally conducted either by mail or over the telephone. You can provide multiple-choice answers for your interviewees, or you may choose to leave the questions open. Each way offers an advantage: multiple-choice surveys and questionnaires are easier for the interviewee to fill out than open-ended ones, and they tend to net a greater percentage of return; open-ended questionnaires and surveys, though more demanding upon interviewees, invite a wider, more interesting range of responses. No matter how you choose to conduct your survey or questionnaire, you should only consider using these methods if you are contacting ten or more people; for fewer respondents, you should conduct formal interviews, which will net you better, more in-depth responses.

If you are sending your surveys or questionnaires by mail:

- Always remember to detail your writing project to the people you contact. Include in your cover letter the name of the publication you are writing for, your deadline, and any other pertinent information.
- Keep surveys and questionnaires as brief as possible. Like formal written interviews, surveys and questionnaires can seem

imposing when too many questions are asked.

- Be specific in the wording of your questions.
- If you're providing answers, be sure to cover as wide a range of responses as possible. People resent being given a choice between two answers. The more answers, the better. When applicable, leave an "open" box ("all of the above," "none of the above," "other, please specify," etc.).
- Enclose a self-addressed, stamped envelope for the return of your materials.

If you're conducting your survey or questionnaire by telephone, follow the first three points on the list. Multiple-choice questions, however, should be avoided; people find it difficult to follow the answers if they aren't written down in front of them, and you will risk trying their patience by giving them multiple-choice answers.

ROUNDUPS

Technically speaking, a roundup — more like a survey than the traditional newspaper or magazine article — is a gathering of facts or sampling of opinions on an issue or topic. Roundups are designed to give the reader a sense of consensus or debate. In the roundup, you are addressing a group of people with common interests, jobs, or personal characteristics. You ask them identical questions and use their responses to establish your feeling of consensus or debate. The published article can read like a stark "Voices on the Street" survey (such as the roundups published every day on the *U.S.A. Today* editorial page), or the voices can be incorporated into a full-blown magazine article that reads like a round-table discussion. Both formats are popular with editors and readers alike.

For novices, the roundup is an ideal way to break into print. Local and regional publications are always on the lookout for roundups on provocative topics, and editors of national publications will trust an unknown or untested writer with this type of article more readily than with longer, more complex articles. Since interviews for roundups tend to be limited to a handful of questions, this kind of article is an ideal testing ground for a developing interviewer.

Like any other nonfiction article, the roundup has a slant, but the slant has to be covered in a mere question or two, whereas in an article the slant is developed in much more space. To find your slant, all you need to do is find a topic, question, or idea for your interviewees to address.

The list for such topics, questions, or ideas is almost endless. You might solicit the opinions of local citizens on a recent city council action. You might contact a number of celebrities about the way they celebrate Christmas. You could talk to a group of veterans about their memories of their time in the service. You could poll hockey players about their choice of the toughest goalie in the game. Wherever there is a point to be debated, there is a slant for a roundup. You could find dozens of roundup topics in any newspaper. Your only major concern is to stay fresh. You won't market roundups on topics that have already been covered.

Find a topic and try to come up with a fresh angle to it. Research thoroughly — a roundup may appear to be an uncomplicated pursuit, but you must research your topic as thoroughly as you would the subject of an article. Check periodical guides and indexes for the possibility that the topic has recently been covered, and if it has not, develop the questions for your roundup interviewees.

When you are designing questions, remember that the success of your roundup will depend upon the sense of agreement or disagreement that a reader will pick up from the article. Design questions that invite discussion and opinion; focus on those questions that seem to be logical points for debate. Try to determine where people would think alike or differently on a topic, and develop questions along those lines.

When you are deciding upon whom to interview for your roundup:

■ *Keep the number of interviewees to a reasonable limit.* For a roundup you need more than two voices, but for articles of this nature there is never safety in numbers. In fact, the opposite is true: the more voices in your roundup, the more likely is the reader to be confused by who's saying what. In a short roundup, you shouldn't have more than three or four voices; in the longer roundup, no more than five or six.

■ *Aim for as much variety in the voices as you can get, given the slant of your roundup.* If you're writing for a national publication, you should find people from different parts of the country. Get a sampling of male and female voices. Find people with varying opinions and outlooks on issues not necessarily related to the subject of your roundup. Roundups don't pretend to be representative of a strong cross section of the country, but they should represent a variety of people and outlooks.

Writing the roundup, like writing any other nonfiction work, is a matter of choosing and editing the best quotes. In a short roundup in which each person is speaking only once, this is a simple task; in longer roundups, you will need to gather the two or three best, most diverse quotes for each point that is being addressed. Each quote should differ decidedly from the others: people can agree in roundups, but they should never echo one another. Remember, a roundup is designed to look like a panel discussion, and what makes the best panel effective is its diversity of voices.

GHOSTWRITTEN AUTOBIOGRAPHIES AND "AS TOLD TO" ARTICLES

It takes a large amount of skill to successfully execute the "as told to" feature or autobiography; regardless of whether your name will appear in the by-line (as co-author) or be left off (as ghostwriter), your major task will be in applying the first person singular to someone other than yourself. In essence, you are sacrificing your own ego to accommodate someone else's.

This is no easy feat, for several reasons. For openers, one of the major attractions to the wrting profession is the by-line itself. Writing satisfies a person's ego. Writers want readers to know who wrote the article, and whose ideas and creativity went into the making of the story; they want readers to notice them. Any writer who tells you that a by-line is unimportant is either 1) lying to you; or 2) not a working professional; otherwise, he or she would be writing anonymously or using a pen name.

In a sense, the writer is sacrificing his or her identity when taking on a ghostwritten autobiography or an "as told to" article. The writer will still be using the first person singular (*I got up and walked to the front porch for the newspaper*), but the "I" in the words will represent someone else's voice. Granted, writers are accustomed to using the first person when it does not apply to them, but those occasions are usually set off by quotation marks ("I got up and walked to the front porch for the newspaper," said Mrs. Smith). The quotation marks indicate that someone other than the narrator is speaking, and in using these marks, the writer is not sacrificing any of his or her ego. This may sound like a minor distinction, but it is an important one.

Most professionals know how to get beyond the ego issue. They learn to take their by-lines for granted (as long as the by-lines are published, that is), and they have little trouble using the first person in quotes, which is all part of the nonfiction business in the first place. Every time a writer puts together a profile, interview, or feature focusing on someone else, a certain amount of ego is voluntarily sacrificed.

This idea is different in ghostwritten autobiographies and "as told to" articles, however, mainly because, to write the intimate details of someone else's thoughts and experiences, it is necessary for the writer not only to accept but also to empathize with the other person's story. Without such empathy, ghostwritten autobiographies and "as told to" articles will not be convincing and, therefore, cannot succeed.

Such empathy requires give and take on the parts of the writer and the person whose story is being told. Two egos, rather than one, will have to be accommodated. For instance, your subject may tell you that a certain event is important and meritorious of a long, detailed passage, while you, the author, feel that the event is incidental and almost not worth mentioning. Who has the final say? How do you say that an event is unimportant to a reader, even if it seems earthshaking to the subject?

In cases such as this, the subject will probably have the final say, but you are compelled to discuss the issue with the person, which brings us to the most important rule of the "as told to" article or ghostwritten autobiography: before you agree to be a part of such a project, be absolutely certain that 1) you and your subject are in agreement as to how the material will be handled; and 2) you have a story that can be extended to the length of an article or book (and not merely a few interesting anecdotes). If you're both honest with each other about these two points, the ego issue will become secondary to the project that you're working on.

Once again: be honest with yourself and your subject. Don't kid yourself. Don't tell yourself that you will be able to bring the person around to your way of thinking after you've begun. And don't be so egotistical that you place yourself or your writing skills above the person's story; without that person's experiences, you have no story.

The task of interviewing for these projects is much more intense and detailed than the interviewing you do for reportage or shorter pieces. In all but extremely rare cases, you will be conducting many hours of interviews over many interviewing sessions. You will have to be well organized in your approach, with a strong ear for details. Nothing should go undiscussed.

To conduct interviews for these types of writing projects, you can choose between two basic approaches:

■ *The Chronological Method.* In this interviewing approach, you gather your story's details in chronological order — you start from the beginning and work your way to the end. This approach works nicely if your interviewee is the type of person who can slowly "work" a story, who remembers details and is in no rush to offer them.

■ *The Circling Method.* In this approach, you first discuss the main events of the story, and then you go back and fill in the blanks. This approach is useful if your interviewee tends to see events in outline, as opposed to detailed, form. As the interviewer, you get the skeletal structure established, and afterward you proceed to flesh out your story with details and less important events.

With either approach, you must gather facts and emotional detail directly from your interviewee, and since you won't be filling in the narrative with your own words, you must be thorough. You should research your interviewee as you would for any nonfiction interview, though sometimes what you don't know might work in your favor when you're interviewing for these types of writing projects.

"I found that my ignorance really turned out to be an asset," says Lawrence Linderman, who worked with opera star Beverly Sills on her autobiography. "Before I did the book, I had never seen an opera, and I had never seen Beverly perform. I had absolutely no knowledge of opera. The publisher felt I was a perfect candidate to write the book because I would ask questions that opera experts would neglect to ask or take for granted."

To prepare for his interviews, Linderman read ghostwritten autobiographies of other opera notables. He tried to gain an understanding of how other writers approached similar projects. Once he had an idea of what the other writers did and what he wanted to do, he began an intensive period of researching the life and career of Beverly Sills.

"I sat for more than a week in her publicist's office, going through old scrapbooks and photocopying material," Linderman remembers. "I read reviews and feature stories—I read a whole lot of stuff. By the time Beverly and I sat down to talk, I knew a lot about her."

The actual interviewing stage of the book took six to eight months, Linderman says. Although she had retired from singing in the opera, Beverly Sills kept a busy daily schedule, and Linderman had to work around it in any way that he could.

"I'd meet her for breakfast at her place, and she would make coffee and toast and, every once in a while, these wonderful jams. She'd sit down and say, 'It's seven-thirty; I can talk to you until nine.' That kind of thing. She gave a *wonderful* interview, but it took a long time because her time was so terribly locked up."

Linderman also worked closely with Sills on the piecing together of the autobiography, gaining her approval on the way he worked their interviews into a text. This kind of cooperation is essential in autobiographies and "as told to" articles. In general nonfiction articles, granting an interviewee script approval is frowned upon, but in autobiographies and "as told to" articles, where the interviewee's name will be appearing on the finished product, such approval is mandatory. Some writers even have their subjects sign release forms when the work is completed.

When you're putting the person's story together, be a tough critic. Make sure your subject's story is complete, that it reads as smoothly as one of your own articles. If you need further details or material to use as background or transitional material, conduct follow-up interviews. Take nothing for granted—your reader won't. Air out any disagreements *when* they occur, and be sure that they are completely resolved before you move on to the next portion of the writing. These projects are very demanding, but for those who like the challenge, the rewards are satisfying.

ORAL HISTORY

The most ancient and traditional form of storytelling, oral history, dates back to a time when tribal or cultural experience was passed down from one generation to another through the spoken word. Even today, there is something quiet and sacred about the telling of experience and myth, a seriousness of intent that seems deeper than the words we speak in everyday conversation or even in formal interviews.

Like autobiography, an oral history passage is a first-person account; in oral histories, however, the feeling of the published piece is less formal — more *conversational* — than the autobiography. Oral histories tell stories in a way that has both a spontaneous and structured sense to it.

To be effective, the published oral history passage must look as if the speaker has offered, without great effort in recall or statement, a passage as self-contained as a short story. The person's words must be well-chosen and exact, even as the passage preserves the rhythms and flows of the interviewee's speech. Like a traditional work of fiction, the oral history has a beginning, middle, and end.

As we've seen throughout this book, people rarely think or speak in this succinct fashion. Their memories fail at times and have to be jogged or refreshed. People speak in phrases or half-sentences; their stories meander, moving from point to pointless. They need to be guided at times and let alone at others.

With all the other uses for interviews, why would one bother with oral histories? What is their main attraction? When successful, oral histories are warmer and more direct than articles, profiles, and other kinds of published interviews. They are filled with anecdotes and stories. They carry greater emotional impact than anything that could be written by another person. They deliver a sense of urgency.

Consider the following passage, taken from *Just A Nurse*, Janet Kraegel and Mary Kachoyeanos's collection of oral history interviews in which nurses talk about their experiences, hopes, and frustrations in the nursing profession. In this passage, the speaker recalls his decision to turn off the respirator of an old man who has no hope of recovery and whose family is suffering emotionally from watching his slow dying process:

> *The other nurse was outside at the nurse's station where the monitors were located. I disconnected the alarm on the monitor. I remember disconnecting the breathing tube with*

one hand and stroking his arm with the other. In nursing school, we were taught that hearing goes last. If he could hear, I wanted him to know what I was doing and why. I talked to him. I told him, "I am disconnecting the breathing tube. You will feel no pain. Soon your suffering will be over." I watched to see if there was any sign that he heard me or knew what I was saying. There was none . . .

Without the embellishment or intrusion of a narrative, this speaker's words are stark and packed with emotion. It is doubtful that his story would have been as effective within the structure of the article, profile, or feature.

For interviewees who haven't been interviewed often, if ever, the idea of recording their words for posterity can seem overwhelming. Some interviewees might be tempted to "perform"—to give exaggerated or embellished accounts—while others might freeze up. To prepare oral history subjects for the formal conversation, many interviewers like to conduct an unrecorded session prior to the main interview. In these "preinterviews," the interviewer outlines the purpose of the project and tries to set the interviewee at ease. There can be a brief "dry run" of the interview, during which an interviewee can get a feeling for how the recorded interview will be conducted. However, these preinterview sessions can have a mixed effect on the actual interview itself: an interviewee might indeed warm up to the interviewer, but there is also the risk of rubbing off some of the shine of spontaneity in the process. A person might tell you his or her best version of an anecdote the first time around.

When you are conducting your formal interview, employ the usual warm-up techniques to get the conversation started, but move to the main point quickly. Gather anecdotes and as much specific detail as you can. Insist upon first-hand or personal experience. Put yourself in your reader's place; you will want as much sensory detail as you can get, to bring the person's story into focus, and you'll need a strong feeling of emotional attachment coming from the interviewee. Since every word in the published piece will be attributed to the speaker, you must coax your interviewee into giving you all this information in his or her own words.

Eliciting the information requires a soft touch and, on some occasions, a sense of diplomacy. Oral histories must sound voluntary, not forced; the best oral histories read like smooth statements rather than reactions to hard-line questioning. To achieve this effect, you must know when to listen and when to gently prod, especially when you are working around the edges of the emotional heart of the interview. Interviewer empathy is required.

Studs Terkel, one of the best oral historians in the business, attributes his success to a chameleon-like quality he exudes during a conversation.

"I become a lot like the person I'm talking to," he says. "I may even take on that person's character. To give you an idea: I was once writing a radio show, years ago, for Mutual Radio Broadcasting. We'd do sketches of the lives of different people. One was about Jimmy Durante — of his memories of his boyhood on the East Side of New York in an Italian community, of his mother's telling him about a figure in Italian folklore named Umbriago. One day, I was reading the script to Durante on the phone. He's saying, 'Yeah, dat's good, yeah.' " (Terkel executes a near-perfect Durante impression.) "And I said — again the raspy voice — 'How 'bout dis, Jimmy?' So I became Jimmy Durante while I was talking to him.

"Or Nelson Algren would call. Nelson had this kind of slow, nasal tone, and I'd talk to him in the same tone. My wife would call later on the phone, and as soon as she'd hear me — even though she didn't know I'd been talking to him — she'd say, 'Give my best to Nelson.'

"I don't do it intentionally. It just happens. You know, the person's character determines the tenor of our conversation. If *I* determine it, it's of no value. A person's style determines the interview, and for me, it happens to work out."

This chameleon-like quality is an important quality to bring to an oral history interview. Interviewer intrusion must be kept to a minimum; you should try to preserve the feeling of selective memory, the sense of a story's being extemporaneously told, and the more you intrude upon the flow of the conversation, the less you get of these sensations. In this interview format, you may prod but you should never challenge. Allow the interviewee to tell his or her story.

Piecing together the oral history is accomplished in the same manner as the "as told to" article or autobiography. Some interviewers will insert a question to further establish the conversational feeling of the piece, or to create a transition when there appears to be a "hole" in the story. The published article, however, should be free of any narrative, unless you wish to include a brief introduction to set up the oral history.

ORAL BIOGRAPHIES

A book critic once complained that the oral biography was a lazy writer's way out of having to go through the hard work of actually writing the traditional biography. This form of biography, the critic intimated, was little more than the publication of a person's research.

This may be true of poorly compiled or edited oral biographies, but the well-organized and executed oral biography offers benefits unavailable in the traditional biography. Oral biographies have a greater sense of immediacy and, because the person's life story is recreated only through the voices of the people who knew him or her, there can be more passion in the narratives. Oral biographies don't pretend to be coldly objective; instead, they honor the subject through a series of recollections.

Oral biographies are similar to traditional biographies in the way they are put together. You choose a subject, research his or her life, interview the people who knew the subject, and recreate the life in a way that is interesting and informative to readers. (If the subject of your oral biography is still alive, you may want to interview him or her, though the subject's voice should be used sparingly; otherwise, the book will seem to be too much autobiography and, perhaps, too manipulated by the subject.) With oral biographies, the focus is more on the interviews than on the author's interpretation of what is learned from the interviews. The final product is a combination of oral history and biography, and writing the oral biography involves your employing the skills necessary in both forms.

In selecting a subject for an oral biography, you must find a person with an almost mythological tinting to his or her personality, a person who is or was almost larger-than-life. Recent oral biography subjects include Ernest Hemingway, Norman Mailer, Edie Sedgwick, Jack Kerouac, and Truman Capote — all of whom share this larger-than-life quality. Their lives have been of a largely anecdotal nature; books could be — and have been — created just by the retelling of the more interesting anecdotes.

When you are interviewing people for an oral biography, take the same approach you take when you are interviewing for a traditional biography. Be as thorough as possible, with the realization that you will be gathering much more material than you will possibly be able to use.

"I would guess that about one-tenth of the interviews done for *Edie* were acceptable and maybe another fifth were really extraordinary," says George Plimpton, who edited the Edie Sedgwick oral biography and is presently completing one about Truman Capote. "You have to be very lucky. For example, in *Edie*, there was a male nurse who spent some time with Edie in an apartment, and his stuff was so good it would make a play. It's a very touching story about two people who collapsed from the normal world and found a sort of retribution in themselves, and it was done as well as any short story. But you have to be lucky to come across people like that."

Your research will help diminish the importance of your relying on this "luck" factor. By thoroughly researching your subject's life *before* you conduct your interviews, you will have a strong feeling for your book's cast of characters and their significance in your story. You'll also be able to draw up a list of people who are qualified to speak about a particular event in your subject's life. With several sources talking about the same anecdote or event, you will be in the position to choose the best voices, rather than the only voice, to tell your story.

Piecing together the oral biography is essentially a two-part process: first, you edit each interviewee's words, and then you assemble the best passages into a chronology of the subject's life. The editing process is the same as the editing procedure for oral history. You boil down each passage into a tightly organized, well-stated unit. In the case of the oral biography, however, you cannot allow your interviewees quite as much leeway in their statements as you can give oral history interviewees. The passages must be better detailed and more to the point, or your oral biography won't proceed smoothly. Each passage depends upon the one preceding it, so without a tighter structure to the statements the book's continuity will suffer.

LEGALITIES AND ETHICS

I n matters of interviewing and writing, legal and ethical principles are not necessarily one and the same. A writer can stay within the parameters of the law and still behave unethically or irresponsibly. Journalism scholars continue to debate the acceptability of such practices as ambush journalism and the use of hidden tape recorders. Invasion of privacy, as a legal concept, continues to be developed and fine-tuned. Checkbook journalism, at one time almost universally scorned, has become a regular practice. A panel discussion with a handful of reporters or freelance writers will produce varying opinions about the ideal of fair play.

If you were to examine any legal or ethical issue connected to the daily practice of interviewing and writing, you would probably find two basic principles at the core of each issue:

- a writer's sense of honesty and fair play; and
- the reader's best interests vs. the interviewee's best interests.

In terms of textbook ideals, neither of these principles would appear to pose much of a dilemma for the conscientious writer. We'd all like to believe that interviewing is an open, honest exchange that is fair to readers and interviewees alike. However, in day-to-day practice, these principles are often ignored or compromised. On many occasions, compromises are necessary for the welfare of the article being written; in these cases, the actions taken by journalists and writers are measured against the public's right to be informed as opposed to the interviewee's right to withhold information. On other regrettable occasions, the compromises are indications of lapses in standards that threaten the perception of the integrity and professionalism of writers and interviewers in general. In far too many instances, writers are perceived to be bottom-line mercenaries willing to lie, bend the truth, trash objectivity and fair reporting, and generally do whatever it takes to see an article into print.

In his book, *The War Against the Press, Time* magazine correspondent Peter Stoler sketched a grim picture of the public perception of today's journalists:

> *As far as a great many Americans are concerned, journalists meddle in politics and the affairs of government; they harass businessmen, educators, and religious leaders. Nor is this all. In the view of a significant number of Americans, journalists invade the privacy of individuals, exploiting them for their own ends, then move on without so much as a thought for the pain and chaos they may leave in their wakes. Journalists, many Americans feel, are not always patriotic; they are generally cynical, arrogant, and self-righteous. . . .*

This public perception is unfortunate because it places the writer/interviewer in the defensive position of having to apologize for the sins of a tiny minority responsible for such public sentiment. On occasion throughout your career, you will find yourself having to explain to an interviewee that you are not one of those callous, bottom-line people; you will have to convince your interviewee that you practice with the kind of writing and interviewing standards that should be taken for granted.

WHOSE BEST INTERESTS?

Whenever you sit down to prepare for, or write, an article, you will have a certain attitude or predisposition toward the subject of that article. It cannot be avoided. Your feelings or opinions might not be strong enough to greatly affect your work, but they will exist. By definition, the concept of objective reporting does not require your being emotionally detached from the subject you're writing about; it does demand, however, that you segregate your feelings from your work, that you present as fair and impartial a picture as possible. To be objective is to place your faith both in your readers' intelligence and in your own writing abilities. You must believe that, upon reading your objective, well-written article, a reader will draw the same conclusions you formed when you set out to write it. You must also believe that your writing is truly reflective of the best interests of your readers.

The task becomes complicated when you pit the best interests of your readers against the best interests of your interviewee. There may be a conflict between what readers *should* know and what readers *could* know, and you will be at the center of such a conflict. It is not an enviable position, since you will be making judgments that you might have to defend long after your article has appeared in print. What you write could have great bearing on the lives of your readers or the people you interviewed for your article, so you should feel a strong sense of responsibility to readers and interviewees alike.

I faced this dilemma, on an admittedly small scale, when I interviewed a controversial, often outspoken young author for a newspaper. The author had been under a lot of fire by the press and critics alike, and his behavior had been reported to such a degree that he had reporters and photographers camping out on his doorstep. At one point during the course of our interview, he unloaded a volley of angry invectives toward his critics and the press. His tirade lasted for quite a while and well exceeded the kind of challenge anyone would want to pose to those who, in the future, could do him a lot of good — or damage.

I went home, transcribed the tapes, and worked up the interview. A couple of weeks later, the author called and rather sheepishly asked if I'd turned in my piece. I told him that I had. He then wondered if his tirade had been presented in its entirety. I answered that I had cut all but the earlier part of the discussion, that I'd kept the rational conversation and cut the rest. In the finished article, he was still addressing the critics and press — and angrily at that — but not to such a damaging degree. I'd made the cuts, I explained, because in my judgment the latter part of the conversation represented an exaggeration, fueled by his anger, of his true feelings. He was relieved by my decision, agreeing with me that his display of temper, along with his statements, were out of character.

Was I being dishonest by not reporting this author at his worst? Does a readership have the right to see a person at his worst, as well as at his best? The answers to these questions are not easy, and there is no truly correct way to address them. I do not feel that the press has an obligation to show *everything*—especially the nega-tive—if the qualities don't affect the issue at hand. We're all human and we've all made mistakes, and as long as those mistakes affect no one other than ourselves, why publicize them? On the other hand, negative qualities and characteristics say a lot about the per-son in question, and readers deserve to see as full a picture of an individual or topic as feasible.

When you're writing your article, you'll have to determine whose best interests need to be honored in each declarative sen-tence that you write. In the case of the young author, I felt that I could protect his best interests while serving those of my readers. It was a decision that was debated at the time, and similar decisions will always be debated.

FAIR PLAY

The principles of fair play are among the most important legal and ethical concerns you will face as a nonfiction writer. These principles separate good, solid reporting from yellow journalism, and without a sense of fair play, truth and integrity in nonfiction writing are merely concepts rather than reality.

Fair play involves several key elements:

- Reporting a story in its entirety, as it has been given to you;
- Allowing all crucial voices the opportunity to tell their sides of the story; and
- Remaining unbiased and objective in the researching and writing of your article.

Ordinarily, it is not difficult to employ these three principles when you're researching, interviewing, or writing. With most of your articles, you won't even consider or be aware of them. You will look at all sides of a story, report it in its entirety, and do so without your feelings being a factor at all. Employing these princi-ples will seem as natural as the writing itself.

However, there may be occasions—especially if you're inter-viewing or writing about people you don't like or agree with—when you will have to almost consciously remind yourself to play fair. You'll find yourself reaffirming your faith in your readers' intelligence, as well as your faith in your ability to connect with that intelligence. You'll find your patience and sense of objectivity tested to their limits.

When this happens, you're tempted to exaggerate or tilt your article in a way that precisely fits your own disposition. During your interviews, you'll be tempted to ask leading or biased questions. You may even find yourself wanting to hurt or "show up" the person you're interviewing. In these circumstances, it isn't difficult to lose your perspective or sense of objectivity.

I experienced some strong feelings when I was working on an article about a small band of Chicago-based nazis. Over the course of several months, I attended their meetings, read their literature, and talked to their members. I conducted over ten hours of taped interviews with their leader. The more I listened to their sickening racist diatribes and observed their bullying tactics, the more I grew to resent the fact that they were protected by the Constitution. I saw them as pathetic, if not hateful, figures, and I secretly hoped they would receive some kind of retribution at one of their rallies. There was no question that my personal feelings were getting in the way of my objectivity as a writer, and I had to remind myself constantly that what made these people so frightening and dangerous was not the fact that they were members of a radical fringe group committed to destruction, but that in almost every other respect the members of the group were average people, not all that different from the nonracists you encounter every day. By keeping this in mind, I was able to contrast their extremism with their more normal attributes—a contrast that gave the article a greater sense of urgency than it might have had if I'd only presented these men as extremists.

Employing the basic elements of fair play will help you avoid many of the legal and ethical pitfalls facing nonfiction writers. When you interview a person, remember that there is usually an entirely opposite viewpoint to the one being expressed; if the other viewpoint is critical to a well-rounded article, be sure to interview the appropriate person for that viewpoint. When necessary, play the devil's advocate. Challenge your interviewee for his or her feelings about conflicting viewpoints. Be skeptical of generalizations ("Most pro-lifers are Republican religious fanatics"); ask for specifics when an interviewee gives you a controversial or inflammatory statement or opinion.

By keeping the three principles of fair play in mind, you will not only avoid legal or ethical problems, but you'll also be giving your readers the kind of completely rendered article they deserve.

THE TRUTH AND LIBEL

"You don't believe everything you read, do you?"

This question, or a variation of it, has always been a sort of put-down, a sneer at the reader's naiveté. As a society, we humor ourselves with the vanity that we're intelligent enough to discern the difference between what is true and what is not. Nobody's going to pull the proverbial wool over our eyes.

However, we tend to believe much, if not most, of what we read. When we read direct quotes in newspaper or magazine articles, we belive them to be precise, accurate reproductions of what people said. When we look at a photograph in a newspaper, we assume that the people named and the actions described in the caption are accurate. When we read accounts of events in newspapers or magazines, we believe that what we're reading is nonfiction rather than fiction.

This is no small irony, given today's public attitude toward journalists and nonfiction writers; people might believe what they read, but they're also quick to accuse writers of laundering or altering facts, misquoting their interviewees, slanting articles for their own ends and generally playing fast and loose with the truth. Hence the question: "You don't believe everything you read, do you?" Such a contradictory attitude is probably the basis for the unprecedented number of libel suits filed against writers over the last decade or so, and it certainly gives a strong indication of why over half of the libel cases are decided in favor of the plaintiffs in jury trials, while nearly two-thirds of these same decisions are overturned in the appellate process. On the surface, at least, there appears to be a disparity between the ethical and legal aspects of libel, as perceived by the public and by the legal system.

Libel laws differ from state to state, but by general definition, libel is a false published statement that opens up an individual to hatred, contempt, or ridicule, resulting in that person's being mentally or physically damaged either on the job or in society. A person suing for libel must prove that he or she was clearly identified in the false statement, that the statement was published or communicated to third parties, that the person or publication publishing the statement was negligent, and that the statement actually resulted in injuries to the person's reputation or ability to earn wages or to function normally in society.

For public figures, the negligence factor differs from that of a private citizen. Private individuals need only prove that the writer or publisher showed *negligent* disregard for the truth when publishing a libelous statement; they need to prove that the writer made no strong effort to verify the false statements in the article. Public figures, on the other hand, must prove actual malice, or *reckless* disregard for the truth, on the part of the writer or publisher, in order to win a libel suit. The distinction is subtle, yet important: Private citizens must only show that the writer was negligent in verifying statements, while public figures must prove that the writer's *intentions* were to publish the statements with no regard for their truth.

Obviously, the truth is the best defense against claims of libel. If you are accused of libel and you can prove your statements to be true, you will be safe from prosecution. The key is your ability to *prove* your statements. For example, you may know something is true, or another person may know something to be true and may pass it on to you, but if you cannot supply the necessary evidence of the statement's truth, you could still be successfully sued for libel. In the past, journalists and nonfiction writers have had the concept of "privilege" in their defense—the idea that a statement *believed* to be the truth, but not necessarily *proven* to be the truth, was reported for the public good—but this concept is continually being tested in court. The only solid defense against libel is the truth itself.

MAJOR AREAS OF CONCERN

Since people have different ways of gauging how they are perceived by the public, it's difficult to make a definitive statement about "problem areas" that might result in libel suits. A simple misstatement might cause great embarrassment to one person, while it might be waved off by another. One person's job might be threatened by a disclosure, while another might not feel any pressure.

Ideally, you should check each declarative sentence or quotation in your article for accuracy, but you should be especially cautious when you're dealing with:

■ *Criminal Behavior.* In court a person is presumed innocent until proven guilty, and the same principle applies in print. To call a person a murderer or thief or drug addict or rapist *prior* to his or her conviction of any charges is a surefire way to wind up in court. Even more dangerous is your accusing an uncharged person of committing crimes. In recent years, reporters have used the word "alleged" (as in"alleged murderer") as a shield against libel claims when they were writing about criminal behavior, but even this is not ironclad protection. If the person has been *formally charged* with a crime, you are safe in using the word alleged in connection with your reportage of the crime, the person's trial, etc.; if, however, the person has not been charged—if, say, the person was picked up for questioning, or is an uncharged suspect—the word "alleged" will not necessarily protect you from a libel suit.

■ *Mental Illness.* Right or wrong, people automatically associate mental illness with a disability to function in a totally normal fashion. People shrink away from people with professionally diagnosed mental illness; they doubt their credibility. To publish statements about a person's mental health is an invitation to possible litigation. If the statements are false—or if the person hasn't been medically diagnosed as suffering from mental illness or defect, you can be sued for libel; if the statement is true, you may be sued for invasion of privacy, depending upon the context of your statement.

■ *Sexual Behavior.* Most people prefer to keep their sexual practices and preferences private—and rightfully so. If you obtain information about a person's sexual behavior, you should ask yourself if that information is essential to your article, and if it is, you'd better be able to prove everything you write.

■ *Physical Illness.* You should avoid writing about those illnesses or conditions that cause public alarm, fear, or other negative reactions—unless the person involved openly discusses them with you. To mention that a person has cancer or venereal disease or AIDS would be injurious and open to a libel suit (if this were not the case) or an invasion of privacy suit (if it were the case).

The last three entries on the list are especially tricky for nonfiction writers because of the privacy issues involved. Even if you don't libel a person, you may be invading his or her privacy in writing about sexual practices, or physical or mental illnesses. Profile writers and biographers may uncover a wealth of material that falls into these categories, but they must be cautious about publishing what they learn. Even fiction writers, who often use real-life people as models for their fictional characters, are not exempt from libel guidelines.

If, during the course of an interview, you're given information that falls into one of the above-mentioned categories, insist upon documentation for your interviewee. Get exact information, not generalizations. Above all, be certain that the information is critical to your article and not merely an interesting aside. Why risk costly court proceedings if they can be avoided?

LIBEL IN INTERVIEWS

As far as libel is concerned, interviewers must concern themselves with two major areas when they are conducting interviews:

- How information obtained during an interview is used as background for an article; and
- How information obtained during an interview is used in direct quotations.

When you're given information about a third party during an interview, it's essential that you obtain evidence that supports the information. You cannot simply publish such information as if you assume it is true. People lie, embellish the truth, and spread rumors as much to reporters as they do among private citizens. They have axes to grind, interests to protect. To accept a statement at face value, particularly a statement that could damage another person, is to invite legal problems.

Let's suppose you're interviewing an employee who has accused his boss of embezzling money from the company. The employee's statements would fall into the caution area we just detailed: the charge is serious enough to jeopardize the boss' job — it would surely result in the launching of a full-scale investigation of the allegations — so to publish such an accusation, either as a declarative sentence in your article or within the confines of a direct quotation, without strong evidence to back it, would surely place you in the position of being sued for libel. (Remember: you can be sued for repeating libelous statements just as easily as if you initiated them.) To be safe, you would need more proof: records of the thefts, corroborating statements from other employees, etc. Besides the evidence, you would have to confront the boss with the statements so you could get his side of the story. Fair reporting standards demand as much. In short, you would have to be fair as well as accurate. You would have to make every effort possible to substantiate the employee's claim. In an age of libel suits, no editor would publish your article if you couldn't provide enough evidence to satisfy the publication's legal department.

How you quote an individual is also important. Earlier in this book, we examined the importance of accurately quoting an interviewee. In the context of libel implications, this is a crucial idea — and one that continues to be hotly debated.

A recent Circuit Court of Appeals in San Francisco decision has fueled the debate. The ruling focused on Janet Malcolm, a *New Yorker* writer, who had been accused by a prominent California psychoanalyst of libel through misquotation. According to the plaintiff, Malcolm had fabricated quotes that placed him in a bad light. There was no doubt that Malcolm had used considerable license in the way she reconstructed the man's quotes, but the court ruled that the objectionable quotes were "rational interpretations" of the man's remarks. In other words, the journalist may not have quoted her interviewee accurately, but she nevertheless maintained a verisimilitude that remained within a reasonable distance of the psychoanalyst's statements. An examination of the text of the man's remarks — which had been tape recorded, no less — pitted against the direct quotations Malcolm drew up from them, presents a number of legal and ethical questions. Even if the man's statements were ambiguous — as was claimed in court — why did she not go back to him for clarification? Why were the published quotations more colorful than the original remarks? At what point does artistic license fade into libel? These and similar questions will be debated for years to come.

When you edit or clean up an interviewee's statements, you must be cautious about tilting your subject's intentions or changing the meaning of what he or she told you. Avoid filling in the blanks, especially if you're dealing with controversial material. If the statements aren't clear, have them clarified. Keep all quotes in context. People may not believe everything they read, but they do tend to place more faith and value on direct quotes than they do on narrative. Readers expect writers to take some artistic license in the way they slant their articles, but they tend to believe, despite outcries to the contrary, that the direct quotes are accurate and within context. By being cautious with the material you gather and the ways you quote your interviewees, you'll lessen your chances of having to defend your writing in court.

INVASION OF PRIVACY

All people—including the famous—have a right to be let alone, as long as their actions aren't newsworthy or directly affecting the public. Private individuals are entitled to go about their private lives without having their every move scrutinized and reported upon by the press. People should not have to worry about the prospect of opening a book and finding the most intimate details of their private lives explicitly detailed, in fiction or nonfiction form, without their prior consent to the publication of such a book.

In the past, the right to privacy was largely determined by the degree of a person's newsworthiness. People who willfully placed themselves in the public eye forfeited many of the rights to privacy that they would have enjoyed as unrecognized individuals. However, the issue of privacy was not limited to the idea of one's voluntary movement into the public awareness; a person connected to a news event, even if involuntarily so (such as an accident victim), lost some of his or her rights to privacy. In these cases, the public's right to know superseded the individual's right to privacy.

From a legal standpoint, there are four ways to invade a person's privacy:

- Intrusion;
- Misappropriation of name or image;
- Presenting the person in a false light; and
- Publishing private and embarrassing information.

Interviewers almost never have to consider the "misappropriation of name or image" point on this list; that provision usually applies to advertisers who might invade a person's privacy by using his or her name or image in the advertising or promotion of a product. The other three provisions, however, do apply in varying degrees to the interviewer.

When we talk about intrusion, we're referring to the method

one uses when gathering information, and it is an issue that figures prominently in investigative reporting. The law says you may not misrepresent yourself in order to gain access to the private individual. You may not steal and publish a person's files. You are forbidden to secretly photograph people in their homes or offices, and publish the photographs without their consent. You may be intruding upon a person's privacy if you initiate and tape a telephone call without the person's permission.

For most reporters and freelance writers, staying within the letter of the law is not difficult because it is rarely an issue. Despite books, television shows, or movies that depict a cloak and dagger aura around their writer characters, the average reporter or freelancer would never dream of sneaking into someone's office and stealing papers, or employing hidden cameras to photograph a person at home. Those myths belong to the fictional superheroes who somehow manage to regularly circumvent the law in the name of justice.

However, from the law rise ethical issues that writers in general — and investigative reporters in specific — should regard. For example, consider the following scenario: You're a male reporter. Your city editor has assigned you to write an article on male prostitution in your city. You realize, even as you drive to the section of town where these activities reportedly take place, that it is unlikely that anyone — male prostitute or his customer — will talk to you, so you decide to pose as a potential customer. By assuming this cover, you will at least be able to obtain minimal information about the type of person involved in male prostitution, the type of "services" performed, and the fees involved. You park your car and begin to walk the strip. It isn't long before you're approached by several men who ask if you're interested in "going out." They're suspicious of your hesitancy, and while none will talk about their services or fees (you could be a cop, for all they know), they do talk to you for a long enough period of time for you to gather some general background material, as well as some basic, quotable material for your article. At no point do you inform these people that you are a reporter, or that you intend to use their words for publication. After spending a couple of hours on the strip, you head back toward your car. Just as you're getting near the area where you parked the car, you notice one of the men you talked to earlier stopping his car next to another parked car. After a brief conversation, a man slips out of the parked car and into the male prostitute's car; you instantly recognize him as being a well-known clergyman who hosts a popular radio show in your city. . . .

A number of legal and ethical questions present themselves in this scenario:

- Is the reporter guilty of intrusion if he uses the male prostitutes' words in an article — even if he doesn't use names?
- What does the reporter really *know*? Can he assume that a crime is being committed every time he sees someone get into a car with one of these people? Would publishing such assumptions be honest reporting?
- What is the value of the information he gathered in his brief, informal conversations?
- By posing as a potential customer — and thereby giving at least an outward sign of approval for this lifestyle — is the reporter guilty of entrapment, which is a form of intrusion? Can he, with good conscience, express disapproval of actions he pretended to condone while he was gathering the information? In order to get material for an article, can he (at least outwardly) *encourage* the commission of a crime, even if he himself does not engage in illegal activity?
- What, if anything, may the reporter write about the minister? Would this fall into the category of publication of embarrassing or private information? Can the reporter assume that the minister was guilty of breaking the law and therefore forfeiting his right to privacy?
- In an article of this nature, does the public's "right to know" justify any method used to gain information? How important is this particular story? Does one sense an importance to the general welfare in the publication of such an article, or is its publication a matter of "breaking" a story that will sell newspapers?

The legal departments of newspapers, magazines, and publishing houses address these types of issues and questions every day. In a scenario such as the one just depicted, where both libel and invasion of privacy may be concerned, legal departments — and writers — must approach with caution. The lines between intrusion and undercover journalism can be very fine ones.

For most freelancers, the major, most common concern is not so much illegal intrusion as it is the less harmful, yet equally unethical, issue of misrepresentation. In both cases, the writer is lying to the interviewee, and while the two cases seem separated by only the finest of lines, the difference is comparable to the perceived difference between the bold-faced and the little white lie. With intrusion, you are using stealth in order to get your story; you are hiding the fact that you're a writer at work on an article. With misrepresentation, you are not disguising your profession, but you are not telling the truth in regard to how you intend to use your interview.

The two most common forms of misrepresentation find the interviewer:

- Lying about the publication he or she is working for; and
- Distorting or lying about the way the interview will be used in print.

In both cases, the writer, uncertain about being able to secure an interview by telling the truth, alters the truth to create a situation that will be more likely to meet a potential interviewee's approval. A writer on assignment for a supermarket tabloid might claim to be working for a more widely respected publication. A novice reporter, eager to secure a difficult-to-obtain interview, might tell the potential interviewee that he or she has an assignment when, in fact, no such assignment exists. A freelancer might give a potential interviewee the impression that the information obtained in an interview will be used as background, when in fact the writer intends to use the interview as a centerpiece in a hard-hitting investigative report.

The above kinds of behavior are not only unethical, but depending upon your circumstances, could also be illegal; while victims of such misrepresentations rarely take offending writers or reporters to court, you have little to gain by being dishonest with your potential interviewees. You may get your story, but you might also gain a bad reputation, which could repeatedly harm you in your future attempts to gather information or secure interviews.

FALSE LIGHT

The "false light" provision of the invasion of privacy issue focuses on the perceptions or impressions readers may draw as a result of what you've written about a person. For an example of this, let's go back to my earlier anecdote of the undercover reporter writing about male prostitution. In that scenario, the reporter witnessed a clergyman entering the car of a suspected male prostitute. The obvious conclusion that the reporter could draw from witnessing this would be that the minister was engaging in an illegal activity. However, for the reporter to state or imply as much in the article, without obtaining further and much more convincing evidence, and without interviewing the minister, could be very dangerous. To state that the minister was engaged in illegal activity could be a basis for a libel suit; to even place the minister at the scene of the illegal activity could be an invasion of privacy by reason of presenting the minister in a false light. For all the reporter knew, the minister could have been attempting to persuade the other man to change his lifestyle. Or the minister could have been attempting to line up an interview for his own radio show. Or the minister's car might have broken down and he was merely accepting a ride. . . . In short, the reporter's conclusion could have been entirely off-base, and to publish the fact that the minister was at the scene of a suspected crime would be to invite readers to draw false conclusions.

An an interviewer, you have to consider false light when you're taking statements from others. A controversial or colorful quotation may look good in print, but it could get you in a lot of trouble if your interviewee's statement were to place another person in a false light. You cannot use the fact that you're only reporting another person's words as a defense against invasion of privacy or libel accusations, especially if you don't allow the "injured party" the opportunity to challenge or rebut your interviewee's remarks.

PUBLISHING PRIVATE OR EMBARRASSING INFORMATION

Just because someone offers you—or you obtain on your own—certain factual information does not mean that you are free to offer it to the public. This applies to celebrities as well as to unknowns. As is the case when you're testing your material for libel, you should be cautious about publishing an interviewee's remarks about another person's physical or mental illness, private sexual practices, or other private issues. To repeat something you're told, even if it is true and accurate, can be every bit as much an invasion of a person's privacy as it would be if you were to break the news yourself.

I encountered this issue while I was researching a book on poet Allen Ginsberg. To help me with my research, Ginsberg allowed me to examine the hundreds of diaries, journals, and notebooks he had kept since his youth. In these private documents, Ginsberg kept detailed accounts of his dreams, activities, and fantasies, as well as early drafts of poems and lists of the books he'd read. The diaries also contained accounts of Ginsberg's sexual activities and uses of illegal drugs, as well as those of his friends. Since many of the people involved in the diaries are still alive, Ginsberg was understandably and correctly concerned about my invading the privacy of his friends by publishing information about events that occurred decades ago. After all, these were private journals, unintended at the time of their writing for public consumption. Even in the journals Ginsberg has published, names have been changed to protect private individuals.

Public documents must also be approached with care, as biographer Ian Hamilton learned when he was writing his book about J.D. Salinger. At first glance it appears that Hamilton, a respected biographer and critic, went out of his way to honor his reclusive subject's privacy. Before he so much as began to research his book, Hamilton contacted Salinger and told him of his intentions. He assured Salinger that he would only be writing about the period of the author's life *prior* to his going underground. He further promised not to bother Salinger's family or friends with requests for interviews or information. Instead, Hamilton sought out public documents. He found numerous letters, written by Salinger and kept in university libraries, that offered telling information about the thoughts and actions of the writer in his youth. However, when Hamilton attempted to quote portions of the letters in his biography — excerpts limited to what is generally acceptable within the constraints of the "fair use" provisions of the copyright law — Salinger sued to prevent the publication of the biography. When Hamilton tried to rework the biography by paraphrasing the letters in question, Salinger rejected the revisions and continued to seek the blocking of the book's publication.

Though the issue was technically debated as a copyright case, there is little question that it actually boiled down to an invasion of privacy case. In many cases, the letters of Salinger's youth were embarrassing and anything but complimentary, and even Hamilton's careful paraphrasing could not have altered a reader's perception of Salinger's youthful arrogance. The author's letters may have been accessible for public viewing, but Salinger didn't want their contents made available in a book that would certainly be read by far more people than those who would have gone to the trouble of reading them in the universities where they were stored. The courts agreed with Salinger, setting a disturbing precedent about the ways writers may or may not publish otherwise public documents about private citizens.

As an interviewer, you must be careful with both the research you accumulate prior to the interview and the material you gather during the interview. You must use good judgment when you consider publishing—or even repeating in the context of direct quotes—any of the potentially private or embarrassing information you've learned. To help you decide whether you're publishing private or embarrassing information about a person, ask yourself the following questions:

- If I were the person in question, how would I feel about having the information published? Would I consider it private or embarrassing?
- Would the publication of such information seriously affect the way the person performs his or her job, or lives his or her life in society?
- How essential is this information to the public welfare or the public's right to know?

The answer to these questions will give you a strong indication about the feasibility of publishing the remarks under consideration. As a general rule, you should avoid publishing any information, no matter how interesting or compelling, that is not 1) crucial to the article you're writing; and 2) important to the public knowledge. When in doubt, you should either discuss the information with the person involved or refrain from writing about it.

CONFIDENTIALITY

Earlier in this book, we briefly addressed the issue of using un-named sources and off-the-record quotes in your articles. As noted, these types of sources and remarks can be problematic in the inter-viewing and writing processes. They can also have built-in legal aspects that you should consider before you decide upon their in-clusion in your work.

When you agree to protect the identity of a source, you are making a solid, binding commitment. You are agreeing to keep a source *entirely* confidential, and as we all know, keeping secrets can be quite difficult, especially when the pressure is being applied to reveal the secret. If you are not the type of person who can withstand pressure to reveal sources (or secrets), you should avoid agreeing to the confidentiality of your sources.

In theory, this sounds simple, but the issue has received strin-gent tests in court, in libel cases where reporters or freelance writers have been subpoenaed to testify. Courts have demanded writers' notes, taped interviews, and research materials, and in many in-stances, writers have been forced to choose between protecting their sources' identities or going to jail on contempt of court charges. It is a dilemma that will test even the most stouthearted or self-righteous writer.

The complexity of the writer/confidential source relationship with the law is perhaps best illustrated by the variety of existing "shield laws" that address the issue of writers' being forced to re-veal confidential sources in court. In general, a shield law is an escape window for journalists, a law that protects them from having to reveal the identity of confidential sources in court. However, shield laws vary from state to state, and the range of protection moves from almost complete protection to almost none. Further-more, many of these laws draw a distinction between journalists and freelance writers, with newspaper reporters being the recipi-ents of the shield, while freelancers are left unprotected. Before you take on a freelance investigative piece or agree to provide confiden-tiality to a source, you should be familiar with the shield laws, if any, in your state.

Of ethical concern in any discussion about confidentiality is the American tradition of allowing a person to directly address his or her accuser. It's easy to say something—*anything*—under the protection of anonymity, so you have to be leery of any confidential statements that accuse others of criminal behavior or other wrong-doing. When an anonymous source delivers serious charges against another person, you will have to ask yourself why that source is insisting on anonymity. In some cases, the answer will be obvious. An employee would insist on anonymity before agreeing to give you information about a boss engaged in sexual harrassment. A government official might not blow the whistle on the improper behavior of a superior if he or she felt the heat of possible recrimination. But some of history's biggest and most important stories have been broken as the result of anonymous tips or confidential sources.

In other cases, the reasons for your interviewee's request for anonymity will not be as apparent, and you must try to determine the benefits of the confidentiality to that person. People have axes to grind, debts to pay, and by hiding behind the shield of anonymity, they feel safe to say whatever is on their minds. In these cases, the interviewer might be placed in jeopardy, and you will have to regard their remarks with caution, if at all. If you give such people anonymity, you'll experience difficulty when you ask another person to respond to the remarks or accusations. That person would quite naturally wish to know the identity of the accuser. By protecting the identities of your sources, you're denying the accused their opportunity to address their accusers. It's an ethical consideration that merits attention, mainly because your objectivity may be questioned in the process.

ALTERNATIVES TO GRANTING CONFIDENTIALITY
As we've already seen, there are times when you will have no choice but to agree to protect your interviewee's identity.

However, on other occasions you might be able to avoid this by:
■ *Persuading the person to go on record.* Requests for anonymity are not always set in stone; there will be occasions when you might be able to use your powers of persuasion to convince an interviewee that going on record won't be as harmful as it's expected to be. You might tactfully suggest as much, or if you suspect the person is wavering between going on the record and standing firm on a request for confidentiality, you might nudge the interviewee by stating that your editor or publication has a policy against anonymous sources. (If you choose to employ the latter method,

you should be confident in your ability to persuade the person to change his or her mind, because if the subject stands firm on anonymity, you'll lose the interview.)

■ *Finding alternate sources willing to go on record.* Alternate sources can be either interviewees who will replace the person you originally hoped to interview, or they can be people who will corroborate, for the record, the information your unnamed speaker is giving you. Either type is preferable to the anonymous source. Corroborating sources go a long way in shoring up an article. For instance, let's say that you're writing an investigative report on corruption in a government agency, and that your main source is a high-ranking government official who is afraid to go on the record for fear of losing his job. Your unnamed source will probably give you information that can be verified by other sources. In fact, one of the main questions you should ask such a source is "Who else knows about this?" When you get other names, you have other potential sources—though you still must find a way to approach them without violating the confidentiality of your main source. These other sources may be willing to go on the record with their remarks—especially when they realize that the proverbial cat is out of the bag—and their statements will fortify and corroborate the statements supplied by your major source.

When you're dealing with reluctant sources, bear in mind the difference between off-the-record and not-for-attribution quotes. Not-for-attribution means that you may use the quote but not the identity of your source; off-the-record means that the information is not for public consumption. Despite the built-in problems in not-for-attribution quotes, you're always better off with that type of quotation than you are with off-the-record information, and you should attempt to "upgrade" your off-the-record quotes if you can. Even so, you might find yourself facing an editor who is reluctant to publish anonymous quotes, but at least you'll have a starting point that would be denied by completely off-the-record material.

AMBUSH INTERVIEWS
This type of interview, popularized by the "60 Minutes" news magazine television program, is conducted just as its name implies: without warning or prior agreement between interviewer and interviewee, an interviewee is confronted by a reporter and asked a

number of questions that he would otherwise be disinclined to answer. The interviewee has no time to consider or prepare responses to the interviewer's questions. Tape recorders take down the interviewee's astonished or angry responses. If the interview is for television broadcast, a camera captures a person's every nervous tic or gesture.

Ambush interviews present numerous ethical questions, the main issue focusing on the extent to which we will go to bring home an important story. The public may have a right to be informed of all things newsworthy, but at what journalistic cost? When does ambush journalism cross over into invasion of privacy? Is it possible to be fair and objective when this type of interview is employed? Is this just an extension of the basic principles of investigative reporting, or is it a manifestation of journalistic arrogance and disregard for fair play?

The answers to these and other questions are complex. There is no question that, without ambush journalism, some important news stories would never see the light of day. Reporters are all too familiar with the skill with which politicians, corporate executives, and other powerful figures avoid the press. Ambush interviews may be the media's only recourse in getting statements from such people.

When asked about ambush journalism, members of the "60 Minutes" broadcasting group gave *Playboy* interviewer Morgan Strong a variety of responses. Not surprisingly, all of those questioned defended the practice, although Mike Wallace, the correspondent most often associated with this kind of confrontational interview, was quick to point out that the program had backed off the practice in recent years.

Don Hewitt, the program's creator, arguing that a person is not "entitled to privacy while committing malfeasance," defended the practice of the confrontational interview. "There is a tendency to look askance at what is called confrontation journalism," he admitted. "Confrontation, as we practice it, is good journalism."

Diane Sawyer, working for the program at the time of the interview, took a pragmatic stance: "I think there are times when what they call ambush journalism—I'd call it a surprise encounter—is the only way to get a story. I think that in every case you have to weigh the importance of this information that you will or won't get against the importance of seeing the person at the center of the story. If it is an important story and you think seeing him is a critical piece in it, then I think it's justified. When it's done for theatre . . . I'm as opposed to that as anyone else."

For print journalists and freelance writers, the paparazzi element in this kind of interviewing is not nearly as effective. Without the intimidating presence of a camera capturing their images and expressions for thousands or millions of viewers, interviewees find it much easier to refuse an interview, snarl their "no comments," or avoid the press. You might spend all day waiting outside an interviewee's home or office, only to be told to "buzz off" when you encounter the person. As we've noted before, an interviewee has no obligation to talk to you, and only the most powerful journalists have the leverage to make the ambush interview an effective tool on a regular basis.

CHECKBOOK JOURNALISM

Depending upon whom you are talking to, the idea of checkbook journalism — the payment of a source for an interview — is either a pestilence or an occasionally cruel necessity in the business of getting otherwise reluctant people to talk. Rivalry between the print and broadcast media, coupled with the inordinate value we place on the word "exclusive" have brought ethical questions and the unpleasant matter of greed into a spotlight that most journalists would prefer to avoid.

As its name indicates, checkbook journalism focuses on the dollar and its relationship to the news — or the public's thirst to satisfy its curiosity — and while it would be tempting to issue a blanket condemnation of the practice, the argument is more complex than a simple purchase agreement.

Generally speaking, you should avoid spending your own money on an interview. If payment is demanded for an interview, and your editors have decided that such an interview is so meritorious that it is worth paying for, ask your publication for the necessary funds. Agree to checkbook journalism only as a last resort: if word gets around that your publication is willing to pay for interviews, you may find yourself confronting this type of journalism on more occasions than you ever bargained for. Furthermore, the fact that you paid for an interview does not assure you of obtaining useful information or a good interview. You may find yourself the unhappy recipient of a worthless interview — and one you paid good money for, to boot.

A FINAL WORD

The best way to avoid being accused of illegal or unethical behavior in your work is to develop a kind of "defensive" posture when you're researching, interviewing, and writing. Check each of your statements or quotes for truth and accuracy. Check for balance and fairness. Never rush an article into print; you're better off honoring accuracy more than a deadline. If you have questions or need clarification, contact your interviewees. Be wary of "hot," controversial quotes that might read well and sell copies, but might also land you in court. In short, be skeptical of your own work. If an article passes your own thorough, honest, rigorous scrutiny, it will probably pass an editor's.

Interviewing can be tough, demanding work requiring every bit of your perception and creativity, but it is ultimately one of the most rewarding tasks you can undertake as a writer. You will meet interesting, if not famous, people. You'll learn about the people, events, and ideas that influence the way we live today; you will be an insider, a witness to history-in-the-making. As a result of what you see and learn firsthand in your interviewing experiences, you will be able to help inform others and, in your own modest way, assist in the formation of public opinion. In short, you will be in the vortex of what's happening *now*.

Developing strong interviewing skills takes time and practice, and you will probably learn as much from a few early failures as you do from all of your successes. Few reporters or freelance writers pick up a notebook or tape recorder and conduct the perfect interview the first time out; instead, they parlay their interviewing experiences into a skill that seems to grow with each subsequent interview. The key is to allow your patience and curiosity to work for you. Applying your own creative touches won't hurt, either.

Lawrence Linderman has worked on both sides of the desk — as an editor and a freelance writer — and he may be speaking for all freelancers when he mentions his reasons for choosing the challenging, often difficult life of the freelancer.

"It's really fun," he says. "It doesn't feel like drudgery because you keep learning and you're always being exposed to different ideas. You can really see something that piques your interest and then go after it."

As you'll see, the interview provides a path to those feelings of creative and personal fulfillment.

APPENDIX

Figure 1: To help organize and prepare for your interview, you might draw up an outline of the questions you intend to ask your interviewee. The process is usually twofold: first, sketch out the general question areas you hope to cover in the interview, then begin to write out the specific questions you'll be asking. This illustration is a sample page of the notes for my interview with author Bobbie Ann Mason.

Figure 2: The first part of a verbatim transcript of a conversation I had with author Kurt Vonnegut. I've already begun my initial workup of the interview.

Figure 3a, b, and c: Three excerpts from an interview with Raymond Carver. In the first, I'm working with an initial workup of the conversation. In the second, I've sent a rough draft of the conversation (as per agreement) to Carver and he has penciled in his comments and changes. The third excerpt represents the final draft.

Figure 4: A sample page of the questions drawn up for a mail interview with John Clellon Holmes, the late novelist.

Figure 5: A section of text from a mail interview with John Clellon Holmes. On each page, I typed a single question, which Holmes answered beneath.

BOBBIE ANN MASON INTERVIEW

Question Areas

Inspiration/origins of works   Dialogue in Fiction

Short Stories, Novels   Characterization

Influences   Regionalism in Fiction

Writing Habits   Pop Culture in Fiction

Biographical Information
Spence + Lila screenplay
In Country: the movie

Regionalism

1.   How does place influence the way you write? In other words, you live in
     PA, yet you always return to your native Kentucky. What does Kentucky
     offer that other locations do not?

2.   Region's influence on dialogue, the way a story is written (its tone,
     natural rhythms, etc.) *How does writer get this flavor in his/her fiction?*

3.   Importance of location/setting in short stories and novels.

4.   In the past, you've referred to yourself as a writer in exile. Isn't
     that what a journalist is? (Vonnegut: insiders, outsiders)

How does a writer collect
details that make up a
strong character?

Characterization

1.   Where do you get your characters? How do you develop them?

Figure 1

Kurt Vonnegut (March 12, 1988/NYC)

1- In your Paris Review interview, you were talking about your being a scout
during World War II, and you mentioned that your job was "to go out and look
for enemy stuff. Things got so bad that we were finally looking for our own
stuff." Sounds like an interesting summation of your career.

What, that I've collapsed like the Battle of the Bulge? (smiles)

2- No, I'm saying that writers, especially the ones just starting out, are always
looking for stuff out there, and the successful ones seem to find it within
themselves. Don't you think that writers are much like scouts?

It all depends. My son, ~~for instance~~, is a writer ~~Mark~~. ~~He~~ wrote because he
had something very much on his mind. It was as though he had been attacked,
rather than looking for a place to attack, ~~because~~ he was responding to a
whack from life. A lot of people, particularly readers of writers' magazines,
are looking for stuff to write about, (you know) because they want a job. They
want this kind of job: they don't want a boss; they want to be free to travel,
and all that. So, yea, they're like scouts looking for something--anything.
But there are a lot of writers--my son included--who felt a necessity to
respond to life and not to start a new professional career at it.

3- Has he written anything since The Eden's Express?

No, he's a pediatrician. He's very busy and has a family and pediatricians
work long hours. . . But, no, I don't agree with you. Some people are looking
for work. During the Depression, everyone was a scout looking for any kind of
work. So I guess there are a lot of people who want to become writers who are
out looking for any kind of job, you know, that would get them into the
profession. I've customarily responded to life as I've seen something that
made me very much want to write about it--not that it made me very much want
to get into the writing profession.

4- In another interview, you said that you had to have an ax to grind. . .

You've also said that you have to have an ax to grind
Well, you've got to have something to write about.

Figure 2

RAYMOND CARVER INTERVIEW--January 29, 1986 (telephone)

When your name comes up in literary conversation, it's generally in connection with your work in the short story form. However, your last two books have been collections of poetry. You've published more poetry volumes, at this point, than you have published short story collections.

. . . I had a short story and a poem accepted on the same day. This was

truly a red-letter day. [And I continued to write. . . This would have been,

probably] in the early-60's . . and I continued to write both short fiction

and poetry in a more or less hit-or-miss fashion, given the circumstances of

my life at the time. Finally, I decided, consciously or otherwise, that I

was going to have to make a decision as to where to give what energy and

strength that I had, what time I had to devote to the writing, to one or the

other. And I did come down on the side of the short story. *Q. you continued to write poetry, though* / And so, for many *Yes.*

years, I feel that I was an occasional poet, but that, to me, was better than

being no poet at all. I just wrote a poem where I could or when I had the

chance, and the earlier books of poems were small press publications.

They're now out of print. Most of those. . . the best of those poems are

preserved in this collection, _Fires_,

Figure 3a

*Back when I began to write, or send things out, I gave
poetry pretty much equal amount of time to short stories
and poems.*

RAYMOND CARVER INTERVIEW--January 29, 1986 (telephone)

1— When your name comes up in literary conversations, it's usually in connection
with your work in the short story form. However, your last two books have
been poetry collections and you've published, to this point, more volumes of
poetry than short fiction. How did your career as a poet evolve? *"I used to write both poetry and stories..."*
Can you fill in the sphere?

There was a sentence used to lead into this but it was garbled on tape. Something like:

In the early-60's, I had a short story and a poem accepted on the same day.
The letter of acceptance from two different magazines, was in the box on the same day.
At this time,
This was truly a red-letter day. I wrote both short fiction and poetry in a

more or less hit-or-miss fashion, given the circumstances of my life ~~at the~~
~~time~~. Finally I decided, consciously or otherwise, that I was going to have
put the *the*
to make a decision as to where to ~~give what~~ energy and strength I had, ~~what~~ *other.*
—I had to decide to give it to one genre or the other.
time I had to devote to writing, ~~to one or the other~~. And I came down on the

side of the short story.

2— You continued to write poetry, though.

Yes. For many years, I was an occasional poet, but that, to me, was better
whenever *whenever*
than being no poet at all. I ~~just~~ wrote a poem ~~where~~ I could, ~~or when~~ I had
2nd wasn't writing stories. *that are*
the chance, ~~The~~ earlier books were small press publications, ~~They're~~ now
√These *of poems* *the*
out of print. The best of those poems are preserved in ~~this~~ collection,

Fires, which **is** in print. There are, I think, about 50 poems that I wanted

Figure 3b

RAYMOND CARVER INTERVIEW

When your name comes up in literary conversations, it's usually in connection
with your work in the short story form. However, your last two books have
been poetry collections and you've published, to this point, more volumes of
poetry than short fiction. How did your career as a poet evolve?

Back when I began to write and send things out, I gave pretty much equal

amount of time to short stories and poems. Then, in the early-60's, I had a

short story and a poem accepted on the same day. The letters of acceptance,

from two different magazines, were there in the box on the same day. This

was truly a red-letter day. At the same time, I was writing both short

fiction and poetry in a more or less hit-or-miss fashion, given the

circumstances of my life. Finally I decided, consciously or otherwise, that

I was going to have to make a decision as to where to put the energy and

strength I had, the time I had to devote to writing--I had to decide to give

it to one genre or the other. And I came down on the side of the short

story.

Figure 3c

conventional;
conservative

(4) It seems that ~~It seems that~~ The nucleus of beat writers came from turbulent family backgrounds. The result of this seems to be an inner struggle between the adolescent desires to rush madly at life and the more adult needs--~~perhaps very strong in some cases~~ to have "normal" family lives. You, Kerouac, and Neal Cassady especially seemed to be torn between the two. How did your backgrounds initially affect your writing?

(5) World War II also played a major role in the origins of Beat writing. Kerouac saw ships being sunk; Ferlinghetti had the horrible misfortune of being at Normandy and then at Nagasaki shortly after it was bombed. In your case, the war's effects were more subtle. Could you expand on what you said (in Jack's Book) about your feelings about the war?

I ask this because I never participated in Vietnam. I felt almost hypocritical protesting the war, and I have been haunted ever since by the fact that I never felt the terror--only the anger. . . I feel almost inadequate discussing the war with vets against war, though Vietnam affected me in a way which will never be altered.

(6) It seems ~~to me~~ that the Beat Generation's "motor" was fueled by danger, that taking real risks separated you from the Middle Class kids just partying for a weekend or two, danger in terms of hurling lightning bolts into the tranquil skies of the Fifties. The pursuit of "nakedness" (as it was called) carried with it an awful price. The message of On the Road and Go implies that total celebration and reckless pursuit of indefinite ideals disappoints the individual in the end, that one finds only an ocean (natural barriers) at the end of a continent or a shambles when the party's over.

    e - a. Was Norman Mailer correct in his thinking that the hipster, like the Black American, lived the life of a psychopath? What differentiated your group from Mailer's hipsters?

    c - b. What was the fascination with the underworld all about? (Your explanation in Go was good, but do you have any further insights now that you are more removed from the scene?)

    d - c. What were your first impressions of william Burroughs and
The "reincarnation
of Poe" Herbert Huncke? Did the intelligence of these two "Underground" types (please excuse the Time categorization) cause you to question your formal education (literally and socially) as a youth?

Figure 4

9A.

<u>Go</u> was the victim of the McCarthy Era and publishers' fears of obscenity trials
and hassles. Do you recall your feelings when you heard that Allen Ginsberg's
<u>Howl</u> was being tried for obscenity in San Francisco? Were you asked to testify at
the trial?

That small-minded and mean-spirited showman, McCarthy, can't be blamed for the
timidity and fear-of-change that characterized the American scene then. If
anything, he was a product of it, and more of a symptom than a cause. Censorship
was a longtime fact by that time. If GO was a victim of anything (and I rarely
think of it that way, and didn't then), it was a prevailing mood of fear & unease
incomprehension. The book was raw, in some ways ugly, and it spoke out of an
older and then-unpopular tradition of the novel. It was the material that was
odious to most of the first reviewers. They could see nothing redeeming in the
characters or their behavior. When HOWL went on trial, I was not surprised at
all. If the use of certain words is obscene, the poem was obscene. The question
to me was always, "So what?" Obscenity, as Henry Miller had stated for decades,
is a legitimate form of literary expression, and always has been. Being mostly

Figure 5:
(Raymond Carver's handwriting has been recreated for legibility.)

INDEX

Other Books of Interest

Annual Market Books
  Artist's Market, edited by Susan Conner $19.95
  Children's Writer's & Illustrator's Market, edited by Connie Eidenier (paper) $15.95
  Humor & Cartoon Markets, edited by Bob Staake (paper) $15.95
  Novel & Short Story Writer's Market, edited by Robin Gee (paper) $18.95
  Photographer's Market, edited by Sam Marshall $19.95
  Poet's Market, by Judson Jerome $18.95
  Songwriter's Market, edited by Mark Garvey $18.95
  Writer's Market, edited by Glenda Neff $23.95
General Writing Books
  Annable's Treasury of Literary Teasers, by H.D. Annable (paper) $10.95
  Beginning Writer's Answer Book, edited by Kirk Polking (paper) $13.95
  Discovering the Writer Within, by Bruce Ballenger & Barry Lane $16.95
  A Handbook of Problem Words & Phrases, by Morton S. Freeman $16.95
  How to Increase Your Word Power, by the editors of Reader's Digest $19.95
  How to Write a Book Proposal, by Michael Larsen $10.95
  Knowing Where to Look: The Ultimate Guide to Research, by Lois Horowitz (paper) $15.95
  Make Every Word Count, by Gary Provost (paper) $9.95
  On Being a Writer, edited by Bill Strickland $19.95
  Pinckert's Practical Grammar, by Robert C. Pinckert $14.95
  The Story Behind the Word, by Morton S. Freeman (paper) $9.95
  12 Keys to Writing Books that Sell, by Kathleen Krull (paper) $12.95
  The 29 Most Common Writing Mistakes & How to Avoid Them, by Judy Delton $9.95
  Word Processing Secrets for Writers, by Michael A. Banks & Ansen Dibell (paper) $14.95
  Writer's Block & How to Use It, by Victoria Nelson $14.95
  The Writer's Digest Guide to Manuscript Formats, by Buchman & Groves $16.95
Nonfiction Writing
  Basic Magazine Writing, by Barbara Kevles $16.95
  Creative Conversations: The Writer's Guide to Conducting Interviews, by Michael Schumacher $16.95
  How to Sell Every Magazine Article You Write, by Lisa Collier Cool (paper) $11.95
  How to Write Irresistible Query Letters, by Lisa Collier Cool (paper) $10.95
  The Writer's Digest Handbook of Magazine Article Writing, edited by Jean M. Fredette $15.95
  Writing Creative Nonfiction, by Theodore A. Rees Cheney $15.95
Fiction Writing
  The Art & Craft of Novel Writing, by Oakley Hall $16.95
  Best Stories from New Writers, edited by Linda Sanders $16.95
  Characters & Viewpoint, by Orson Scott Card $13.95
  The Complete Guide to Writing Fiction, by Barnaby Conrad $17.95
  Cosmic Critiques: How & Why 10 Science Fiction Stories Work, edited by Asimov & Greenberg (paper) $12.95
  Creating Short Fiction, by Damon Knight (paper) $9.95
  Dare to Be a Great Writer: 329 Keys to Powerful Fiction, by Leonard Bishop $15.95
  Dialogue, by Lewis Turco $12.95
  Fiction Is Folks: How to Create Unforgettable Characters, by Robert Newton Peck (paper) $8.95
  Handbook of Short Story Writing: Vol. I, by Dickson and Smythe (paper) $9.95
  Handbook of Short Story Writing: Vol. II, edited by Jean M. Fredette $15.95
  How to Write & Sell Your First Novel, by Collier & Leighton (paper) $12.95
  One Great Way to Write Short Stories, by Ben Nyberg $14.95
  Manuscript Submission, by Scott Edelstein $13.95
  Plot, by Ansen Dibell $13.95

Revision, by Kit Reed $13.95
Spider Spin Me a Web: Lawrence Block on Writing Fiction, by Lawrence Block $16.95
Storycrafting, by Paul Darcy Boles (paper) $10.95
Theme & Strategy, by Ronald B. Tobias $13.95
Writing the Novel: From Plot to Print, by Lawrence Block (paper) $10.95
Special Interest Writing Books
The Complete Book of Scriptwriting, by J. Michael Straczynski (paper) $11.95
Editing Your Newsletter, by Mark Beach (paper) $18.50
Families Writing, by Peter Stillman $15.95
Guide to Greeting Card Writing, edited by Larry Sandman (paper) $9.95
How to Write a Play, by Raymond Hull (paper) $12.95
How to Write Action/Adventure Novels, by Michael Newton $13.95
How to Write and Sell Your Personal Experiences, by Lois Duncan (paper) $10.95
How to Write Mysteries, by Shannon OCork $13.95
How to Write Romances, by Phyllis Taylor Pianka $13.95
How to Write Tales of Horror, Fantasy & Science Fiction, edited by J.N. Williamson $15.95
How to Write the Story of Your Life, by Frank P. Thomas (paper) $11.95
How to Write Western Novels, by Matt Braun $13.95
Mystery Writer's Handbook, by The Mystery Writers of America (paper) $11.95
Successful Scriptwriting, by Jurgen Wolff & Kerry Cox $18.95
Travel Writer's Handbook, by Louise Zobel (paper) $11.95
TV Scriptwriter's Handbook, by Alfred Brenner (paper) $10.95
The Writer's Complete Crime Reference Book, by Martin Roth $19.95
Writing the Modern Mystery, by Barbara Norville $15.95
Writing to Inspire, edited by William Gentz (paper) $14.95
The Writing Business
A Beginner's Guide to Getting Published, edited by Kirk Polking $11.95
The Complete Guide to Self-Publishing, by Tom & Marilyn Ross (paper) $16.95
How to Sell & Re-Sell Your Writing, by Duane Newcomb $11.95
How You Can Make $25,000 a Year Writing, by Nancy Edmonds Hanson (paper) $12.95
Is There a Speech Inside You?, by Don Aslett (paper) $9.95
The Writer's Friendly Legal Guide, edited by Kirk Polking $16.95
A Writer's Guide to Contract Negotiations, by Richard Balkin (paper) $11.95

To order directly from the publisher, include $3.00 postage and handling for 1 book and 50¢ for each additional book. Allow 30 days for delivery.

Writer's Digest Books
1507 Dana Avenue, Cincinnati, Ohio 45207
Credit card orders call TOLL-FREE
1-800-289-0963
Prices subject to change without notice.

Write to this same address for information on *Writer's Digest* magazine, Writer's Digest Book Club, Writer's Digest School, and Writer's Digest Criticism Service.